"I HAVE NOTHING TO HIDE"

AND 20 OTHER MYTHS ABOUT SURVEILLANCE AND PRIVACY

HEIDI BOGHOSIAN

BEACON PRESS
BOSTON

BEACON PRESS
Boston, Massachusetts
www.beacon.org

Beacon Press books
are published under the auspices of
the Unitarian Universalist Association of Congregations.

24 23 22 21   8 7 6 5 4 3 2 1

This book is printed on acid-free paper that meets the uncoated paper
ANSI/NISO specifications for permanence as revised in 1992.

Text design and composition by Kim Arney

Library of Congress Cataloging-in-Publication Data
Name: Boghosian, Heidi, author.
Title: "I have nothing to hide" : and 20 other myths about surveillance
    and privacy / Heidi Boghosian.
Description: Boston : Beacon Press, 2021. | Includes bibliographical
    references.
Identifiers: LCCN 2021006674 (print) | LCCN 2021006675 (ebook) |
    ISBN 9780807061268 (trade paperback ; acid-free paper) |
    ISBN 9780807061275 (ebook)
Subjects: LCSH: Electronic surveillance—United States—Miscellanea. |
    Domestic intelligence—United States—Miscellanea. | Civil
    rights—United States—Miscellanea. | Privacy, Right of—United
    States—Miscellanea. | National security—United States—Miscellanea.
Classification: LCC TK7882.E2 B64 2021 (print) | LCC TK7882.E2 (ebook) |
    DDC 363.1/0630973—dc23
LC record available at https://lccn.loc.gov/2021006674
LC ebook record available at https://lccn.loc.gov/2021006675

For my parents,
Marilyn and Varujan Boghosian,
with love

CONTENTS

INTRODUCTION

Do you know where your data is?

Most of us do not.

It's astounding how we've embraced the digital age without such an awareness. Late-night television news watchers from the late 1960s through the 1980s remember what became a parodied catchphrase: "It's 10 p.m. Do you know where your children are?" Celebrities like Andy Warhol and Grace Jones even appeared on screen to invoke the public service announcement mantra, urging parents to keep track of their kids.

Fast forward to the electronic age. Youngsters—the so-called iGeneration—spend hours online each day. Virtual forays can be as sinister as walking unattended in the streets after dark. A public service warning about the perils of electronic mass surveillance is long overdue.

That's because most Americans are unfit as digital parents. They let the family's personal information roam far and wide, through electronic devices and social media platforms. Hundreds of data trails remain, like breadcrumbs in a forest. In this epoch of data-as-commodity, these crumbs give strangers—commercial data aggregators who mine and analyze our habits—a means to monitor us 24/7 and to influence our thinking. When we don't take precautions to secure our personal information, such intruder entities exercise more and more control over our lives.

When third parties control our information, we are vulnerable to discrimination by landlords, employers, or service providers based on age, race, disease and mental health history, and other qualities. Autonomy and personal freedoms perish when private data is up for grabs. Gone is the option of being anonymous when we want to voice an unpopular opinion or share a tip about fraud. Also harmed is freedom of expression and personal agency over our thoughts, actions, and self-perception.

And that's why we must demand to know where our data is and how it serves as the keystone of the surveillance state.

WHO'S GUARDING THE CROWN JEWELS?

Northridge, a data analytics firm, suggests that in the "data economy," data is more valuable than oil. "Like oil, raw data's value comes from its potential to be refined into an essential commodity."[1] And what is the refinement process for our data? It is the linking of different information sets to create dossiers on every American to sell to third parties.

The US data brokerage industry is estimated to be worth over $200 billion, while the European Commission, as of 2020, estimated the European data market to be worth €106.8 billion.[2] Mining, summarizing, and analyzing data are also politically useful. The British firm Cambridge Analytica (CA) is a case in point. During its brief life, from 2013 to 2018, the conservative political consulting group claimed it had amassed enough data points on American voters to construct targeted political ads and influence elections.[3] The firm paid Dr. Aleksandr Kogan of Cambridge University to develop a personality quiz app, "thisis yourdigitallife." Touted as being for academic use, the app scraped data from Facebook users' friends, without the social network's knowledge.

Algorithms then combined this data, according to former CA staffer Christopher Wylie, "with other sources such as voter records to create a superior set of records . . . with hundreds of data points per person."[4] The firm also purchased data from giant aggregator firms such as Acxiom, Experian, and Infogroup. It was then easy to personalize direct political advertising to unsuspecting individuals. Disinformation and fear-based messaging were sent to people whom CA identified as emotionally unstable or who might make snap decisions, to dissuade them from voting, according to whistleblower and former CA staffer Brittany Kaiser. Kaiser says there are hundreds of other "Cambridge Analyticas" out there.[5]

Despite practices like this, Madison Avenue advertisers aren't creating PSAs urging data protection. Slogans like "If You See Something, Say Something," addressed later in this book, in Myth 19, convince civilians that spying on one another is a civic duty. Apps like Neighbors and Nextdoor are popular vehicles to share information about home repair recommendations, attempted auto thefts, or suspicious activity. And for $2,000 a year, Flock Safety will install a private license plate reader on a pole to track the comings and goings of all cars on your street. These apps, cameras, and social media platforms influence profit and politics, while marketing a false sense of benign community.

The prevailing message is clear: share your personal information for convenience and total connectivity. Tech companies market the tools of electronic surveillance as our friends, while disguising the lucrative business of gathering and selling personal data as essential for security: "Smart" homes are more secure. Biometrics are unhackable. Surveillance makes the nation safer. And so on.

Preferences expressed on Facebook, as the Cambridge Analytica scandal shows, purportedly enliven exchanges with friends but can also reflect, and affect, our choices in the voting booth. The masters of the surveillance state—marketers, contractors, and government agencies—make it easy to enlist but quite difficult to get answers about what they do with our information. That's like stashing the crown jewels in a motel room safe, and then leaving the code on a Post-it. Yet we do it daily.

TECH ILLITERATES ON HIGH

Every two seconds a new victim of identity theft is born in the United States. Experian estimates that more than 30 percent of data breach victims will have their identity stolen.[6]

Why is that? Once they amass our information, aren't big corporations and the government safeguarding it in their databases?

Lawmakers aren't doing enough to learn about cybersecurity and hold large database managers accountable for data breaches. Sloppy security practices—both by corporations and government agencies—expose wide swaths of credit card numbers, social security numbers, passwords, and other personal information to hackers.

Another reason identity theft is an epidemic in the US is that federal law enforcement agencies (the FBI, NSA, and others) handle data under the illusion that they are computer geeks, super sleuths able to avert threats to national security with the press of a computer key. In fact, the entire government suffers from tech illiteracy that was exposed when the FBI tried to force Apple to provide access to a terror suspect's iPhone in 2016. A 2020 audit of the FBI's information security program and practices identified weaknesses or "control deficiencies, in five of the eight domain areas that need strengthening to ensure adequate protection of the Bureau's information systems and data."[7] As Emily Dreyfuss noted in *Wired*: "Digital illiteracy at every level of government endangers the security of the nation and the functioning of democracy."[8]

Errors abound, corrupting the dossiers held on millions of Americans. The mundane task of entering data incorrectly can be life altering. That happened to Muslim graduate student Rahinah Ibrahim. She was stranded in Malaysia for nine years after the United States barred her reentry in 2005. An FBI agent had mistakenly added her to a terror watch list by checking the wrong box on a form.[9]

The National Crime Information Center (NCIC) database has also been susceptible to errors in profiles of individuals. This database is a central resource for more than eighty thousand law enforcement agencies. Defying common sense, the FBI, in 2019, exempted the NCIC database from provisions of the Privacy Act of 1974's mandate that federal agencies keep all records used by the agency accurate, relevant, and complete.[10] This means that more than thirty-nine million NCIC records, relied on by law enforcement, may include errors.

Each day new privacy intrusions come to light. During the upsurge in online learning due to the 2020 COVID-19 pandemic, hackers set their sights on e-learning portals such as Unacademy. More than sixteen billion sensitive records were exposed in data breaches between 2019 and the summer of 2020, according to the blockchain startup SelfKey.[11] The company claims that the first quarter of 2020 was one of the worst in the history of data breaches—with eight billion records exposed. OneClass, a Canadian class note-sharing platform for students, was breached after an unsecured Elasticsearch database exposed the personal information of more than one million students across North America.[12]

Breaches of online classes are just the tip of the pandemic-related data breach iceberg, whose impact will likely be far-reaching. Efforts to quell the novel coronavirus have sent tech companies and public health officials scrambling for ways to track its spread. Left unchecked, valid public health objectives may pave the way for more insidious and permanent means of government surveillance. "We could so easily end up in a situation where we empower local, state or federal government to take measures in response to this pandemic that fundamentally change the scope of American civil rights," says Albert Fox Cahn, head of the Surveillance Technology Oversight Project in Manhattan.[13]

SENTINELS OF SURVEILLANCE

Concerns about data privacy and its effects on fundamental rights are filtering into the mainstream. Many realize that what we thought were truisms are in fact modern myths.

What if national security is hindered, not helped, by our massive surveillance apparatus? Historian Matthew Guariglia explains that mass surveillance—and the overflow of data accumulation that comes with it—has posed a problem for intelligence services since the 1800s. "Aided as much by innovations like the vertical filing cabinet as spy software such as PRISM, government agencies in the United States have repeatedly struggled with the problem of using information produced by over-surveying and over-retaining."[14]

Bruce Schneier, whose website Schneier on Security is a go-to source for analysis on electronic surveillance and cybersecurity, concurs. In 2014, he noted, "It is unclear how effective targeted surveillance against 'enemy' countries really is. Even when we learn actual secrets, as we did regarding Syria's use of chemical weapons earlier this year, we often can't do anything with the information."[15]

Others on the vanguard of the digital age continue to sound the alarm.

For example, the *New York Times* Privacy Project regularly identifies threats to individual data privacy and gives suggestions for how to keep more of our data private. Organizations such as the Electronic Frontier Foundation educate the public about threats to privacy and challenge intrusive practices in court. The Institute for Technology Law and Policy at Georgetown Law provides training and resources for attorneys and legislators, in part to reframe how we think about regulating new technologies in the networked era.

In popular culture, a host of myths blind us to these facts: an all-seeing state is not inevitable; the threats such a state poses to democratic institutions are not inescapable; and there are better alternatives to the way data is handled.

DEBUNKING THE MYTHS

This book debunks twenty-one myths about surveillance and privacy. It shows how believing these myths hastens the forfeiture of privacy and personal agency, and tarnishes fundamental freedoms.

The first section relates to personal and national security. Many believe that encryption and anonymity tools are the domain of criminals, even though they help prevent ransomware attacks and other cyber intrusions. Millions invest in "smart" homes equipped with newfangled security devices, blind to total connectivity's portal into their intimate lives.

The second section, on protections and immunities, discusses myths that lead us to believe in the good faith of authorities and others. Societal rules will protect children, we assume, because of their youth and innocence. We trust that institutions and leaders will safeguard democratic norms such as a free press or the right to legal counsel, and that the courts, the Constitution, and Congress will assure fundamental notions of privacy.

The third section lays out the impact that surveillance has on autonomy, communities, and society. We change how we act, according to numerous studies, when we know we're being watched. Do we have a civic duty to watch and report on our neighbors? Who suffers the most in a mass surveillance state?

The insecurity of our data is political, a threat to our fundamental human and constitutional rights. But the reason that privacy is imperiled has less to do with political forces than economic ones. This "crude oil of the information age" has earned billions for companies like Facebook and Google, whose customers deal in massive amounts of user information to tailor advertising, profile consumers and voters, and manipulate unsuspecting people through the content they deliver.

STEALTH BY DESIGN

Product design is informed by data's value in the digital economy and political sphere. And, by design, everyday devices reinforce the myths that carve out the space in which the surveillance industry operates. Integral to breaking down myths is understanding how the tools of convenience—Apple iPhones, Ring doorbells, Alexa, Siri, and so on—are engines of intrusion.

We school designers in "captology," the psychological and technological tricks that capture users' attention and hook them into continuing to use a given product. Like cigarettes from Philip Morris labs, apps are made to be addictive, as creators find novel ways to monopolize their customers' attention. In designing new products, there's little incentive to build in privacy protections—and every incentive not to. The result is a factory farming of our personal data: apps with few privacy protections manipulate us into spending more time and giving more information, feeding the insatiable corporate hunger to amass information about every aspect of our lives.

The combination of captology and lax design is a powerful cocktail: whether inadvertent or intentional, product design today has the power to influence our behavior and control what we say and do. Captology was at the heart of outside interference from all sides in the 2016 presidential election. It wasn't just Cambridge Analytica's massive stolen cache of Facebook data; it was also Russia's sweeping disinformation campaign to manipulate political debate—and the body politic.

Government spying—an accumulation of power over its citizens—
is made more effective and more insidious by the data collection that's
going on in the private sector. There are legal limits on how government
agencies can gather data on individual citizens, but they don't apply to
corporate snooping. Some practices, for example, have done end runs
around the law. In the years following the attacks of September 11, 2001,
AT&T furnished millions of Americans' call logs to the NSA. Authorized under the USA PATRIOT Act, this surveillance was conducted
without warrants or subpoenas. Despite the 2006 testimony of whistleblower Mark Klein, a former AT&T employee, at the time the story got
little media—much less congressional—attention.[16]

DISENGAGING FROM DIGITAL DOMINANCE

It's time to undo the compromises made since September 11, 2001. There
is no reason, for example, that we can't expect the design of tech products to keep our privacy in mind. Sensible regulations have been proposed, akin to what we apply in areas ranging from trading stocks to
driving cars, that would build privacy protections into the emerging
digital fabric of society. A different online world is still within our reach.

But first we must understand and challenge the ways we've been
convinced that privacy is unimportant, unattainable, or even dangerous. In deflating the myths surrounding digital surveillance, we pave
the way for reasonable changes in how companies can access our personal data, and in what we expect by way of modern privacy rights.

Read on, and explore the movement for privacy: the core of liberty
in the online age.

PART ONE

PERSONAL AND NATIONAL SECURITY

MYTH 1

"SMART HOMES
ARE MORE SECURE"

"Clap on! Clap off!"

The Clapper, a sound-activated light switch, debuted in TV ads in 1985. Soon millions of delighted Americans were clapping their lights on and off like children with a new toy. Decades later, more sophisticated "smart" devices have insinuated themselves into domestic life in much the same way. Around the globe, the market for these items increases about 12 percent annually and is estimated to reach 125 billion devices by 2030.[1] Residential security monitoring devices are among the most popular of these. It's no wonder: In one survey by Safety.com, 74 percent of those polled said home security technology makes them feel safer.[2]

A smart home is one equipped with internet-connected appliances, devices, and systems that can be turned on or off remotely by phone or computer. They are based on a concept familiar to anyone who has channel surfed with a wireless remote control, invented in 1898 by Nikola Tesla. Thermostats, lights, televisions, window blinds, toothbrushes, doorbells, refrigerators, and vacuum cleaners are some of the products that can be smart. Public energy and water utility operations and metering are also being increasingly digitized in urban areas.

Among the proclaimed benefits of automated homes are convenience, improved security, energy savings, and resale value. Smart homes often include sophisticated security cameras, motion sensors, and direct connections to private security companies or the local police station. By employing key cards or biometric identification rather than traditional locks, they can make illegal entries more difficult.

Because smart homes employ cutting edge technology, many assume that they are more secure than non-automated ones.

That is a myth.

Smart homes are invasive hives of electronic sensors. They gather, store, and transmit data to third parties—including manufacturers, marketers, and government agencies—about residents' activities and proclivities. They don't just track user habits or energy consumption; they also enable eavesdropping on conversations. In 2017 many were shocked to learn that not only did Samsung smart televisions record conversations in a room, but that Samsung then sent those recordings to government agencies including the CIA. Former CIA director Michael Hayden told TV host Stephen Colbert, "There are bad people in the world that have Samsung TVs, too. You want us to have the ability to actually turn on that listening device inside the TV to learn that person's intentions. This is a wonderful capability."[3]

Smart home surveillance has been likened to a "private security dumpster fire."[4] Gadget providers often link third-party companies to each device, including marketing firms. Data gathered isn't necessarily secured in its new repositories. Researchers from the UK consumer organization *Which?*, in a 2018 report, exposed a flaw in a smart home camera application that provided access to more than two hundred thousand passwords and device IDs. Live video feeds of other users were exposed, and direct lines of communication opened to those users through camera microphones.

One couple in Wisconsin told how a hacker accessed their smart home devices, harassing them over a 24-hour period by setting their Google Nest thermostat to 90 degrees and talking to the family through a camera. Google Nest is a brand of smart home products that includes smoke detectors, doorbells, locks, security systems, and speakers, among others.

Google's response was that users needed to employ two-factor verification to avoid this kind of hack. It claimed that Nest itself was not compromised but rather that the users' passwords were exposed through breaches on other websites. The difference, for many, is just semantics. For Google, the solution brings in even more company-reliant customers, given that for Nest users to access the additional security protections, they would have to migrate to a Google account. As Google added, "Millions of users have signed up for two-factor verification."[5]

ENTER AMAZON

Despite these vulnerabilities, the business of home automation systems—also called *domotics*—is expected to grow in value to more than $17 billion by 2024.[6] Amazon has staked claim to a huge corner of the market. Central to its efforts to become a smart home security provider is its smart doorbell Ring, which it acquired in 2018. When one is not at home, a smart doorbell camera pings your phone when it senses motion or when someone rings the doorbell. Ring films and records all interactions and movement at the threshold, then alerts users' phones. Matthew Guariglia of the Electronic Frontier Foundation notes that Amazon's foothold in the smart home/smart appliance world banks on the strategy of integrating security with surveillance. It behooves the company to feed into fears of crime, even though, nationally, crime stats are on the decline.[7]

With Ring's neighborhood surveillance capability, Amazon began aggressively pursuing video-sharing partnerships with law enforcement, even hosting parties at their conferences. As of 2019, more than four hundred police departments across the nation had potential access to homeowner's video recordings, according to the *Washington Post*.

Guariglia says Ring has created a CCTV network that belongs to Amazon. The company cooperates with police by providing surveillance data, circumventing the search warrants required for government agencies seeking such information.[8] Ring officials focus their marketing on a shared community value of safety while ignoring civil liberties violations. Many public officials are contractually obligated to promote Ring products. At least fourteen US cities, and one in the UK, have paid Amazon up to $100,000 in matching funds to subsidize cameras that police then sell at a discount to residents. An interface allows police to access Ring cameras with the touch of a button. Users can opt out, but the unspoken message is that if you do, you're a bad citizen, uninterested in helping to stop crime in your neighborhood. This incentivizes residents to cooperate with police by signing away their privacy. Many police departments have maps of Ring device locations. Footage is stored in Amazon's cloud and Amazon can use that footage for pretty much whatever purpose it wants.

"Every time a delivery person comes to the door. Every time a dog walker comes by you get a notification on your phone. Suddenly it seems like your house is under siege," says Guariglia. "People think they're getting peace of mind and security, but they are getting paranoia. What they're not thinking about is how all these cameras are networked together. You're not just watching your own porch. You're helping police and Amazon watch every house in your neighborhood."[9] Ring has used camera footage showing alleged criminal offenders in sponsored ads on social media, without permission from the subjects or the homeowners. In an August 2019 Electronic Frontier Foundation post, Guariglia notes that Ring's terms of service allow for unlimited right to reuse, modify, display and create derivative works.

Ring and other home security devices can also have a chilling effect on speech. Guariglia asks how comfortable political canvassers would be if they knew their interactions were being recorded and could be shared by Amazon with the click of a button. In addition to creating a permanent record of community organizers, comings and goings, this Big Brother aspect of Ring networks can manifest a chilling effect on neighborhood interactions.

SPY CHIPS AND THE INTERNET OF THINGS

Let's step back. How did smart devices enter our lives?

In 2000, Kevin Ashton needed a way to track lipstick inventory. He consulted with two MIT researchers who had been seeking to miniaturize radio frequency ID technology, or RFID chips. The three devised a way to put a chip with a unique identification number on each lipstick tube, which would be more specific than bar codes that only identified product types. These chips, the size of a grain of rice, can be implanted into clothes, electronic devices, and even human beings.[10]

Soon, the technology had developed enough so that additional information could be stored. Credit card companies began embedding the chips to track users' activities. RFID technology enabled the development of appliances, households, pets, and even human bodies that are increasingly internet-connected or "smart." From stoplights and sewage plants to electric and nuclear grids, the nation's critical infrastructure systems are also being connected to the internet.

Thus was born the Internet of Things: all the devices embedded with software, sensors, and network connectivity—including the home security devices we've just discussed. Connected devices monitor physical objects, extract certain data, and communicate that data through IP networks to software applications. Rice-sized RFID implants enable machines' communication with other machines.

For corporations, the Internet of Things (IoT) is their cash cow of the near future. Cloud-connected sensors—including cameras, microphones, fingerprint readers, gyroscopes, motion detectors, and infrareds—collect virtually endless data about Americans' movements, preferences, and habits. This data is used by marketing companies to feed the needs of an equally hungry populace, providing convenience to consumers and suggestions of new or related products they can consume. Thus, the IoT opens new vistas of profits for the corporations that gather this information and use it to better market their products to increasingly segmented and well-targeted audiences.

Including to children.

"We're indoctrinating our youngest members of society to accept this technology," warns Liz McIntyre, coauthor of *Spychips: How Major Corporations and Government Plan to Track Your Every Move.* "RFID chip technology is creeping into everyday items. Several toys can identify the food children are eating. We see cooking sets, Little Tykes, that can talk to you," she recites with encyclopedic knowledge. "This mirrors plans in society to have RFID ubiquitous in the things we buy, wear, and carry. Reader devices [are] in public places and in our kitchens, in our stoves, so that information is shared in vast databases in public places as well as in our private spaces."[11]

Corporations and futurists extol the efficiency of the Internet of Things, when our devices can communicate independently to fulfill our needs. The vision they spin out is one of homes that take care of themselves, freeing us from the daily toil of existence, spreading freedom and leisure through a technologically interconnected future—and filling shareholders' pockets.

What was once the province of the futurists of an earlier age is increasingly becoming an expectation of the masses.

But the IoT promises to be more than just a threat to individual privacy.

Vulnerable points of access exist in each connection. Cybersecurity expert Nadir Izrael described the effect of the popular Amazon product Alexa: "As we make everything smarter and more connected, we end up creating a huge attack surface on devices."[12] Alexa insinuates her way into our homes, connecting with hundreds of devices. This all-facilitating virtual assistant can offer music and pizza; she can dim the lights and arm home security systems. Giving would-be attackers such a broad surface to target not only exposes private citizens, but it also exposes emergency services and national security as more devices afford multiple service providers and vendors with access to handle software and service upgrades.

Private communications service providers put profit before protection with the IoT. The Federal Trade Commission, whose mission is to promote consumer protection, acknowledges this. With an eye to cybersecurity risk reduction, in 2017 it looked at this growing "exposed attack surface"—picture an intergalactic dart board—created by connected consumer devices on privately owned and managed communications networks.[13] There were thirty thousand private sector communications service providers, all prioritizing profit over security.

CYBER CITIES

Having found a home for their devices in residential security, Google and other tech titans are on to bigger pursuits: smart cities.

It was bound to happen. These cities are designed with connectivity from the ground up. Personal data informs and determines how all city functions and resources are managed. Also called wired cities, they use different electronic data collection sensors to supply information used to deploy resources. Data from residents and devices is processed and analyzed to monitor and manage water, power, policing, education, hospitals, traffic, and transportation systems. By merging information and communication technology, proponents claim they will maximize efficiency, safety, and economic growth. Smart cities essentially become the conductors of the orchestra of life. Corporations tout them as models of efficiency, safety, and economy.

"Dystopian techno-capitalist hellscapes." That's how *New York Times* columnist Farhad Manjoo describes big tech's interest in building cities.[14]

Sidewalk Labs, backed by Google's parent company, Alphabet, announced plans in late 2017 to design a smart city on twelve acres in Toronto's industrial district of Quayside. The test site was supposed to host a "microgrid" to power driverless electric cars, include mixed-use spaces to bring down housing costs, and employ "sensor-enabled waste separation" to aid recycling. It would have become a "global hub for urban innovation." Yet partnering with an American colossus in this way is not in itself innovation, say critics. They assert that the practical elements have not been well thought out.

Tech activist Bianca Wylie is one such critic: "We're twenty years into this idea that technology happens to us. Socially, it's important that we begin to exert human agency and not let corporations define us."[15]

Around the time of Sidewalk Labs' announcement, Wylie and three other activist entrepreneurs launched Tech Reset Canada. They urged long-term responsibility in tech planning, notably focusing on how corporations will collect and sell personal data. For them, the Quayside project raised more questions than its proponents could answer. For example, would it discriminate against those who opt out of private data collection? Would they be given non-data-driven limits on water consumption and other public goods? What would it all mean for visitors?

"Lines between market and state blur. When you start to have input about privatization, and a new interface, there are a whole host of new issues," says Wylie. She saw Toronto's smart city as a test bed for new technologies rather than what is best for residents. "It's not the place to be having a research and development lab because you're seeking profits globally. Hype around innovation is one thing, but who gets stuck with the tab to maintain it and keep it secure? That should be public infrastructure. When you begin to entrench corporations into the functioning of a municipality, it's hard to get those out."[16]

In 2020, Sidewalk Labs announced the cancellation of their billion-dollar smart city plan. While it cited the COVID-19 pandemic as the reason for abandoning the project, had the company not run into community opposition, it might well have proceeded.[17]

The problems inherent in smart cities also plague smart homes and the neighborhoods they capture on camera. In addition to bringing surveillance devices into homes, they can end up threatening vulnerable communities.

Matt Guariglia mentions the case of an African American real estate agent walking through a neighborhood, as agents do, appraising the real estate. One person opened their Ring app and reported that someone was casing the house in order to come back and burglarize it later. "This can put people in danger who have done nothing wrong other than taking a stroll through the neighborhood," says Guariglia. "Amazon Ring is a digital superhighway for racial profiling," the privacy expert continues. "If every person that walks by your camera is a potential criminal, a lot of implicit or real biases surface. When you can share that footage with police and everybody in the neighborhood that has the app, suddenly racial profiling gets outsized. What looks suspicious to some comes to the surface."

"Part of what is so nefarious," concludes Guariglia, "is when you buy a Ring to keep your house safe, it's hard to conceptualize it as part of a large, state-accessible surveillance network. As people start to realize that their domestic decisions have national and community implications, I'm hoping we'll start to see some pushback."[18]

"I HAVE NOTHING TO HIDE, SO I HAVE NOTHING TO FEAR"

Shortly after 12:30 a.m. on March 13, 2020, three plainclothes police officers descended on Breonna Taylor's apartment in Louisville, Kentucky. The twenty-six-year-old EMT and aspiring nurse was asleep with her boyfriend, Kenneth Walker. They awoke suddenly to a loud bang.

"Who is it?"

"Who's there?"

As if to answer, the door flew off its hinges, felled by a battering ram. Sergeant Jonathan Mattingly and Detectives Brett Hankisonn and Myles Cosgrove entered forcefully without identifying themselves.

A licensed firearm carrier, Walker fired a shot in self-defense at the non-uniformed officers, hitting one in the leg. Police returned fire, unleashing a battery of rounds into Taylor's home. Taylor was struck five times. Detective Cosgrove fired the lethal shot.

What had young Breonna Taylor done to warrant this frenzy of lethal bullets?

What was she hiding?

It turns out, she'd done nothing wrong. And she was hiding nothing.

Police, on the other hand, had botched a search-warrant execution. Taylor wasn't even the target of their investigation. A detective alleged that two months earlier he spotted a former boyfriend of Taylor's leaving her apartment with a package, before driving to a known drug house more than ten miles away. A judge signed a no-knock warrant permitting police to enter Taylor's home. The fact is, the former boyfriend was sitting in police custody before the warrant was even executed on Taylor's home.

As Walker sat in the squad car, a plainclothes official arriving on the scene in an unmarked SUV said to him: "I just want to let you know right now that all of this was a—they had a misunderstanding."[1]

PLENTY TO FEAR

As the Taylor tragedy shows, the popular myth "I have nothing to hide, so I have nothing to fear" misses the mark. Individuals with a clean criminal record can't expect to be immune from overreaching police and prosecutors. Did racism play a role in this situation? Of course. The officers were white and the victims were black. But white people should not assume they will be exempted from a similar overreach, which may have tragic results.

Of equal concern are the number of obscure laws on the books for which people can be arrested. Anyone may run afoul of laws they don't even know exist. New laws are passed annually. Cyberstalking, hate crimes, inappropriate workplace comments, and certain kinds of animal abuse are examples of activities that were not criminalized until the late twentieth century.

As former defense attorney James Duane, a professor at Regent Law School, notes: "It has been reported that the Congressional Research Service cannot even count the current number of federal crimes. These laws are scattered in over 50 titles of the United States Code, encompassing roughly 27,000 pages." And that, Duane notes, doesn't even include regulations put forth by federal agencies and authorized by Congress. The American Bar Association estimates there are nearly ten thousand.[2]

Prosecutors have indicted outspoken activists on unrelated charges as reprisal for challenging government policies, just to disparage their reputation. For example, the New York City Department of Education's Office of Special Investigations opened an investigation into a public school principal, Jill Bloomberg, who had critiqued the education system for discriminating against students of color. She was investigated for Communist organizing. The year was 2017.[3]

In 1985, New York chief judge Sol Wachtler said that prosecutors could convince a grand jury to indict a "ham sandwich."[4] Modern surveillance makes their job even easier. Personally identifying information gathered on millions of Americans by many corporate and government actors is readily accessible by law enforcement. If the authorities want to pursue someone in criminal court they have plenty of data at their fingertips from which to cobble together specious charges.

PRIVACY, EVEN FOR LAWBREAKERS

The "I have nothing to hide" myth suggests that people who break the law do not deserve privacy.

They absolutely do. Anyone who has watched a television police procedural knows the extent to which investigators must go to secure search warrants to enter a suspect's home to conduct a search for evidence supporting criminal activity. If they can't show probable cause, or specific reasons suggesting a crime is afoot, they are barred from entry.

The rule of law imposes such constraints on police powers to ensure that a suspect's rights are respected during a criminal investigation. That's because our justice system is based on the principle that everyone is innocent until proven guilty in a court of law. The Breonna Taylor murder is an example of what happens when constraints on policing go awry. It also demonstrates that judges can be complicit; the judge granting the no-knock warrant essentially signed Taylor's death warrant by not requiring police to show their suspect was likely to be at Taylor's apartment.

The innocent-until-proven-guilty precept has been around for centuries, dating as far back as the 1500s, when it was used to protect people from torture. It was codified in the 1894 Supreme Court case *Coffin v. United States*, when it held that, in a criminal trial, the trial court had improperly refused to instruct the jury on the presumption of innocence.[5] Since then, numerous international treaties and legal systems protect the principle. The presumption of innocence—the companion of privacy—is crucial to ensuring a fair trial and preserving the integrity of the justice system. That's why the "I have nothing to hide" myth fails in suggesting that some deserve more privacy than others.

The "nothing to hide" myth also demonstrates a lack of understanding of how Americans' data is stockpiled. It presupposes that if you have a clean slate, no one will be interested in you. Information gathered is stored indefinitely and for use at any future time—no matter how benign one thinks one's life is—in ways most people do not fathom. Vast quantities of data bring an increase in errors. Misspelled names and incorrectly entered information—such as when the FBI agent checked the wrong box and landed Rahinah Ibrahim on a watch list—in health, police, and other administrative records have resulted in grave miscarriages of justice.[6]

PRIVACY MATTERS

"I have nothing to hide" adherents assert that minimal intrusion exists if the person monitored has committed no crime. Their thinking may stem from a sincere desire to be a dutiful citizen, with the rationale being: "Giving up a small amount of privacy is worth it if it keeps us safe from terrorism."

It's a fallacy that we must choose between safety and privacy. We can have both. Unquestioning faith in state and corporate power may jeopardize rather than protect long-cherished freedoms.

Privacy is important in ways that are not immediately obvious and, in some instances, can mean the difference between life and death. The nature of privacy, however, is such that we can't turn it on and off like a light switch, nor can we apportion it and give it away in incremental amounts.

Privacy advances several societal interests. One interest is sustaining public health and welfare. Victims of domestic abuse who have escaped life-endangering relationships, for example, are at greatest risk of homicide. Government databases and other public records are carefully regulated to ensure the safety of victims. Without confidentiality, these individuals would be at great risk of experiencing bodily harm—or death.

The National Suicide Prevention Lifeline allows callers to be anonymous if they wish. The hotline answered more than two million callers in 2018, likely saving countless lives. Certain tests, as for HIV, can be conducted confidentially or anonymously. If confidential, results are part of one's medical records but are protected by state and federal privacy laws. Early knowledge of HIV infection is crucial in reducing mortality rates; privacy can encourage more people to get tested and, if need be, treated.

Most people are probably familiar with the importance of privacy in reporting official malfeasance, waste, and abuse, or helping police solve crimes. Callers—or electronic filers—to the federal Government Accountability Office's FraudNet hotline are given three choices of privacy: standard, confidential, or anonymous.[7] Many states have similar hotlines. And law enforcement hotlines for tips related to criminal activity also offer anonymity. The New York Police Department's Crime Stoppers hotline, for example, doesn't trace or record calls, nor does it ask for names. Email and IP addresses are not captured, tracked, or saved. As of 2019, tips to police helped solve more than 1,500 murders or attempted murders and solved nearly 2,500 robberies.[8]

A bedrock of American society is respect for individual autonomy. Autonomy is manifested in different ways. We exercise it regarding medical, legal, and education matters as well as intimate relationships and other facets of life when we decide what and when we reveal to others. We desire control over what we consider socially appropriate in varying contexts. For example, with an intimate partner we may wish to exchange texts or images that we wouldn't necessarily want shared with anyone else or added to an electronic dossier about us. Or we may want to share images from social events that we would prefer to keep private from employers—even years into the future. Without privacy, we lose autonomy.

Exercising autonomy includes freedom of expression, especially when one's ideas rub against the grain of the status quo. Just knowing we're under surveillance, even if we don't object to it, changes how we act. We alter our behavior, usually trying to conform or put our best face forward.

Researchers discovered this when they commissioned a series of studies in the 1920s on worker productivity. At Hawthorne Works, a

Western Electric Factory outside Chicago, they examined the impact of coworkers and different lighting levels in the workplace. Researchers found that subjects altered some of their behavior—to be on their "best" behavior—when they knew they were being monitored.[9] They called this the Hawthorne effect.

In general parlance, we call this reaction "the observer effect." In 1986, UK psychologists stationed in eighteen different homes welcomed costumed children on Halloween. In half of the houses they placed a mirror and left the children alone with a candy bowl, secretly recording the children. The researchers' theory was that kids near the mirrors would be less apt to sneak a handful of candy if they saw their reflection. They were correct. Even in costumed faces, those children exercised restraint in treat-taking.[10]

Acting differently when we know we are being watched impedes freedom of association and expression. This is true even with constitutional protections for political and religious views, what we read and write, and who we gather with. The simple fact is that when people perceive that their actions and preferences don't align with mainstream views, they tend to forgo the things in life that are important to them. This includes the essence of who they are as human beings.

Everyone has an expectation of privacy in the sanctity of their homes, even to be able to withdraw from family members for quiet thought. That expectation is so strong that twenty-three states have castle laws, also called defense of habitation laws, designating a person's home a place worthy of protection and legal immunity.[11] Several countries, including Australia, Canada, Germany, Italy, and Sweden have equivalent laws. The need for and reliance on privacy is built into the DNA of life. Doors on bathrooms, shower curtains, shades or curtains in windows, and locks on doors and apartment mailboxes guard against unwanted intrusion. It's a form of privacy Americans take for granted.

SECURITY VS. INDIVIDUAL RIGHTS

Tensions between state desires and individual rights date back to the aftermath of the American Revolution.

Protections against intrusive spying were enshrined in the Bill of Rights in 1789. Also protected was the notion of private property as a place to exercise personal liberties. Both were measures to guard against humanity's authoritarian tendencies. Despite this, courts from then and up until the present day have rarely held in favor of individual rights in cases involving government and corporate surveillance. After the attacks of September 11, 2001, dozens of legal challenges to government civil liberties intrusions were lost with two conversation-stopping words: national security.[12] That should concern us all.

There's not much evidence that surveillance makes us safer, as we'll explore in greater detail in Myth 7. Weak computer and database security has far-reaching implications, leading to whole-system hijacking by ransomware, which can impact the health and welfare of millions. Because of that, one of the major underlying presumptions of the myth of "I have nothing to hide" is false.

BLIND FAITH IN STATE AND CORPORATE POWER

While automation of records and mobility of citizens have advanced since the nation's early days, more abstract fears of government overreach remain constant. An overarching problem with the "I have nothing to hide" myth is its implicit trust in how government officials treat the personal data they gather. Unfortunately, federal agencies and their corporate partners have proven that they cannot be trusted to operate in good faith. Civil rights leaders and antiwar activists are just a few of the values-driven people that both government and big business have monitored, infiltrated, and harassed for opposing the status quo. With the rise in popularity of social media platforms controlled by corporate monoliths, Americans' privacy choices impact others. The privacy needs or desires of friends, family, and community may be harmed by one's decisions to be unconcerned about one's own digital privacy. And how the self-proclaimed guardians of our data protect it is equally troublesome. Massive data breaches have exposed millions of individuals' private information, opening them up to identity theft and fraud.

The US voter database, the Office of Personnel Management, and the Department of Veterans Affairs are some of the agencies whose inadequate security resulted in exposing millions of sensitive data records. Corporate data breaches occur on a regular basis, with Equifax, LinkedIn, and Adobe being a few examples. Human error was to blame for most of these breaches, whether from improperly configured databases, device theft, or misplaced hard drives.

By now, the United States and other countries are far enough into the surveillance state that proponents of these myths should question the integrity of government motives. Daily news reports reveal how government agencies and corporations misuse Americans' data. The public should understand how surveillance furthers the interests of those motivated by profit, and those with an interest in suppressing voices of dissent. Blind trust in the government and its corporate partners—especially around high-tech mass surveillance initiatives—seems naive in the twenty-first century.

As for the myth, "I have nothing to hide"? It greatly underestimates the potentially repressive nature of the all-seeing state.

MYTH 3

"ENCRYPTION AND ANONYMITY TOOLS—THOSE ARE FOR TERRORISTS!"

American and British intelligence agents disguised themselves as wizards and sorcerers to spy on players of the wildly popular fantasy game World of Warcraft.[1]

That didn't happen in the movies; it happened in real life, according to leaked classified documents from 2008. Unsubstantiated fears that terrorists may communicate through games played by millions around the world led the FBI and CIA to monitor, collect data, and even recruit informants from the virtual world. Similar fears surfaced after the 2015 attacks in Paris, when Belgium's Minister of the Interior at the time, Jan Jambon, speculated that ISIS terrorists might have used Sony's PlayStation 4 to orchestrate their lethal attacks.[2]

Police see any form of communication that disguises one's identity, including online video games, as a potential enabler of crime. If you don't expose yourself to public view, their theory goes, you must be hiding something. Using this logic, lawmakers and law enforcement equate encryption and other online privacy tools with criminal activity.

This myth facilitates spying on Americans.

Using this myth, law enforcement pressures: (1) lawmakers to allow mass surveillance, and (2) tech and telecommunications companies to build "backdoors" for police access to equipment. Backdoors are secret ways to bypass encryption in a computer, router, or cell phone. They afford remote access to a device and enable access to plain text communications prior to encryption. It's like a locksmith handing police a special house key to use whenever they want to look around when you are out, without your knowledge or permission. As for encryption, this is how it works: an algorithm scrambles information, then uses an electronic key for the receiver to unscramble, or decrypt, that jumbled information.

It's true that many lawbreakers hide their communications with anonymity technology, including the Tor browser. Tor—it stands for "the onion router," suggesting layers of protection—is a digital tool that allows users to keep secret their browsing activity by routing internet use through thousands of relay points. Far from being for lawbreakers, however, Tor's development was funded largely by the United States Department of Defense and the Navy to protect national secrets.[3]

Contrary to myth, lawbreakers comprise a small percentage—just three percent—of the population who connect to hidden services or illicit websites. Most Tor users visit public websites for legitimate reasons. They just do so privately. And the most popular site frequented by Tor users? Facebook. In 2014, responding to demand for a way to privately communicate on the site, the social network added a way for Tor users to directly access it. As of 2016, it's been reported that more than one million people use Tor on Facebook on a monthly basis.[4]

In debunking the myth that encryption is for terrorists, consider the case of one privacy advocate in a small New England library.

As a youngster, Chuck McAndrew got into trouble when he saw an option for "Robot" on his father's computer. What child wouldn't react in delight? He excitedly pushed the button. What the youngster saw as "Robot" was actually "Reboot." His father lost an entire day's work.[5]

Years later, in 2015, a red-bearded McAndrew eased his car into the parking lot of Kilton Library in West Lebanon, New Hampshire, population 13,522. His technical acumen, much improved since the Robot incident, had landed him a job there as an IT librarian. The thirty-eight-year-old former Marine from Texas was about to learn that an agent from Homeland Security had tipped off local police about his latest handiwork. Police wanted to meet with library staff.

When McAndrew began working at Kilton Library in 2013, his first order of business was to secure the library's computer systems from external surveillance. He nixed Microsoft Windows because it is easy to hack into, and thus less able to protect users' privacy. Revelations would surface not long after that the tech company had participated in PRISM, the government's mass surveillance program. McAndrew installed Linux, an open-source operating system that is more difficult to hack. Open source means its source code is available free to the public to analyze and improve. Thousands of computer programmers globally have examined and refined Linux over years of use.

After switching to Linux, McAndrew made it even harder to spy on library patrons. Partnering with the Philadelphia–based nonprofit Library Freedom Project, in 2015 he installed Tor browser software on Kilton's computers. With this move, Kilton became the nation's first library to provide patrons with anonymous Web surfing. When a teenager looks up typical issues of concern that might be embarrassing if made public—say about relationships, sex, or depression—no one else can track his or her viewing activities. Without this protection a significant number of citizens, whose only way to access the internet is through the library, are vulnerable to surveillance by the government or third parties.

From his office in the modern and airy library, McAndrew explains the importance of this seemingly modest initiative, "We need to make strong encryption the default, not the exception. People would be shocked to see a car without locks on the doors and an alarm these days. They should be just as shocked when they find out about bad encryption practices."[6]

The Tor installation attracted the attention of an agent at the Department of Homeland Security's (DHS) Boston Bureau, when he read a news article about it. With the DHS tip-off, local police came to warn library staff that summer day that Tor might be attractive to persons conducting nefarious activities such as selling drugs or sharing child pornography. They asked: "Did library administrators want to grease the wheels of lawlessness?"[7]

That question was not without foundation, given how agents are indoctrinated. Fears of unmonitorable online activities preoccupy people like former FBI Director James Comey who want special access to encrypted devices. Intelligence officials call lack of access "going dark." In late 2014, Comey delivered remarks titled "Going Dark: Are Technology, Privacy, and Public Safety on a Collision Course?" at the Brookings Institution. Comey's focus was on an oft-repeated theme: bad guys will murder and terrorize if the Bureau can't read their communications.[8]

But Comey highlighted three homicide cases that had been solved without needing access to electronic devices. In one, a known sex offender in Louisiana, Brian Douglas Horn, posed as a teen girl who lured a twelve-year-old out at 3 a.m. and then strangled him to death. Horn was seen driving his taxicab to pick up the boy. When he ran out of gas a sheriff's deputy ran Horn's license and saw his sex offender registration. The boy was later reported missing; deputies found muddy footprints between the cab's location and the murder scene, where Horn had dropped his keys. That's how they apprehended him.

Comey confessed during the question-and-answer session that he had searched for examples hinging on cell-phone data but had none. In other words, one of the top law enforcement officials in the country could not find cases in which the solving of a crime hinged on access to the suspect's technology.

Comey wrote about his pet peeve in A Higher Loyalty:

> The leaders of tech companies don't see the darkness the FBI sees. Our days are dominated by the hunt for people planning terrorist attacks, hurting children, and engaging in organized crime. We see humankind at its most depraved, day in and day out. Horrific, unthinkable acts are what the men and women of the FBI live, breathe, and try to stop. I found it appalling that the tech types couldn't see this.[9]

This is not a healthy perspective from which to institutionalize laws enabling near total police access to Americans' communications. It distorts the reality of the relatively small number of lawbreakers using encryption.

Law enforcement's framing of surveillance and cryptography shapes how the mainstream sees it. Privacy and national security are depicted as irreconcilable, with emerging technology a setback to security. "It is a brilliant discourse of fear: fear of crime; fear of losing our parents' protection; even fear of the dark," observes computer science professor Phillip Rogaway.[10]

Intelligence and law enforcement agencies try to solve the "going dark" problem by lobbying to mandate backdoors in hardware. The Communications Assistance for Law Enforcement Act (CALEA) of 1994 was an early legislative effort to address "going dark." The law requires telecommunications carriers to offer police ways to comply with court orders for real time interceptions and call-identifying information.[11]

THE REALITY: ENCRYPTION HELPS SOCIETIES REMAIN FREE

Encryption protects many government systems, including those used by intelligence and law enforcement. Attorneys seeking confidential communications, the military, human rights activists avoiding repressive regimes, and others also rely on encryption.

Noted technology security expert Bruce Schneier observes, "Encryption protects our officials working at home and abroad. During the whole *Apple vs. FBI* debate, I wondered if Director James Comey realized how many of his own agents used iPhones and relied on Apple's security features to protect them."[12]

Prompted in part by widespread concerns about surveillance, many companies are creating communications services with built-in encryption, like Signal and Protonmail. These programs, along with Tor, have become popular as the public understands more about surveillance and seeks ways to avoid it. SecureDrop, launched in 2013, is Tor-powered software enabling anonymous and secure communication between journalists and sources. The *New York Times, Washington Post,* and other global news organizations all use SecureDrop.[13]

Shari Steele knows a lot about privacy tools. The California-based lawyer has served as the director of the Electronic Frontier Foundation and the Tor Project. She reflects on the effect of sensationalized stories about anonymity software and suggests a level of cluelessness on the part of law enforcement. Their leadership doesn't get this: if they are able to access encrypted communications, malicious hackers are also likely able to access them.

"It's unfortunate because the Dark Web is kind of sexy for journalists to pick up on. So a lot of times there are stories that demonize Tor as being the way, the channel, that's being used for criminal activity," she notes. "But Tor is much, much more than that. In fact, if you talk to any of the people who work on Tor, or see who the developers of Tor are, they're all freedom fighters. These are people who actually are doing it because they care passionately about making the world a better, safer place."[14]

During the Cold War, Steele explains, the US and allied nations tried to limit access to encryption by both the American public and other countries. They sought strong access limitations to thwart foreign intelligence agencies' efforts to decrypt and thus read American intelligence. At the same time, academics, researchers, computer engineers, privacy advocates, and others wanted to protect their user data and communications with encryption. The conflict became known as the Crypto Wars.

"Because it was only being used as a weapon during World War II, one thing that gave us a great advantage over Germany was our ability to decrypt the messages that they were sending back and forth. So that was a closely guarded secret," Steele notes. She also sees the impetus for change: "As technology developed and companies started to realize that to perform electronic transactions, they needed to protect the data going back and forth, classifying encryption as a munition limited their ability to do things."[15]

Financial institutions were not the only ones seeking to use encryption. A shift to personal computing and digital commerce made strong encryption necessary to protect financial and other data. The financial institutions won, and other industries followed, especially social media platforms and technology companies. Today, with the level of electronic communications performed by the average American—through cell phones, computers, and "smart" connected devices—regular citizens have a practical need for strong encryption technologies to keep even a minimal level of security over our information.

Two cases reveal continuing tensions between law enforcement and tech companies.

The first followed the mass shooting in San Bernardino, California, in December 2015. After police killed shooters Syed Rizwan Farook and his wife in a shootout, agents seized Farook's Apple iPhone while searching his Lexus. On February 9, 2016, Comey announced that the FBI lacked technical capability to access the phone and went to court to compel Apple to decrypt it. Apple refused. A month later, Azimuth, a cybersecurity firm, unlocked the phone. This "end run" around Apple, while troublesome, is preferable to forcing industry to change its principled stand.[16] In the second case, a gunman opened fire at the Pensacola Naval Air Station in Florida on December 6, 2019. The FBI again asked Apple to create tools to crack a newer iPhone model. By then, Apple had strengthened the phone's encryption, limiting its capacity to be broken.[17]

Also in 2019, Attorney General William P. Barr reiterated the encryption myth. He asserted that technology companies should stop using advanced encryption or other security measures that convert personal devices into "law-free zones."[18]

Shari Steele calls the Apple cases a new chapter in the so-called Crypto Wars, the battle between industry and the government over commercially available strong encryption: "It's a new angle of these crypto wars that have been going on for years and years. There is a natural tension between law enforcement [that] wants to be able to get access to everything easily, and our rights and our civil liberties. That tension has always existed and probably always will. The key is finding the right balance and making sure that as new technologies develop that we don't get out of balance."[19]

A 2018 *Washington Post* report found the FBI exaggerated the number of devices it says it can't open by at least four times.[20] This cast doubt on "going dark" claims, according to Greg Nojeim, director of the Center for Democratic Technology's Freedom, Security, and Technology Project. He urged the inspector general to investigate the FBI's inflated claim.[21] The *Post* report noted that private companies' technical solutions enable the FBI to access the content of iPhones, further compounding credibility concerns.

Tech industry leaders resist the myth that Tor and encryption are the domain of criminals. In response to William Barr's 2019 comments criticizing encryption, a coalition of 102 organizations and individuals wrote to senior officials in the US, the UK, and Australia (part of the Five Eyes alliance, which shares intelligence, along with Canada and New Zealand) explaining how compromising encryption would hurt the privacy and security of billions of individuals. The letter called out the FBI's exaggerated claims to Congress in 2017 that it had seized 7,800 encrypted and inaccessible phones. In fact, the number was 1,200.[22]

POLICYMAKERS' LEARNING CURVE

As for the New Hampshire library, what happened after the police visit? The library gave in to Homeland Security's wishes and stopped using Tor. But when residents got wind of what had happened, they responded in protest. Library officials soon restored the anonymity software.

On the issue of policymakers' siding with law enforcement on the encryption debate, IT librarian Chuck McAndrew is adamant: "We need to demand a level of technical competency from political leaders who legislate these matters," he says, citing subpar computer literacy in the nation's capital. "When politicians who make the rules don't understand these issues, you get government agencies that are largely unregulated by the political oversight that is supposed to prevent their excesses. You get laws that weaken security and endanger the average citizen while claiming to do the opposite."[23]

He raises an important point. Until prosecutors, defense attorneys, judges, and jurors understand the workings of the wired world, the enactment of ill-advised laws will continue. In the 2019 Facebook congressional hearings, for example, one senator had no idea how the platform was funded. Many federal judges know nothing about how technologies communicate, yet they cite national security concerns and summarily dismiss legal challenges to unconstitutional surveillance practices.

The privacy-protecting librarian continued, "The key is making people understand that strong encryption is not something that terrorists and criminals need. It is something that we all need in every aspect of our daily lives." A more secure information network requires a government commitment to shore up existing weaknesses of the internet's infrastructure. It also requires that they not further weaken it. Security experts have said this for years: Governments can't have it both ways. An internet that's resilient against fraud, criminal activity, and espionage is incompatible with backdoors for government surveillance.

Tor, says Steele, is a critical part of the infrastructure of internet freedom. "It is what freedom fighters around the world use to be able to communicate with one another and to be able to get the word out about the things that are happening in their countries."

Anonymity software and encryption allow activists to stand up to authoritarian rule. Government suspicion and surveillance—in places such as China and Iran, but also the United States—make the Web more dangerous for all if encryption is forbidden. Privacy is a keystone for those challenging authority and seeking accountability. As is clear from lawmakers' and law enforcement's disdain for encryption and software like Tor, ordinary and ancient desires for privacy cannot be conflated with covert criminal intent.

Librarian Chuck McAndrew puts it in context: "Saying someone has access to information is meaningless if societal pressure prevents that person from using that access. We may say that we don't censor authors, but if they make clear that your library records are subject to surveillance, then people won't read controversial books, and authors who write them won't get published."

On the issue of anonymity, he draws on history: "When Thomas Paine published *Common Sense* he did so anonymously. Having the privacy to explore the concepts embodied in this pamphlet and to write them down allowed him to write one of the most influential works in American history."[24]

MYTH 4

"WE SHOULD WORRY ABOUT GOVERNMENT, NOT CORPORATE, SURVEILLANCE"

The specter of government mass surveillance is ominous. But it's a myth that we should fear Uncle Sam more than Google. Corporations conduct massive surveillance as government contractors and for their own purposes. Profit is behind all. As we saw in Myth 1, they gather information on consumers through "smart" devices to sell to third parties. Corporate espionage, in order prevent employee theft of trade secrets, is its own multibillion-dollar market. Corporate spying also keeps tabs on, and silences, activists who criticize corporate malfeasance. With lucrative government contracts, corporate partners conduct much of the government's intelligence work. A two-year *Washington Post* investigation revealed that under the banner of counterterrorism, approximately 1,931 private security companies and 1,271 government organizations are currently engaged in intelligence gathering.[1]

As contractors, corporations skirt constitutional protections in ways that government agencies cannot do themselves. When it comes to surveillance, think of corporations as "butlers to the billionaires."

They do the dirty work for the one percent, helping maintain the power of the world's wealthiest people. Amanda Hess describes how privacy is monetized in the digital age. "We can either trade it for cheap services or shell out cash to protect it. It is increasingly seen not as a right but as a luxury good." She describes how after Congress voted in 2017 to allow internet service providers to sell users' data without consent, the issue of premium products arose. They would allow people to pay to protect browsing history from resale. When someone asked about those who couldn't afford to pay, one congressperson replied, "Nobody's got to use the internet." Hess points out the reality that nearly everyone must use it. "Tech companies have laid claim to the public square: All of a sudden, we use Facebook to support candidates, organize protests and pose questions in debates. We're essentially paying a data tax for participating in democracy."[2]

Disparities in monitoring have historic roots. After a slave revolt in 1712, New York City required slaves to carry lanterns if they went out after sundown unaccompanied by a white person. They had to be visible, and thus controllable. Corporate-run automated surveillance equipment performs similar functions in low-income neighborhoods. Barton Gellman and Sam Adler-Bell write: "Technology and stealth allow government watchers to remain unobtrusive when they wish to be so, but their blunter tools—stop-and-frisk, suspicionless search, recruitment of snitches, compulsory questioning on intimate subjects— are conspicuous in the lives of those least empowered to object."[3]

Another reason to be wary of corporate spying is the blurry distinctions between government and corporate monitoring. Corporate contractors conduct what we traditionally think of as government functions. Private security contractors, according to Big Data expert Kalev Leetaru, can include "quasi-employees who sit side-by-side with government employees at desks in government buildings."[4] We saw this in AT&T's collaboration with the NSA, revealed in 2006, and with Project Hemisphere, a covert program that began in 2007. Responding to DEA subpoenas (instead of court orders), the project granted agency personnel access to AT&T databases storing decades of phone calls.[5] Peace activist Drew Hendricks exposed Project Hemisphere in 2013 when his Freedom of Information Act requests revealed a Hemisphere PowerPoint training.

CONTRACTOR SPIES

Technological advances have reshaped some government functions. The National Security Agency's (NSA) original mission was to make and break code. Until 2013, most Americans believed that NSA targets were international. However, the Foreign Intelligence Surveillance Act (FISA) Amendments Act of 2008 authorizes the agency to monitor Americans' electronic communications and international phone calls under the guise of targeting international subjects.[6]

When whistleblower Edward Snowden disclosed covert government and corporate surveillance programs in 2013, he made clear the extent to which the NSA was abusing its mandate and scooping up troves of domestic information. The former CIA employee and contractor also exposed how private contractors conduct surveillance for the NSA and other agencies.

As for its code-breaking role, as Phillip Knightley wrote in 1986 in *The Second Oldest Profession*, the NSA's "usefulness has been declining in direct relationship to the rapid development of computers and their manufacture."[7] Knightly notes that as a result, the NSA morphed into producing intelligence community packages by "vacuuming the entire electromagnetic spectrum," with emphasis on "economics and trade."

In addition to Snowden, NSA employees Thomas Drake, Bill Binney, Ed Loomis, and J. Kirk Wiebe blew the whistle on widespread invasions of Americans' privacy. In 2002, they criticized a multibillion-dollar program called Trailblazer, the supreme failure of a pet contractor named SAIC, even though a better in-house program that they had designed in the 1990s, ThinThread, protected privacy and cost only $3.2 million. It was the perfect example of government cronyism gone awry. According to former NSA employee Bill Binney, contractors working on ThinThread were warned not to embarrass giant security contractors like SAIC, which failed to warn of the 9/11 attacks.[8]

The ThinThread/Trailblazer case is not a solitary one in the corporate–government symbiotic relationship. In general, federal agencies spend far too much on contracting out national security functions to fill the pockets of government cronies. The constant loser—because corporate contracting falls under the radar of the Constitution—is individual rights.

CORPORATE–GOVERNMENT PARTNERSHIPS

Contractors are among the first to acknowledge that they are not hindered by the Constitution as government agencies are. Eric Prince, the founder of military contractor Blackwater (the company has since been renamed due to bad publicity), has called for private mercenaries to fight in Afghanistan. Commentators noted that his army would operate freely. "The Bill of Rights would not constrain Prince's army from violating U.S. citizens' constitutional rights. . . . Federal statutes that limit government conflicts of interest and mandate transparency would not apply by their terms, either. Nefarious activity could occur in the name of the U.S. Government and there would be little the American electorate could do about it," writes Kimberly Wehle in *The Hill.*[9]

Such implicit corporate immunity from constitutional strictures and liability emboldens them to engage in surveillance and infiltration operations. An intricate surveillance network of police and private business is less accountable than the federal government is to the public.

When improper data-gathering by corporations *is* revealed, penalties lack teeth. Some court settlements or regulatory fines are no more than a slap on the wrist. In March 2012, for example, Google (with a net worth in 2020 of approximately $632 *billion*) reached a $7 *million* settlement with thirty-seven states and the District of Columbia to destroy personal data it collected from unsecured Wi-Fi networks—in violation of the Federal Wiretap Act, from its Street View project from 2008 to 2010.[10]

Fines have not deterred goliath Google's data accumulation and tracking activity. In 2020, appeals judges overturned a $5.5 million class-action settlement over alleged privacy violations from Google's use of cookies—text files with small bits of data used to identify your computer as you use a computer network—to track user data.[11] Despite some users' configuration to stop tracking, the cookies still worked. The Third Circuit judges expressed concern that the settlement eliminated the chance for millions of consumers to bring future cases against Google.[12] Theoretically, this is good for consumers concerned about surveillance. But how many consumers even know what Google is doing? Let alone have the wherewithal and funds necessary to sue for privacy breaches?

By joining forces with private information technology corporations, government authorities multiply surveillance's invasive properties. Through lucrative government contracts, or even just for their own intelligence operations, corporations amass and store troves of personal information on individuals easily retrievable by other corporations as well as state and military forces globally.

Federal agencies sought to partner with corporations possessing spying capabilities around the time COINTELPRO, the government's covert counterintelligence programs (described in the next chapter), were exposed in the 1970s. From 1972 through 1977, the Law Enforcement Assistance Administration of the Department of Justice commissioned the Private Security Advisory Council to study the relationship between private security systems and public law enforcement, and to create programs and policies concerning private security "consistent with the public interest."[13] A multifaceted working relationship between public and for-profit policing grew over the next two decades. But consonance with the public interest is negligible.

MITIGATING THE RISK

Today, dissent is threatened as much as privacy by private surveillance.

Companies that specialize in "risk mitigation," or "threat assessment," are paid handsomely to conduct domestic surveillance of people, organizations, and communities. Corporations engage such companies to produce briefing documents that include names of ordinary people, advocates, organizers, legislators, and special interest groups that may or may not be "friendly" to their interests. The profit margins of these businesses depend on identifying "threats." In this case, the term "threat" does not refer to hazards to safety, health, or environment, but to anything that hinders corporate earnings.

The CEO of SeaWorld admitted in 2016 that its maritime theme park employees had posed as animal rights activists to spy on People for the Ethical Treatment of Animals, or PETA.[14] The animal welfare organization was raising awareness of harsh behind-the-scenes treatment in forcing SeaWorld animals, like orcas, to perform tricks. One SeaWorld staffer, concealing their identity, posted social media messages urging others to "burn [SeaWorld] to the ground" and "drain the new tanks at #SeaWorld," in order to encourage unlawful sabotage.

When exposed, SeaWorld wrote this on its blog:

> Following the completion of an investigation conducted by independent outside counsel, the board has directed that the company's management team end a practice in which certain employees posed as animal rights activists in connection with efforts to maintain the safety and security of company employees, customers, and animals in the face of credible threats that the company had received.

This and other industry responses when spying and infiltration are made public tend to describe activist efforts as "credible threats," while downplaying corporate-sponsored acts of infiltration, impersonation, and unlawful incitements to violence.[15]

Contractors also spy on and sabotage corporate critics by hacking them. In 2020, authorities investigated a large hacking-for-hire scheme that included efforts to steal confidential communications from thousands of sources fighting climate change—including investigative journalists, advocacy groups, and short sellers. Among those targeted were hedge funds like Coatue Management and Blue Ridge Capital; journalists from several news outlets; and nonprofit groups who opposed the telecommunications companies trying to gain control over the internet, according to several cybersecurity researchers, including the research group Citizen Lab in Toronto.[16]

The hackers were paid to attack on behalf of third parties and were typically hired by private investigators and other middlemen in the US, Europe, and Israel. Clients are often law firms or corporations that may receive stolen material under the guise of corporate intelligence or as evidence in preparation for litigation.

Apparent beneficiaries included the German tech firm Wirecard AG, a company that processes financial transactions over the internet. It was one of Germany's most successful technology companies until critics and financial analysts alleged accounting improprieties. Hedge funds, short sellers, journalists, and investigators who looked into claims of market manipulation by Wirecard were targeted by the hacking-for-hire operation, according to Citizen Lab. The group reported that "some individuals were targeted almost daily for months, and continued to receive messages for years."[17]

In a 2017 blog post, the Electronic Frontier Foundation detailed cyberattacks on their own activists fighting for net neutrality, which telecommunications companies have aggressively lobbied against. One of the targets of the alleged attacks, Evan Greer, told *Bloomberg News* that she was alerted when she realized someone was trying to hack her email.[18] For several weeks in 2017, EFF's colleagues at Fight for the Future, an advocacy group fighting over the internet rules, had been receiving "phishing" emails—fake messages appearing to be from trusted senders but that seek to trick users into giving up their passwords. Citizen Lab linked the EFF hack to the BellTroX hacking operation, and said another net neutrality advocacy group, Free Press, was also targeted.

Canadian scholar and law professor Joel Bakan likened corporations to "institutional psychopaths" in his 2005 documentary film, *The Corporation*. More recently he noted that "corporations are collecting ever more data, triangulating it, graphing our every move and emotion, especially as all the hardware in our lives becomes internet-connected (through the "Internet of Things") and the software becomes more sophisticated at monitoring and predicting our behavior."[19]

Bakan reminds us of the great control corporations wield over lives and democracies: "The problem is often thought about in terms of privacy—that our privacy is being invaded by the collection of all this data. But the real problem is control: how the data is likely to be used to control how we act, think, and feel in ways that are ultimately profitable to corporations."

MYTH 5

"THE USA DOESN'T HAVE
NATIONAL ID NUMBERS"

A 1981 White House Cabinet meeting included a discussion of whether to establish national ID numbers and cards. One of President Reagan's top domestic policy advisors, Martin Anderson, joked in response to the brainstorming the group had done earlier: "I would like to suggest another way that I think is a lot better. It's a lot cheaper. It can't be counterfeited. It's very lightweight, and impossible to lose. It's even waterproof. All we have to do is tattoo an identification number on the inside of everybody's arm."

Reagan didn't miss a beat.

"Maybe we should just brand all the babies."[1]

This off-color exchange broke the ice in a longstanding national identity debate. Is the US a nation of freedom or one subject to electronic control?

Cabinet members reached consensus after Richard Wirthlin, the Reagan administration pollster, conducted a public opinion survey. Results revealed that an overwhelming majority did not want national identity numbers. They feared they would infringe on individual privacy. Chief of Staff James Baker then wrote a memo to Reagan saying, "The administration is explicitly opposed to the creation of a national identity card."[2]

National ID cards are not your ordinary form of ID. That's why many think they are un-American. Three elements distinguish them from other forms of identification, according to the Cato Institute, a

DC–based think tank. First, the ID number facilitates correlations with other databases and biometric systems such as facial recognition. Through such matches it is possible to infer a person's politics, attitudes, and other inclinations. Second, the ID crosses national jurisdictions. If systems in different agencies and states use the same identifying algorithms, they can operate across the country. Third, these IDs are mandated by law.[3]

A MYTH OF NOMENCLATURE

The myth that the United States does not have national ID numbers is largely one of semantics.

Changing terminology can be a politically expedient tactic. During the George W. Bush administration, the CIA and other defense and intelligence agencies detained persons in so-called black sites around the world. Officials used "enhanced interrogation" to describe the torture contractors and the military inflicted on prisoners. Through language, and creative legal memos justifying practices such as waterboarding, they skirted domestic and international laws. For many, the term normalized the practice.

In 1995, the National Right to Life Committee hatched a new name for the procedure now commonly known as a "partial birth abortion." In the heated and longstanding debate over a woman's right to an abortion, the Bush administration adopted this nonmedical—yet inflammatory—term for the rarely performed "dilation and extraction," or D&X, procedure.[4]

Another example of agenda-motivated terminology lies in how politicians nixed the term "global warming" in favor of "climate change." *Mother Jones* obtained a confidential memo written by a top Republican strategist for George W. Bush's reelection campaign. It acknowledged that the president and his party have "lost the environmental communications battle." The memo suggested replacing "frightening" terms like "global warming" with "less emotional" ones that mask Republicans' "vulnerable" spot, namely science. In this case, climate activists and scientists also prefer not to use the term "global warming," opting instead for "climate change" because "warming" is too narrow. It doesn't, for example, account for other extreme weather changes like severe winter storms.[5]

By not using the term "national ID number," leaders of both parties cast aside partisan differences to coalesce around an omission that furthers the myth that America does not have mandatory national ID numbers. It's just that the nation is not as forthright about its practice as other countries.

The US currently has two different ID systems. They are both described as non-compulsory, but in practice they are necessary to fully participate in modern society. They are the Social Security Number (SSN) and the REAL ID.

Carolyn Puckett, formerly with the Office of Research, Evaluation, and Statistics at the Social Security Administration, has documented the history of the SSN and its shift to additional uses. "[It] has become a number assigned at birth and used by many government agencies to identify individuals and by private industry to track an individual's financial history."[6] Beyond being used for the administration of social security, it is also needed to open a bank account, obtain a credit card, or get a driver's license.

Puckett continues, "In order to share data among government agencies or between commercial firms, a unique identifier to match records is critically important, and the SSN is the one unique tag that follows an individual throughout life. People may change their names and addresses throughout their lives, but their SSNs generally will remain the same."[7]

When Congress established the Department of Homeland Security (DHS) in late 2002, it made clear that the agency would not set up a national ID system. In September 2004, then DHS secretary Tom Ridge reiterated, "The legislation that created the Department of Homeland Security was very specific on the question of a national ID card. They said there will be no national ID card."[8]

But in 2005, Congress changed its mind. It passed the REAL ID Act. Enforceable starting in October 2021, it closely resembles a mandatory national ID program.[9] State drivers' licenses, permits, or ID cards must be "enhanced," or REAL ID–compliant if used to board a commercial aircraft or to enter military bases and federal facilities. Most states include a gold or black star on REAL ID cards. The substantive difference between the old and new forms of identification is that now the federal government, not the state, requires applicants to provide certain documents. Traditional driver's licenses will still be lawful for driving in states that continue to offer them as an option.

Just as the Social Security number had mission creep, it's almost certain that REAL ID is destined to become a universal identifier.

TWENTY-FIRST-CENTURY JUSTIFICATIONS FOR NATIONAL ID NUMBERS

Many people associate mandatory ID schemes with authoritarian regimes and diminished civil liberties.

Yet some called for a national ID system in the wake of the attacks of September 11, 2001. On September 13, attorney Alan Dershowitz asserted in a *New York Times* op-ed that such a card "would make it more difficult for potential terrorists to hide in open view, as many of the Sept. 11 hijackers apparently managed to do."[10]

In addition to the assertion that a national ID system will keep the nation more secure, another commonly cited benefit is that it will reduce racial and ethnic stereotyping. Some claim that police will not engage in profiling of individuals on suspicion of their being illegal immigrants. Proponents also say it will help to increase law enforcement accountability because there will be rules to act on when authorities unlawfully demand to see the cards. Finally, the thinking goes, the cards are difficult to alter or forge, making them safer from identity thieves.

FLAWED ARGUMENTS AND A BAD RAP

Mandatory national identification numbers are bad optics for the nation's image as a free society.

What about claims that ID numbers will reduce terrorist attacks and other crimes?

Little evidence supports that.

A 2004 Privacy International study found no connection between ID cards and thwarting terrorist attacks. It noted that of twenty-five nations that experienced terrorist attacks from 1986 to 2004, 80 percent used national ID cards. And increased accuracy in proving one's identity has nothing to do with knowing if an individual is prone to committing an act of terrorism. Wade Michael Page served in the US Army from 1992 to 1998, first stationed at Fort Bragg in North Carolina, home to the Eighty-Second Airborne Division and the Army's Special Forces Command. On August 5, 2002, Page entered a Sikh temple in Oak Creek, Wisconsin, and murdered six Sikh worshipers.

In terms of personal security, mandatory IDs may create incentives for identity theft and widespread use of false identities. While added security features such as holograms make cards more difficult to forge, rapidly evolving fraud capabilities and the use of biometric data create other risks; the Electronic Frontier Foundation cautions that biometric databases are a "honeypot of sensitive data vulnerable to exploitation."[11]

The administration of ID programs is often outsourced to private companies that are not accountable to the public. Linkages and analyses are made between different forms of identifying information stored in many databases. If hacked, multiple accounts are tainted. It may be safer to store information with service providers, such as utility providers, libraries, and banks. So much for the rationale that mandatory ID numbers keep us safer.[12]

As for the claim that they will reduce racial profiling, national ID systems have been used to discriminate against or categorize people based on race, ethnicity, religion, and political views. In states with voter ID laws, for example, voters must show ID to cast their votes. That practice has been documented to be biased against voters of color, who disproportionately lack government-issued photo ID cards.

On a related note, advocates say that rules will curb illegal state practices. But we know how that works. Rules to restrain police spying on residents in New York City did not stop the NYPD from a decade of secretly monitoring Muslim communities, in mosques and elsewhere, absent suspicion of wrongdoing. It took a 2017 federal lawsuit to fashion more effective oversight of what a judge called the City's "systemic inclination" to ignore rules safeguarding free speech and religion.[13]

The argument that REAL ID cards make holders safer from identity theft doesn't hold up, because there is no way for authorities to tell if someone fraudulently obtained a REAL ID card. Linked state databases can contain errors, any of which could render a person unemployable until they get their "file" corrected. The more officials with access to the database, the more mission creep sets in, just as with Social Security numbers. Law enforcement and other government agencies might soon seek linkages. Employers, landlords, credit agencies, mortgage brokers, direct mail companies and retailers, and other third parties could also ask for access, further eroding the personal privacy Americans expect.

REAL IDs can also function as internal passports. As of October 2021, domestic air travelers must show a REAL ID driver's license, or a state-issued enhanced driver's license or other approved formed of ID. Other locations, including medical facilities and metropolitan transportation, will scan the IDs. Those scans create a permanent record of all transactions. Critics of REAL ID cite additional concerns, notably the federalizing of state functions, as well as a concern for the wellbeing of individuals already fearful for their safety. Victims of domestic violence, along with prosecutors and judges who have sent people to prison, are obvious targets.

NEXT UP: ELECTRONIC IDS

REAL ID cards seem destined to become electronic.

As of 2017, more than 80 percent of countries with national ID cards use electronic IDs, or eIDs.[14] These include a microprocessor for stronger document verification and online authentication and signature. When needed, they can function as biometric identification and authentication because they often contain the owner's fingerprint.

Authorities argue that biometric identification and authentication helps secure borders, verify employment and immigration, prosecute criminals, and combat identity fraud and terrorism. Despite these claims, the citizens of some countries have opposed biometric national

ID schemes, including citizens of the Five Eyes countries: Australia, Canada, New Zealand, the United Kingdom, and the United States.[15]

One reason for opposition is because biometrics-related identity and authentication systems are weak. If compromised, biometric data can't be reissued like signatures or passwords. Annually, up to five percent of national ID cards are lost, stolen, or damaged.[16]

Aggregated personal information invites security breaches, and large biometrics databases are a hive of sensitive data, susceptible to being exploited. Identity thieves can exploit other identifying information linked to stolen biometric data. Privacy remains a concern, as does loss of autonomy with respect to profiling, behavioral targeting, social sorting, dynamic pricing, blacklists, and constant surveillance. This is compounded when a unique identifier is tied to multiple sectors such as financial, insurance, and government benefits.

For a country purporting to place a premium on civil liberties, the adoption of national identity cards in the United States raises a host of legitimate concerns touched on briefly here. But for all the potential risks of spying that come with unique identifying numbers, a more insidious threat is denying that they already exist, which they clearly do.

MYTH 6

"SURVEILLANCE DRONES
ARE JUST FOR WAR"

Drones have many benefits in civilian life, as the following case shows.

Two Australian teenagers were swimming more than a thousand feet out from shore and became distressed. Fortunately for them, lifeguards had been testing drones as part of a multimillion-dollar shark mitigation program.

The lifeguard supervisor affixed a float to a drone, steered it, and dropped it from above to the swimmers as they struggled in the powerful surf that December in 2017. The teens used the float to navigate powerful waves and return safely to shore.[1]

Drones, or unmanned aerial vehicles, can access perilous locations without endangering human life. They can aid search and rescue missions, and, using gas and infrared sensors, aid first responders such as firefighters. They can gather air samples to test for impurities. Mapping remote areas with drones is affordable and safer than flying a helicopter into dangerous locations. Drones are popular for non-lifesaving purposes as well. Photographers and filmmakers can conduct shoots with a five-hundred-dollar drone instead of hiring a costly helicopter and pilot team.

Drones are such a fixture in daily life that tech creators have devised ways to find and confront rogue drones. The company Dedrone has helped planners of events such as the Professional Golf Association tour team to prevent rogue drones from flying in their airspace. A software platform uses sensor fusion technology to enable PTZ cameras—cameras that are able to pan, tilt, and zoom so that larger areas can be monitored by a single camera—to verify radar detection data. It can recognize and classify RF, Wi-Fi, and non-Wi-Fi drones to detect nearby drones before confronting the rogue drone or its operator.[2]

IDEAL FOR SURVEILLANCE

Unmanned aerial vehicles (UAV) have been fixtures of war since Austria filled hot-air balloons with explosives and dropped them over Venice in 1849. It wasn't until a century later that the US military first used UAVs for photographic surveillance, in the mid-1950s. Video cameras became a game changer; drones equipped with them were first used in 1995 in Taszar, Hungary. The remote-controlled "Gnat" gliders could see movement sixty miles away. The Gnat was renamed the Predator and became the military's favorite surveillance tool. In 2004, US Customs and Border Protection launched a fleet of drones for patrol, investigation, and disaster relief. Contrary to myth, surveillance drones are becoming permanent fixtures in civil life, and ideal vehicles of mass surveillance. They can stay airborne for protracted periods, can often fly undetected, and can be equipped with sophisticated cameras and tracking software.

In late May 2020, an MQ-9 Reaper drone looped twenty thousand feet over Minneapolis.[3] Protests were erupting in the wake of police officer Derek Chauvin's public nine-minute-long murder by suffocation of a black man, George Floyd. Also called the Predator B, this frequent fixture in military operations belonged to US Customs and Border Protection (CBP) and came from North Dakota's Grand Forks Air Force Base.

The CPB claimed they deployed the Reaper to capture live video to help federal law enforcement. On the other hand, the Reaper could have been taking images and using facial recognition software to catalogue individual protesters.

For people exercising their First Amendment rights, drones in the skies are a hostile specter. Besides using high-powered cameras, drones can also deploy so-called less lethal weapons such as rubber bullets and pepper balls, projectiles that release skin and eye irritants. This escalation aligns with what American police departments have done for years, deploying military-strength forces against protesters.

Law enforcement agencies in at least a dozen jurisdictions use surveillance drones. In 2011, the FAA Air Transportation Modernization and Safety Improvement Act sanctioned drones for domestic surveillance.[4] In 2013, the federal government allocated $1.2 million for drones that year. Congress appropriated $64 billion to the drone industry and police departments in order to hasten drone deployment.[5]

Orange County, Florida, experimented with two surveillance drones over Orlando in 2012. Sergeant Tim Ehrenkaufer of Daytona Beach, Florida, tested drone capabilities such as taking body temperatures with a Forward Looking Infrared Camera, and in 2020 the city received two loaner drones with this ability.[6]

As of early 2018, there were 910 public safety agencies that owned drones; six hundred of these agencies had surveillance capabilities.[7]

FROM PUBLIC SAFETY TO PUBLIC SPYING

The city of Baltimore launched a controversial wide-area aerial surveillance experiment in May 2020. Its police department contracted with Ohio-based Persistent Surveillance Systems to fly Cessna aircraft, not drones, over the city for six months. Michael Harrison, the Baltimore police commissioner, justified the nearly $4 million project: "There is no expectation of privacy on a public street, a sidewalk."[8]

Maryland ACLU attorney David Rocah disagrees: "This technology is categorically different from the ground-based cameras or one-time flyovers that we are more familiar with in this country. This technology is the most far-reaching surveillance system ever deployed on American soil."[9]

He explains how it works: "It uses a network of very sophisticated wide-angle cameras, which capture in each frame one third of the city. But the resolution of these networked cameras is sufficient to be able to zoom in and distinguish one person from another. The cameras record video at the rate of one frame per second thus creating a slow-frame rate video record of everywhere that everybody in Baltimore goes anytime they are outside while the planes are flying."

The contract calls for three planes to fly twelve hours a day, covering more than 90 percent of Baltimore's land area. The Aerial Investigation Research Pilot Program is limited to monitoring such felony crimes as robberies, carjackings, shootings, and homicides. Images are to be used solely in criminal investigations and are stored for forty-five days. But no oversight agency is enforcing these provisions.

"The net result is a virtual time machine allowing the police to go to any location at any time and trace movements of any person to and from that location," Rocah continues. Identification works by linking to the city's ground-based surveillance systems, including license plate readers and private security cameras if they are registered with the city. "This is game changing technology," says Rocah of aerial surveillance. "No government in the United States has ever had the power to record, store, track, and have at its fingertips the movement data of the entire population. To give the government that power is profoundly danger-ous, and profoundly invasive of privacy. It's the technological equivalent of having a police officer follow you every time you walk out the door of whatever building you happen to be in and record where you are going."

If that happened in real life, we'd all viscerally understand the pri-vacy implications. Rocah notes that it's only because of sophisticated new technologies that surveillance can happen remotely from space. Because of this distance, residents do not have the experience of con-tinuous monitoring.

In the 2018 landmark decision in *Carpenter v. United States*, the Su-preme Court held that the government violates the Fourth Amendment by accessing, without a search warrant, historical records containing the physical locations of cellphones. Chief Justice John Roberts noted that new technologies require the Court to find ways to preserve pri-vacy from the government even when surveillance tools have enhanced the government's ability to "encroach on areas normally guarded from inquisitive eyes."[10]

Rocah echoes the dangers of long-term tracking surveillance: "Because movement data is so revealing of private details of life, and because it's available to almost everyone, allowing acquisition would so alter the balance of power of our society. Here, we're not talking about the acquisition of long-term location tracking information of one person, but of every single person in Baltimore."

Protracted tracking, whether by airplane or drone, enables government agencies to watch sensitive activities and catalog individuals. It is similar to metadata: whom one calls on the phone, or emails—without knowing what is said—can reveal more than the contents of communication. Ongoing monitoring of targeted persons' activities and movements yields abundant information: Everyone entering or exiting an Alcoholics Anonymous meeting, union hall or political gathering, or a lawyer's or doctor's office might be identified and catalogued. Or a drone could zoom in on and scan cars parked outside a medical facility or church and create a list of attendees in just seconds.

Remote-controlled drones come in all shapes and sizes and can be equipped with a wide range of features, such as heat sensors, motion detectors, and license plate readers. Drones can accommodate affordable aerial zoom cameras to give law enforcement the ability to monitor individuals from afar. Some, like the Zenmuse Z30, can provide magnification up to 180x. They can zero in with precision on subjects from two or three miles away.[11] Drones have an advantage over on-the-ground cameras and photographers because a slight adjustment in mid-air can remove viewing impediments such as trees without being noticed.

Affordability of drones adds to their attractiveness. If equipped with an infrared camera, they can be had for less than $20,000, while police helicopters can cost up to $3 million. With this cost differential, a department might purchase a fleet of five hundred drones instead of a single police chopper, giving the department a swarm of devices that can watch individuals without notice from thousands of feet away, use software to identify people in an automated manner, and follow them without human piloting. As technology improves, the potential power of this type of fleet will only increase, creating the possibility of a massive surveillance umbrella buzzing over America's cities and towns.[12]

THE CREEPY SIDE

Onboard technology that allows remote control of drones presents opportunities for other kinds of privacy invasion. Hackers can take control of the drone and access data that it may have collected on any number of individuals. In 2016, German cybersecurity student Nils Rodday found flaws in one drone model, while he was working for its manufacturer to increase its security. He was able to intercept broadcasts sent from a chip (through an XBee channel) and send commands to the drone from more than one mile away.[13]

One of the largest drone manufacturers, DJI, has developed a feature for many of its drones—including models like the Inspire 2, which police often use—that allows drones to lock onto and automatically follow individuals. Such "Active Track" enables the drone to follow moving items, including people, without human control. DJI drones in Active Track operate in a mode allowing the drone to travel at roughly twenty miles per hour, more than enough to keep pace with an individual on foot. Some drones are even programmed to avoid obstacles while continuously tracking their locked-on target.

Developers are creating drones with so-called swarm capabilities that enhance automated flight power by allowing a single pilot to control multiple drones. That could allow a single officer to command a large fleet of drones, inconspicuously identifying and following many individuals for protracted periods.

Drone manufacturers and drone lobbyists have successfully pushed to open the US airspace to drones. And law enforcement agencies also back this, because more and more of them are using drones to "ensure public safety." Over time, however, surveillance tools assume other purposes, some of which are unsavory. Awareness of what goes on in the skies above is a first step to preventing this type of protracted, all-seeing spying.

As the Supreme Court majority wrote in the *Carpenter* case:

A person does not surrender all Fourth Amendment protection by venturing into the public sphere. . . . Society's expectation has been that law enforcement agents and others would not—and indeed, in the main, simply could not—secretly monitor and catalogue every single movement.[14]

Chief Justice Roberts, writing for the majority, acknowledged that new technologies raise constitutional concerns. Roberts gave a nod to past high court warnings: "As Justice Frankfurter noted when considering new innovations in airplanes and radios, the Court must tread carefully in such cases, to ensure that we do not 'embarrass the future.'"

The caution against "embarrassing the future" seems a logical measuring tape for assessing the impact of surveillance tools on privacy and individual autonomy. While the *Carpenter* decision specifically impacts law enforcement, the Court's reasoning points to the need for more effective privacy protections in the marketplace.

MYTH 7

"SURVEILLANCE MAKES
THE NATION SAFER"

Objects that can double as lethal weapons, such as scissors, baseball bats, darts, knitting needles, and utility knives less than four inches long were permitted in airplane cabins before the 2001 hijackings. Since then, the United States has tightened security in several vulnerable sectors. Air travel is safer, with secure cockpits, federal screeners trained by the Transportation Safety Administration, and additional federal air marshals on aircraft. Port and maritime security benefit from modernized technology, including radiation detectors. And federal agencies are more aware of potential biological and chemical threats. Emergency stockpiles include antidotes to such toxins.[1]

One practice, however, has not made the nation safer: mass surveillance.

The myth that "it makes the nation safer" arose after criminal attacks on the homeland occurred on September 11, 2001. A primary purpose of the myth is to justify widespread spying on citizens and residents. Surveillance has become such a profitable industry, and the government has invested so many resources in waging a "war on terrorism," that rooting out real criminal threats is like searching for a grain of rice in a sandbox. No one in government knows the amount of counterterrorism spending, how many staffers or contractors it employs, which agencies are duplicating others' work, or who is reading the fifty-thousand-plus-page annual intelligence reports.[2]

As *Washington Post* reporters Dana Priest and William Arkin wrote in their 2011 book *Top Secret America*, after the 9/11 hijackings taxpayers spent billions of dollars "to turn the machine of government over to defeating terrorism without ever really questioning what they were getting for their money." Priest and Arkin noted that one decade after 9/11, it no longer made sense to cast such a desperate and wide net.[3] Two decades later, dragnet spying on Americans makes even less sense.

Memories are short when it comes to the track record of spying in the name of national security. Throughout history, law enforcement has targeted particular citizens and residents as subversive. Intelligence agents and police have done this even with no suspicion that unlawful activity is afoot. The irony is that in conducting searches for such supposed threats to democracy, leaders ask us to forfeit the qualities that comprise a democracy.

The fact is, surveillance isn't a cure-all for security.

One military source gives an unvarnished assessment of how secure surveillance and other anti-terrorism tactics have made us: the United States Army War College. The college provides graduate-level instruction to senior military officers and civilians to prepare them for senior leadership assignments. Its 2016 report on the effectiveness of anti-terrorism measures is forthright:

> The data suggest U.S. efforts in the war on terror have been largely ineffective in achieving the stated objectives. More Americans have been killed by terrorist acts since 9/11 than before. While still a very small number, the number of Islamist-inspired terror attacks in the homeland has also increased. Additionally, al-Qaeda and terror groups of global reach have not been defeated and destroyed. Rather, the number of such organizations and fighters supporting them has risen substantially since 2001.

What portion of the war on terror relies on surveillance?

The college's report continues:

> One perspective is that since another 9/11—the sine qua non measure—has not occurred, the war on terror has been a success. Another viewpoint asserts while many factors have deteriorated, absent

the muscular U.S. response, the situation would be worse today. To date, those claims have not been supported empirically.[4]

In 2018, two years after that paper's publication, a nonpartisan think tank, the Center for Strategic and International Studies, reiterated statistics about the rise of extremists. Sunni Islamic militants, it found, increased by nearly four-fold since 2001, despite the war on terror campaign. Salafi jihadists number up to 230,000 in nearly seventy nations.[5] A Saudi Air Force cadet perpetrated the late-2019 shooting at the Army base in Pensacola, Florida. It turned out he had been in touch with al-Qaeda leaders.

The cost of surveillance and other initiatives as part of the war on terror has been extraordinary, especially given that they have all been abject failures. While exact numbers are not public, the government has spent an estimated nearly $6 trillion on its global counter-terrorism campaign as of late 2019.[6]

The country's obsession with surveillance often obscures larger concerns. Look at how the nation has dealt with pandemic preparedness. The COVID-19 pandemic, for example, claimed nearly 120,000 American lives in just four months, revealing a public health vulnerability. It is not for lack of warnings over the past thirty years. Scientists and the intelligence community have long cautioned that a virus could cause mass devastation.[7]

In 1998, President Bill Clinton read Richard Preston's thriller *The Cobra Event*, about an attack on the United States using a lethal virus that spreads like the common cold. Clinton then initiated the first federal government pandemic preparedness effort. He created a biodefense czar position and the Strategic National Stockpile, storing vaccines and medical gear in secret locations around the country.[8]

George W. Bush, in 2001, eliminated the White House biodefense czar position that Clinton created, saying it was not a national security issue. He also let the stockpile go dry. But when Bush read a book about the 1918 influenza pandemic, in 2005 he directed the newly created DHS to institute a bio-preparedness unit and devise an early warning system.[9] After two Gulf wars and the attacks of 9/11, however, bioterrorism soon became less of a priority.

Barack Obama was credited with handling the 2009 H1N1 flu outbreak, the deadly 2014 Ebola outbreak, and the 2016 mosquito-borne Zika outbreak. Congressional Republicans praised the CDC for developing a Zika vaccine in seven months. But the Obama administration failed to replenish the federal stockpiles, according to ProPublica and *USA Today*.[10] He sped up the war in Afghanistan against the Taliban instead. And to many, his greatest accomplishment was authorizing the killing of Osama bin Laden.

In 2018, Donald Trump fired his top biosecurity adviser and disbanded the global health unit. Instead, he launched a sixth branch of the armed forces, Space Force, under the FY20 National Defense Authorization Act.[11] When the COVID-19 pandemic arrived in 2020, he recast the coronavirus as an international threat and dubbed himself a "wartime president." Budget numbers reflect federal priorities: the war on terror remains primary despite the fact that these efforts have not made us safer.

Public health spending declined under Obama and a mostly Republican-controlled Congress. In 2008, per capita public health spending, adjusted for inflation, rose from $39 in 1960 to $281 in 2008. It fell by 9.3 percent from 2008 to 2016, according to a 2016 study in the *American Journal of Public Health*.[12] From then on, it continued to plummet. The Centers for Disease Control's budget dropped by 10 percent from 2010 to 2019. Its funding for state and local preparedness was cut by a third from 2003 to 2019, according to a report from the nonprofit, nonpartisan Trust for America's Health.[13]

TWENTIETH- AND TWENTY-FIRST-CENTURY GOVERNMENT INVASIONS OF PRIVACY

The history of US surveillance in the name of national security is not a noble one. Government agents claim it will make us safer, yet time and again the surveillance yields only damage to civil liberties and the ruining of many lives at the cost of a huge drain on public resources and fostering citizens' lingering mistrust of their government.

THE 1950s AND MCCARTHYISM

Other national security initiatives in the twentieth century have failed, with blunt beat downs of personal freedoms. Privacy-invading measures have stigmatized entire communities, with no upsides, and with devastating consequences.

After World War I, and Russia's Bolshevik Revolution in 1917, dictator Vladimir Ilyich Ulyanov (Lenin) murdered about nine million resistors. Shaken by the advent of communism in Russia, legislators in the US began enforcing the Sedition and Espionage Acts to prevent its spread.

In the 1950s, Senator Joseph McCarthy pursued a quest to expose communists and their sympathizers who had infiltrated the State Department, the CIA, and the atomic weapons industry. A Gallup poll found that at the peak of his power, in January 1954, 50 percent of the American public supported McCarthy.[14]

The lives and careers of many law-abiding Americans were ruined. Ten film producers, directors, and screenwriters refused to answer questions about possible communist ties before the House Un-American Activities Committee in 1947. Known as the Hollywood Ten, they were held in contempt of Congress. The industry then blacklisted them.

McCarthy also deemed gay and lesbian people a threat to national security, saying, "The pervert is easy prey to the blackmailer." What ensued was a campaign of rooting out and removing homosexuals from government jobs. When Dwight D. Eisenhower took office, he signed an executive order in 1952 authorizing the FBI and the Civil Service Commission to conduct personal investigations of "sexual perversion" in all branches of the federal government. In the first four months of this campaign, 1,456 employees were fired or forced to resign after being blackmailed with threats to tell their families.[15]

For decades, the government tracked, harassed, and banned thousands more from public service. The so-called Lavender Scare was more private than other politically motivated persecutions because targeted individuals did not want to publicize their status. All-told, it's estimated that up to ten thousand people's lives were ruined. Besides forfeiting chances of career advancement, and with no legal recourse, some ended their lives by suicide. The policy of discrimination continued until 1995, when President Bill Clinton rescinded the Eisenhower executive order.

1950s AND 1960s—COINTELPRO

For nearly two decades the FBI engaged in covert surveillance programs on Americans.

The Bureau's unlawful initiatives, from 1956 until 1971, were called COINTELPRO, for "counter-intelligence program." It used secret informants, wiretaps, mail opening, break-ins, and microphone bugs. FBI director J. Edgar Hoover ordered Bureau agents to "expose, disrupt, misdirect, discredit, or otherwise neutralize" several domestic movements and their leaders. They monitored, infiltrated, and disrupted political and peace organizations that they deemed subversive to the United States. Among those targeted were Vietnam War opponents, feminist organizations, Dr. Martin Luther King Jr., Cesar Chavez and the United Farmworkers, the American Indian Movement, and the Black Panther Party.[16]

In 1971, the press exposed COINTELPRO after seven activists broke into FBI offices in Media, Pennsylvania. Surprised burglars found files detailing the covert program; they mailed copies of the files to several journalists. As a result, in 1976 the Senate conducted hearings into the FBI's actions, and enacted policies limiting law enforcement surveillance. During the hearings William C. Sullivan asserted that but for endless war, the surveillance apparatus and mentality informing its abuse would not exist. The former assistant to the FBI director said, "What works against one enemy will work against another." He posited: "Along came the Cold War. We pursued the same course in the Korean War, and the Cold War continued, then the Vietnam War. We never freed ourselves from that psychology that we were indoctrinated with, right after Pearl Harbor, you see."[17]

Despite the FBI's mission of protecting the American people and upholding the US Constitution, its activities during this time did the very opposite.

1980s—CENTRAL AMERICA ACTIVISTS

The FBI did not stop, however, after the press exposed COINTELPRO. The Bureau simply did a better job covering its tracks.

In another covert campaign, from 1981 until at least 1985, agents infiltrated and disrupted the work of the Committee in Solidarity with the People of El Salvador (CISPES). From CISPES, the FBI investigation spread through the anti–US intervention movement. Agents monitored the United Steelworkers, the Southern Christian Leadership Conference, US senator Christopher Dodd, and US representatives Pat Schroeder and Jim Wright.

A 1989 report of the Senate Select Committee on Intelligence concluded, "The CISPES case was a serious failure in FBI management, resulting in the investigation of domestic political activities that should not have come under governmental scrutiny. It raised issues that go to the heart of the country's commitment to the protection of constitutional rights."

The 1989 report by the committee, then chaired by Senator Joseph Biden Jr., continued to cite collateral damage of surveillance on individuals exercising their First Amendment rights, and who have done nothing to warrant suspicion of criminal activity: "Unjustified investigations of political expression and dissent can have a debilitating effect upon our political system. When people see that this can happen, they become wary of associating with groups that disagree with the government and more wary of what they say or write. The impact is to undermine the effectiveness of popular self-government."[18]

1990s—MUSLIMS AND PALESTINIANS

On February 26, 1993, at about 17 minutes past noon, a thunderous explosion rocked lower Manhattan.

> The epicenter was the parking garage beneath the World Trade Center, where a massive eruption carved out a nearly 100-foot crater several stories deep and several more high. Six people were killed almost instantly. Smoke and flames began filling the wound and

streaming upward into the building. Those who weren't trapped were soon pouring out of the building—many panic-stricken and covered in soot. More than a thousand people were hurt in some way, some badly, with crushed limbs.

Middle Eastern terrorism had arrived on American soil—with a bang.

That screenplay-like account is from the FBI's website.[19]

In 1996, three years after this first World Trade Center attack, President Bill Clinton signed legislation that he said "strikes a mighty blow" against terrorism. The bill afforded government agencies expanded anti-terrorist powers that Clinton had proposed a year earlier on the heels of the bombing of Oklahoma City's Alfred P. Murrah Federal Building. The law made it easier to deport non-citizens suspected of terrorism connections.

The collateral damage in this decade—even though the Oklahoma City bomber was a United States citizen—was the stigmatization of Middle Easterners. Once again, surveillance of this community has not made us safer.

2000s—THE WAR ON TERROR

Days after the hijacking of four airplanes on September 11, 2001, George W. Bush used the term "war on terrorism." He had in mind Sunni Islamist fundamentalist groups, notably al-Qaeda, the Taliban, Tehrik-i-Taliban Pakistan, and others.[20] Three days after the attacks, Bush signed into law the Authorization for Use of Military Force Against Terrorists. It authorized the use of force against countries, persons, or organizations deemed to have planned, authorized, committed, or aided in the attacks.

Critics claim that with this initiative, law enforcement shifted from responding to crimes after they happened to preemptive policing, including increased surveillance. History reveals many examples of US responses to perceived public safety threats that trigger an increase in police surveillance activity. Since the police often lack the resources and technical expertise to keep pace with global terrorists and criminals, they have widened their surveillance capability.[21] This is done by collaborating with private commercial enterprises to obtain personal data or to eavesdrop on the public.

2010s AND BEYOND—EXPOSING BULK SURVEILLANCE

On June 6, 2013, *The Guardian* ran its first in a series of disclosures by an unnamed whistleblower about the NSA's vast surveillance program. The whistleblower was soon revealed as former CIA and NSA–contracted systems analyst Edward Snowden. Over two months of publication, the American public learned how their internet and phone communications were being monitored by the NSA. The programs received assistance from the FBI and the Department of Justice. Internet and telecoms such as Google, Facebook, and Verizon assisted many of the NSA initiatives, as did the United Kingdom and Australia, two other members of the five-nation-strong anglophone intelligence alliance known as Five Eyes.

Snowden says public awareness of surveillance has increased: "The government and corporate sector preyed on our ignorance. But now we know. People are aware now. People are still powerless to stop it but we are trying. The revelations made the fight more even."[22] After Snowden's disclosures, numerous lawsuits challenged mass surveillance and some laws were reformed. In 2015, Congress passed the Freedom Act to reduce mass collection of phone data.

A MYTH WITH LETHAL IMPLICATIONS

A myth is dangerous when it perpetuates tunnel vision.

The myth that surveillance keeps the nation safer has developed over decades. Its targets vary according to the whims of politicians. Public fears fuel the myth until common sense is unable to set it straight. The myth justifies focusing on ideological enemies and investing trillions of dollars to vanquish those enemies, even as military efforts are failing, according to the US Army War College report and other authorities.[23]

Elements of human nature sometimes seem as predictable as mythology story lines. It is easy to find comfort in identifying enemies, assigning blame, and then setting out to vanquish them.

Facts reveal that the more difficult the attempts made by those in power to root out enemies becomes, the more they are likely to get it wrong. That is true when leaders turn mass surveillance justified as necessary for national security on its own citizens.

PART TWO

PROTECTIONS
AND IMMUNITIES

"NO ONE WANTS
TO SPY ON KIDS"

Each day, 170,000 children worldwide go online for the first time.[1]

There, budding encounters with screen strangers seem so benign that parental warnings—"Never take candy from strangers"—don't enter their young minds. With baptismal keystrokes, kids slide into the world of corporate marketing. They are exposed to predators of a type different than those conjured by parental warnings. Temptations are irresistible: Wondrous fantasy creatures and friendly cartoon characters offer up friendships and make McDonald's and Coca-Cola seem like the kids next door asking for a play date.

It's no wonder marketers are cashing in on this fast-growing online user group. KidTech describes technology, software, and infrastructure built to engage and be used by children. Experts expect the KidTech digital advertising market to reach $1.2 billion by 2021.[2]

What's the upshot? Cloaked as fun, the digital ads entice kids to happily share lucrative data—their likes, dislikes, fears, and habits—with their new online friends. Corporate data aggregators and marketers take this information, store it, and sell it to others.

The idea that no one wants to spy on kids is as naïve as childhood itself. It's a veritable myth.

HAPPY PROFITEERS

Quebec resident Antonio Bramante eats at McDonald's about twice a month, urged on by his three young children. The fast food giant's

Happy Meals come with toys that are often linked to blockbuster film releases. Bramante claims that McDonald's Happy Meal advertising is breaking provincial laws against targeting children under thirteen years of age by displaying toys at their eye level. Bramante is the lead plaintiff in a class-action lawsuit against McDonald's (Canada is one of the few nations in the world that prohibits advertising aimed at children).[3]

The website happymeals.com features, in bold letters with cartoon and toy characters, an app, activities, and "play together" options. The words "fun," "magic," "inventor," and "artist" splash across the screen, appealing to youngsters' desire for entertainment. In lettering that requires a magnifying glass to see, on the site's upper left-hand corner are the words "Hey kids, this is advertising."

THE PERILS OF SHARENTING

Reflecting parental ignorance, or apathy, on this issue, most of the other lawsuits against McDonald's have nothing to do with advertising to children. Many parents in the US have a steep learning curve about the nuances of online predation at a time when more than 90 percent of two-year-olds have an online presence, thanks to "sharents" (parents who overshare on social media).[4] And more than 80 percent of babies under that age also have a social media presence.

Proud parents do not think twice when posting a child's name and birthday on social media, exposing them to identity theft before they can say "Mama" or "Dada." They're also easy targets for digital kidnapping, the practice of using other children's photographs as their own. in addition, photos of young children are often doctored and then posted on websites frequented by pedophiles. The Child Rescue Coalition cautions parents that "child predators not only use the internet to distribute pornography, but also to stalk children, share info, and trade tips and techniques on how to seduce and lure them into sexual encounters."[5] The coalition's @KidsForPrivacy campaign urges parents to share with caution and not to use hashtags or geotags when doing so.[6]

That's only one of the flagrant abuses that can come from collecting, storing, and selling private information about underage children. Parents may not be fond of corporations collecting data from their children, but they are not doing much to try to stop it. According to a report by the Pew Internet and American Life Project, an overwhelming number of parents—more than 80 percent—are concerned about the amount of information advertisers can learn about their children's online behavior.[7] Social media platforms are required to gain parental consent for children under thirteen years of age before gathering data on them or affording access to interactive features that let them share personal information with others; but children can and do lie about their ages in order to gain fuller access, clicking through to wherever ads may lead.

COPPA

The primary law protecting children from advertising is the Children's Online Privacy Protection Act of 1998, or COPPA. It is enforced by the Federal Trade Commission and has the goal of letting parents control what personal data is gathered from children under thirteen years of age. It imposes several requirements on operators of websites or online services directed at children in that age group, and on operators of other websites, and programs or apps that collect and share personal information at home or at school. Marketers cannot lawfully target youth under age thirteen with advertising without parental permission. Personal information can be a child's name or screen name, email, telephone number, geolocation, photo, voice recording, or other unique identifier.

The video sharing social networking service TikTok, just like Mc-Donald's, is a flagrant collector of kids' data. Two advocacy groups have complained to the Federal Trade Commission about TikTok's endless feed of jokes, dances, recipes, and "challenges." The Boston-based Campaign for a Commercial Free Childhood (CCFC) and the Center for Digital Democracy in DC call the popular app's business model "one of the most predatory."

In 2019, TikTok's parent company, ByteDance, paid a fine of $5.7 million, and the Federal Trade Commission (FTC) prohibited it from collecting and using data from kids under the age of 13. It also agreed to destroy data already collected.

Attorneys at Georgetown Law's Institute for Public Representation found that TikTok was violating the settlement, scooping up data without parental permission. CCFC director Josh Golin told the *New York Times* that this marketing practice puts millions of underage children at risk of sexual predation. So the groups filed another complaint, supported by twenty leading advocacy organizations, describing TikTok's ongoing violations of children's privacy. It had not deleted the personal data of kids under thirteen—a clear violation of the settlement. The company claims it does not need parental permission because "regular" TikTok accounts are for users thirteen and up. Kids under thirteen, TikTok says, can only sign up for "younger users" accounts, with limited functionality; they cannot upload videos or message other users, two core elements of the app.

The investigation found that the new privacy policy and the policy of allowing only children under thirteen to access new "younger user" accounts lacked teeth. Kids can skirt the limited functionality of the app's "young" version and can lie about their age. And even if children do use the "younger user" accounts, TikTok violated the law with its algorithmically curated video feed anyway. The company gathers data about what and how long kids watch to find ways to keep them interacting longer.

TikTok is so wealthy that a $5.7 million fine is built into their cost of doing business. The FTC complaint calls for holding TikTok executives accountable and for levying the maximum penalties of $41,484 per violation. And until TikTok can adopt an effective age-verification policy and be COPPA–compliant, child advocacy groups are urging the FTC to prevent TikTok from registering any new users in the US. In 2020 President Donald Trump signed an executive order calling TikTok a security threat because of ByteDance's ties to China. A federal judge ruled against a government ban on TikTok's operation in the US, but as of early 2021 litigation was still pending and ByteDance was pursuing a deal with US firms Oracle and Walmart that could skirt the government's attempted ban.

In 2019, Google's subsidiary YouTube agreed to pay $170 million for violating COPPA, the largest claim the Federal Trade Commission has obtained since the law was enacted in 1998. YouTube had failed to divulge that parts of its platform were aimed at children under age thirteen. YouTube then gathered personal data without parental consent, using cookies. New York Attorney General Letitia James said: "These companies put children at risk, and abused their power, which is why we are imposing major reforms to their practices and making them pay one of the largest settlements for a privacy matter in US history."[8] Google and YouTube must create and implement a system by which channel owners can identify child-directed content on YouTube.

With the European General Data Protection Regulations (GDPR), which went into force in 2018, more are waking up to the need to protect juveniles' data. The GDPR calls for special protections for children under age sixteen—compared to COPPA's age thirteen—such as adopting measures to verify a child's age and managing consent. Although legal and regulatory protections haven't kept pace with technological methods used to target and expose children to corporate persuasion, that may be changing.

Despite more protections, it will always be the goal of multinational corporations to prime children to be consumers before they learn what it means to be informed and engaged citizens.

Adam Jasinski, a technology director for a school district outside of St. Louis, Missouri, used to conduct keyword searches of the official school email accounts for the district's 2,600 students, looking for words like "suicide" or "marijuana." In 2018, he learned that tech company Bark was offering schools free automated monitoring software in the wake of the 2018 Parkland, Florida, school shooting, in which seventeen people were killed. The software scans school emails, shared documents and chat messages, and alerts school officials anytime key phrases are found.

Proponents claim such monitoring takes the burden off other students to report on their classmates and lets administrators react in near real time. Officials are looking for cyberbullying, self-harm, and shooting threats. It's cost effective and on the alert twenty-four hours a day. All told, the school surveillance industry is a $3 billion a year industry.[9]

Facial recognition software in schools is being used to avert mass shootings. In 2020, the New York Civil Liberties Union sued the New York State Education Department for its $1.4 million facial recognition system. The Lockport School District was one of the first public schools in the nation to use the technology on students and staff. Alerts pop up under their system when suspended staff members, Level 2 or 3 sex offenders (moderate- or high-risk of reoffending), persons barred by court order from school property, or others deemed to pose a threat are seen on campus.

ARE THE LAWS ADEQUATE?

Advocacy groups try to tip the balance in order to slow down corporate data harvesting. The task is daunting in scope. Groups have asked Congress to enact greater privacy protections for children. In late 2019, the DC-based Electronic Privacy Information Center (EPIC) urged the Federal Trade Commission to reject a "school official exception," which allowed schools to share information with parent volunteers, tech companies, or other vendors for educational purposes directed by the school. It called on the FTC to define the term "commercial purpose" and ensure that children's personal data collected by schools wasn't being transferred to EdTech companies that provide hardware and software to enhance teacher-led learning in classrooms. EPIC also urged the FTC to require notification within forty-eight hours of a data breach by a company subject to COPPA.

A bipartisan group of senators called on the FTC to launch an investigation into children's data practices in the EdTech and digital advertising sectors. They wrote: "The FTC should use its investigatory powers to better understand commercial entities that engage in online advertising to children—especially how those commercial entities are shifting their marketing strategies in response to the coronavirus pandemic and increased screen time among children."[10]

How society treats its most susceptible members is revealing. Rather than sparking curiosity in children about social issues, corporations would prefer children center their worlds around having the latest toys, clothes, and junk food. Monitoring minors' play habits and collecting their personal information does more than shape their future consumer habits as adults—it enables the normalization of a surveillance society.

Corporate spying exploits our earliest innate cravings for excitement and interaction in order to extract private information, and it conditions juveniles to accept surveillance. The business model is lucrative, and because sanctions lack teeth, many tech companies line-item judicial settlements as the cost of doing business. Aggressive and deceptive KidTech marketing techniques speak volumes about societal priorities. When it comes to safeguarding the rights of the young, the United States, like a foul-prone soccer player, is a prime candidate for a red card.

MYTH 9

"POLICE DON'T MONITOR SOCIAL MEDIA"

Monitoring these public social media
posts is simply good police work.

—MEMPHIS POLICE, director Michael Rallings[1]

Mass shooters sometimes post their plans to kill on social media. In 2019, Brenton Harrison Tarrant, a twenty-nine-year-old white supremacist, massacred fifty-one worshippers in two mosques in Christchurch, New Zealand.[2] Before doing so, he posted a lengthy manifesto on Facebook, then livestreamed the attack.

"Mr. Tarrant now appears to have become the first accused mass murderer to conceive of the killing itself as a meme; it seems he was both inspired by the world of social media and performing for it, hoping his video, images and text would go viral," wrote David Kirkpatrick in the *New York Times*.[3]

Law enforcement points to this type of incident to justify monitoring social media posts.

The FBI's Internet Crime Complaint Center (IC3) identifies certain online crimes as increasing. These include confidence/romance fraud, child porn, cyberstalking, hate crimes, and identity theft.[4] The FBI cites this as a basis for increasing monitoring of the public's social media engagement.

Much like the "precogs" who foresaw crime before it occurred in Philip K. Dick's 1956 novella, *The Minority Report*,[5] the FBI says it wants to access a "social media early alerting tool" to anticipate crimes.[6] The futuristic work of fiction reflected Cold War anxieties relating to authoritarianism and the loss of personal autonomy. In the twenty-first century, elected officials exploit the public's fears of "terrorist" acts as propellant for their policing of the virtual world.

A 2019 FBI request for funding asserted, "With increased use of social media platforms by subjects of current FBI investigations and individuals that pose a threat to the United States, it is critical to obtain a service which will allow the FBI to identify relevant information from Twitter, Facebook, Instagram, and other social media platforms in a timely fashion."[7] Its ultimate wish, the document continued, is for "an interactive tool that can be accessed by all headquarters division and field office personnel via Web browsers and through multiple devices."

It's a myth that police don't monitor social media. With budget cuts, and an increase in online crime, proponents view it as a necessary practice.

CONNECTED COPS

Police departments partner with third parties to conduct social media mining. One tool of the trade is GeoFeedia. The platform boasts that it can circumvent privacy options on Facebook and other sites.[8] It creates dummy accounts, as does Snaptrends, that employ such gimmicks as posting provocative photos of women to get "friends" and to track their locations on a range of platforms, regardless of whether they publicly geotag their posts. Geofeedia is funded in part by the CIA's venture capital firm, In-Q-Tel. It has monitored Greenpeace actions, labor protests, and other mass assemblies.[9]

Consider this Geofeedia marketing copy, with the heading "Opportunities: The Freddie Gray Incident Was a Watershed Moment for the Baltimore City Police."[10] Referencing touchstone moments that triggered surveillance, it described public outcry after a twenty-five-year-old black man sustained fatal injuries in 2015 when six officers brutally transported him, unstrapped, in the rear of a van. "The minute his death was announced we knew we had to start monitoring social media at key locations," continued the marketing vignette.

Twitter, Instagram, and Facebook announced their suspension of Geofeedia after the ACLU learned in 2016 that police were using it on their platforms to spy on Black Lives Matter protesters in Baltimore.[11] Twitter later cut off access to other monitoring businesses, Media Sonar and Snaptrends.[12] But dozens of other companies stand ready to provide similar data mining services for police.[13] By contracting out, monitoring can be done by third parties without revealing that law enforcement is behind it.

Tech expert Kalev Leetaru wrote in *Forbes*:

> There is not a big data meeting or contractor expo day I've attended in DC that has not included at least one company offering social media surveillance capabilities extremely similar to Geofeedia's to the law enforcement, intelligence and military communities, with most of them specifically mentioning protest triaging and agitator profiling as key focal areas. The academic community has also focused extensively in this area, both via DOD directly and through other federal funds, including a lot of research on profiling individuals through social media, building psychological profiles or estimating sensitive attributes like sexual preference or political views.[14]

Police typically do not need a search warrant to read social media posts, a practice they refer to benignly as "open-source monitoring." Third-party firms that monitor keywords and hashtags for police include Cellebrite, Snaptrends, Media Sonar, Beware, and Digital Stakeout.[15] Beware assigns a "threat level" to individuals.[16]

One website, Connected Cops, shows how omnipresent police are on social media.[17] It features an infographic using BrightEvent's data on how police use Twitter. There were over 772 official Twitter handles tied to police officers in eight countries as of 2020. The group even gives awards in such categories as "Social Media Investigator" to the investigator at any worldwide law enforcement agency who, as a practitioner, has used social media to solve crimes.

The unstated corollary to this myth is that no harm is done by police monitoring social media. That's also false. Several communities experience negative effects, among them activists, immigrants, and youth.

BULLSEYE: ACTIVISTS

Activists are easy marks for online surveillance. Law enforcement creates inflammatory terms for their monitoring that have no basis in fact, allowing them to cast a wide net. Vacuous labels can falsely incriminate innocent persons or tie them up in the court system at great personal cost.

Mara Verheyden-Hilliard is a constitutional rights lawyer and cofounder of the Partnership for Civil Justice Fund in Washington, DC. She writes, "Law enforcement seeks to obscure the true intent and impact of having the government collect, monitor and aggregate data on individuals and organizations by using demonizing and generalized labels against persons who are targeted based on lawful First Amendment protected activities and affiliations."[18] Since 1995, Verheyden-Hilliard has sued police departments for illegal treatment of protesters, winning changes in policy, and securing multimillion-dollar settlements for activists: "They tell the public that they are protecting against an undefined threat of 'anarchists,' 'extremists,' [and] 'lawbreakers,' and rely on the media to dutifully amplify this message. Using the pretext of 'crime prevention,' the FBI and local police agencies are tracking and targeting people engaged in social justice movements and causing extreme harm to fundamental democratic rights."[19]

Police in Memphis, Tennessee began monitoring social media posts after 2014 protests in Ferguson, Missouri, and the 2016 shooting of officers in Dallas, Texas.[20] They created bogus social media profiles to spy on Black Lives Matter activists. Police kept dossiers—including photos, mental health histories, and addresses—and presentations detailing the lives of Memphis-area protesters and known associates. They distributed those files to local businesses and the county school districts.

In June 2018, a private intelligence firm assembled a report detailing six hundred planned protests of Donald Trump's family-separation policy. The firm tracked Facebook activity for the data and then circulated it to DHS and fusion centers.[21] The fusion centers then shared it with Immigration and Customs Enforcement, which monitored border groups and other protests, including location coordinates, on spreadsheets with data from Facebook pages of the various event organizers.

Verheyden-Hilliard disputes the value of this surveillance: "The vast monitoring undertaken by law enforcement is time and again political policing and has nothing to do with 'crime prevention.' At the PCJF, we have uncovered thousands of pages of government documents demonstrating that the FBI and Department of Homeland Security have targeted movements organizing for racial, environmental, and social justice and abused anti-terrorism authority and funding to do so." The DC lawyer notes that surveillance cuts across party lines. "Sweeping political surveillance and the growth of an unchecked and sprawling network of Fusion Centers have been expanded under Democratic and Republican administrations alike."

Some of the documents the PCJF obtained involved the nationwide crackdown on the Occupy movement showing that federal and local police agencies were functioning as what Verheyden-Hilliard calls "a de facto intelligence and surveillance arm of Wall Street and corporate America." Before the first tent was set up in Zuccotti Park in New York City, federal law enforcement was meeting with Wall Street firms to provide them information on the anticipated political protests.[22]

Fusion center operatives in Boston tracked Occupy activities including yoga classes and teach-ins, diverting their claimed anti-terrorism focus to the peaceful movement during the period leading up to the Boston Marathon bombings.[23] The ATF, charged with investigating crimes related to alcohol, tobacco, firearms, and explosives, as well as terrorist activities and organized crime, diverted resources and taxpayer money to spying and compiling information on protesters.[24] The US Marshals Service—responsible for fugitive operations, prisoner transport, witness and officer protection, and the management of illegally acquired assets—distributed a list of "Known Anarchists and Protestors" compiled and maintained by the Louisiana State Police and State Fusion Center.[25] FBI agents across the country issued a stream of reports on Occupy protesters under their anti-terrorism divisions, while simultaneously acknowledging in those reports that the movement was "peaceful."[26]

"Federal and local law enforcement authorities are never going to announce or confirm that they are undertaking surveillance and monitoring as a tool of political control and disruption of social justice organizing," says Verheyden-Hilliard. "They will always state that they have a crucial crime or terrorism prevention purpose—and they will rely on the mainstream press and majority of the public to accept these assertions unchallenged no matter how often they are exposed as false."

IMMIGRANTS AS SECURITY THREATS

The Department of Homeland Security (DHS) prowls through social media accounts ostensibly to assess security risks of travelers, both foreign and domestic.[27]

In 2020, the DHS upped the ante. All visa applications—for about fifteen million travelers each year—ask for social media handles, allegedly for vetting purposes. But they are stored indefinitely, and the DHS can access them for a wide range of purposes, according to the Brennan Center in New York. From examining religious and political beliefs along with data on friends and family, State Department officials will make assumptions that are often subject to wholesale bias and misinterpretation.[28]

What's the harm?

Harsha Panduranga, counsel at the Brennan Center's Liberty and Security Initiative, says, "We're seeing a broad, unaccountable collection of social media which hasn't been proven to work in terms of determining who might be a security threat."[29] The center, in a 2019 lawsuit, challenged the State Department and DHS's collection and retention of social media handles.[30]

Gross misinterpretation of posts becomes a problem because of language differences, according to Panduranga. Sarcasm, humor, and tendencies to exaggerate or boast are easily misread: "People in groups that have historically been discriminated against as well as folks that speak different languages or are from different cultures."

He says it has to do with how social media analysis works: "You have an American officer who might not be as steeped in the customs or traditions of a range of communities. They might not put remarks in their appropriate context. That can fail to catch things like humor and sarcasm. Anyone not familiar with a social media meme or joke and sees it recirculated can appreciate how lack of context can harm your ability to interpret something."

Panduranga notes that automated tools don't fix the problem. Natural language analysis tools, which attempt to decipher the meaning of social media, often fail to interpret flags more commonly discriminated against at a much higher frequency: it's not a stretch to say that the DHS does not have a great track record when it comes to keeping track of who the real threat is.

Internal reports support this assertion. After US Citizenship and Immigration Services (USCIS) launched five social media monitoring programs in 2016, agency evaluations found the programs largely ineffective in identifying public safety or national security threats. As for three out of the four programs used to vet refugees, "the information in the accounts did not yield clear, articulable links to national security concerns, even for those applicants who were found to pose a potential national security threat based on other security screening results," according to a DHS brief.[31]

SCHOOLS AND CHILDREN AS THREATS

Marketers of surveillance products target K–12 schools. Responding to a surge in school shootings, many school districts purchased social media monitoring equipment to detect and prevent school violence. These products also claimed to detect cyberbullying and threats of self-harm.

Little proof exists that these software tools are effective.[32]

Kids' exchanges on social media are highly contextual and open to misinterpretation. Automated tools have documented failings that are heightened with slang. Companies selling these tools have provided only anecdotes of ostensible threats, many of which are simple misunderstandings while others likely would have been flagged by a concerned parent or peer. When perceived threats on social media lead to punitive measures, students of color are disproportionately punished.[33]

On the misinterpretation issue, Panduranga says, "There's no doubt this has particular salience for teenagers. One way to look at social media monitoring of children, and in schools, it's a way of putting a counter-terrorism oriented approach into a school context. You are casting a wide social net, whereas in reality, schools should be treated as a place kids can learn. Other values—a climate of threat and suspicion—is what's being fostered." Approaching issues that kids might have from a threat-focused lens causes many problems, he says.

One such problem happened in the Bronx in New York, after police monitored teens from public housing projects' social media accounts. They raided several complexes and charged kids under RICO (Racketeer Influenced and Corrupt Organizations Act) laws, which are designed for powerful mobs with sophisticated structures.[34] In one 2016 Bronx public housing raid, teens and young adults were charged with complex white-collar crimes; the young people were poor, some could not afford lawyers, and public defenders lacked experience in RICO cases.[35] They were just kids boasting online.[36] Yet the consequences are long-lasting, with families harmed in the process.

Police treat information they harvest from social media as significant, even if of dubious integrity. They show online photos to witnesses to help identify perpetrators. They create fake accounts to view comments and photos on a private account's timeline.[37] Officers post security video or photos of suspects on their own increasingly popular Facebook and Twitter accounts, asking the public for assistance in catching those they think may be responsible for property damage and other crimes.[38] That practice can encourage vigilantism against innocent individuals.

The Brennan Center addressed information sharing and storage in its lawsuit. Once user handles are collected, the government claims it has broad authority to retain them, sometimes up to one hundred years after a person's birth.[39]

"You never know when your information can come back to bite you in the future," notes Panduranga. He notes that the peril of indefinitely stored information is that such a long duration increases the scope of how it can be used, while also having a chilling impact on free speech.

In late 2020, the Partnership for Civil Justice Fund took a formal step to help counter the escalation of online surveillance. It launched a Center for Protest Law and Litigation, the mission of which is to protect and advance the rights of protesters to organize, assemble, and demand justice nationwide.[40] Mara Verheyden-Hilliard underscores the importance of sharing information with lawyers and activists about online surveillance. "It is critical that communities rein in this vast unchecked authority and restrict access to tools that are used for breathtaking constitutional rights abuses."

Social media surveillance is on the uptick as an investigative tool for law enforcement. But prosecutors often lack a solid grasp of the courtroom uses and limitations of digital evidence. According to a Rand Corporation report, that means they generally ask for more information to be extracted from devices than is necessary.[41] Judges typically lack knowledge about proper removal and processing techniques. Both prosecutors and judges could benefit from training surrounding the use of digital evidence in the courtroom. To promote better preservation of digital evidence, there could be training on digital evidence handling and preservation at the police academy level, and in the training of investigators. This also could limit seizing of devices not relevant to an investigation and result in greater privacy protections than currently exist.

Many people are attracted to social media because it offers an informal outlet for spontaneous speech. Much as in private conversations, social media posters are colloquial, and many of them are not self-conscious about what they write. Few post with an eye toward how police or government enforcement agencies might misinterpret it. As it turns out, there's no safe haven from police monitoring.

MYTH 10

"BIOMETRICS TECHNOLOGIES
ARE FOOLPROOF"

The impersonators wore 3D printed masks of other people's faces. They breezed through facial recognition systems at border crossing checkpoints, point of sale terminals, and airports. They duped Chinese payment and lifestyle apps AliPay and WeChat Pay, a high-speed rail station in China, and security systems at Amsterdam's Schiphol Airport. Using their sham facial features, they also unlocked a popular smartphone model.

The imposters were not lawbreakers. They were researchers from Kneron, a San Diego–based firm that develops artificial intelligence (AI) products and systems. In this 2019 experiment, they were testing the strength of facial recognition security solutions.[1]

Biometric identification (who a person is) and verification (whether a person is who they say they are) systems, such as facial recognition, are hailed as the future of security systems.

But foolproof? That's a myth.

WHAT ARE BIOMETRICS?

Biometric identification uses physical or behavioral characteristics unique to an individual human being to authenticate that person's identity.[2] They can be anatomical or physiological, such as finger and palm prints, iris and retina scans, ear prints, facial recognition, heartbeats, DNA, or brain waves. Behavioral biometrics, on the other hand, include gait, voice, eye-blinking, speech patterns, signatures, handgrip on a steering wheel, and typing rhythms.

After initial imprints from a person are gathered, they are stored in databases or on a card. Identification systems use algorithms to compare a biometric sample to a template in the database to search for a positive recognition, or to disqualify a person as a match.

As identity fraud increases, product developers hail biometrics as a necessary component of identity verification and authentication.[3] They are making biometrics identification systems smaller and more portable, and therefore more affordable. With growing public acceptance, increased rates of accuracy, and a sprawling network of surveillance cameras and sophisticated software to install and interact with biometric systems, the industry is flourishing.[4]

Applications span all aspects of modern life, from police, military, border and travel control to civil identification (think voting and residency), healthcare, public and criminal justice security, physical and logistical access, and commercial purposes.

In 2004, President George W. Bush implemented a directive for a mandatory, government-wide personal identification verification (PIV) card credentialing system.[5] Through this so-called USAccess program, federal agencies issue credentials to employees and contractors after gathering and storing fingerprint and facial images. The credentials are necessary to access federal facilities and systems.

Also in 2004, the Intelligence Advance Research Projects Activity sponsored a Face Recognition Grand Challenge to encourage researchers to create algorithms designed to improve facial recognition technology. The challenge continued annually until 2018. Its website describes this and other initiatives as focusing on "high-risk, high-payoff research programs to tackle difficult challenges of the agencies and disciplines in the intelligence community."[6]

Biometrics would become equally popular among the general public.

POPULARITY, WITHOUT PAUSE

In 2013, Apple made Touch ID available on several iPhones along with its iPad Air 2 and iPad Mini 3 as another way for owners to gain access to devices.[7] After that, several financial institutions followed suit to mitigate fraud and bolster cybersecurity. Bank of America, Wells Fargo, and TSB Bank introduced iris scan authentication for mobile banking.[8] Apple's iPhone 10 model integrated facial recognition.[9] With that move, biometric ID was well on its way to normalization.

A 2016 poll by Veridium, a firm that develops multi-factor biometric authentication technology, showed that 52 percent of individuals polled want biometrics to replace passwords. Eighty percent think they are more secure.[10] That might stem from the perception that because they are uniquely personal and scanned by sophisticated machinery, they are more "scientific," and thus safer.

That perception has fueled the global popularity of biometrics, which are being integrated into many countries' passports and visas.[11] Law enforcement in the US is amassing a massive facial recognition database.[12] Malaysia has a multipurpose smart card, and after India passed its 2016 Aadhaar Act, a twelve-digit unique identity number relies on retina scans and fingerprints.[13] Mexico has a trimodal (iris, fingerprint, and facial data) biometric ID project, and the United Arab Emirates' watch list uses iris recognition. Thailand has an iris biometric visa system, and China's social ranking system—monitoring citizens' behavior and ranking them based on "social credit"—relies on facial recognition.

Facial recognition in casinos helps spot known card counters. Financial institutions use voice recognition to verify patrons over the phone, employees' heartbeats help secure mobile payments or validate them to a corporate network, and hospitals identify patients via unique vein patterns in the palms of their hands. Many high schools use fingerprint technology in cafeterias to speed up long lunch lines and cut costs by avoiding cashiers and ensuring that students entitled to free or discount meals get them.

This rapid assimilation should sound privacy alarms.

More than half of American adults are in a face recognition database accessible to law enforcement for criminal justice searches.[14] Such use gained traction in 2008. At least thirty states permit police to access, or to ask for searches of, driver's license databases. Real-time matches can pinpoint a person's location from a live video feed. Unlike finger-printing, matches can be made remotely, spanning groups of individuals without their knowledge.

Clare Garvie is an attorney and facial recognition expert at the Georgetown Law Center on Privacy and Technology. She explains the technology's ubiquity, facilitated by the vast network of closed-circuit TV (CCTV) cameras in the public sphere. Facial recognition CCTV compares images of individuals from incoming video streams against ones stored in a database. Developers claim they perform well even when parts of the face are covered, or when a person wears eyeglasses or changes facial expressions.[15]

"Cameras are scanning the faces of people walking by, or in a protest, and seeking to identify those people. Our face is something that we can't leave at home, we can't discard, we can't change," Garvie explains. "In some states, we can't cover them up legally." That's because at least twenty states have old "mask laws" on the books.[16] They were originally enacted to ban facial coverings to crack down on the Ku Klux Klan. Civil rights–era laws provide that two or more persons walking around publicly cannot cover their faces. With the 2020 COVID-19 pandemic, mask-wearing for public health has impeded enforcement. In February 2020, for example, officials in Washington, DC, allowed a group of white nationalists to demonstrate with covered faces.[17] But otherwise, covering one's face is not always an option for persons seeking to avoid cameras.

In terms of accuracy and reliability, the devil's in the details, or, in this case, the nodal points. Scanners read certain nodal points that are unique to each face—there are approximately twenty thousand on a single face. According to Garvie, there are neither standards for how many points need to be matched nor for how analysts are trained. This makes facial recognition less accurate than fingerprinting. So-called facial signatures are based on a face's geometry, such as the mathematical distance between forehead and chin. Research has shown that biases and misinformation exist in facial recognition technologies, especially in identifying persons of color. Despite this, Garvie's research reveals that at least half a dozen police departments allow the use of facial recognition searches on forensic sketches, or computer-generated composite faces based on witness descriptions.

"The problem with witness identification is that human errors come into play," says the tech authority. "Because of its relative newness, it suffers from inaccuracies and doesn't meet the scientific rigor to be introduced in court."

DNA DATABASES

In 2018, police used DNA forensics to apprehend the so-called Golden State Killer, Joseph James DeAngelo.[18] The former police officer was a spree killer and serial rapist in California. His case factored into the establishment of California's DNA database, which collects DNA from all accused and convicted felons in California and has been successful in solving cold cases. The FBI and local police identified members of DeAngelo's family through forensic genetic genealogy.

After the DeAngelo arrest, police across the nation uploaded crime-scene DNA to GEDmatch and other databases where purchasers of genetic testing kits share their DNA with companies such as 23andMe and Ancestry. Police do this without the knowledge or consent of customers who submit their DNA. Consumer DNA tests are wildly popular, with more than twenty-six million test kits sold by early 2019.

In New York City, police routinely collect DNA samples from individuals they have arrested, or even just questioned, by scraping material off items that have touched their mouths, such as cups of water or cigarettes.[19] In early 2020, the Trump administration enacted a program requiring Immigration and Customs Enforcement agents to take mouth swabs of persons in their custody for the FBI's DNA database.[20] Internationally, procedures do not exist for how genomic data uploaded through consumer technology should be handled by state officials. But some nations (Kuwait and Kenya, for example), have held that the practice is unconstitutional.[21]

A Pew Research Center study finds division over whether police should use investigative genetic genealogy to solve crimes. In a 2019 survey, 48 percent of respondents said they were okay with DNA testing companies sharing customers' genetic data with police. A third said it was unacceptable, while 18 percent were unsure.[22]

Part of the mixed feelings may be due to lack of standardization in use and privacy regulations endemic to biometrics generally. Consumers hear mixed messages about who can access their DNA. "What we have right now we can call the Wild West. There aren't a lot of rules on the ground," according to Natalie Ram, an associate professor of law at the University of Maryland.[23] "State legislatures are one of the best-situated bodies to engage in rule-making in this area."

The very site that led to serial killer DeAngelo's arrest shut down temporarily in July 2020 after a breach exposed to law enforcement agencies the DNA of more than one million users. GEDmatch announced an attack on its servers that left information searchable by police for approximately three hours.[24]

BIOMETRIC DATABASES ARE VULNERABLE

In 2019, a security flaw exposed fingerprint and facial recognition data of more than one million users of the biometrics giant Suprema's Bio-Star 2 security platform.[25] Companies secured commercial buildings with the system in the US, UK, Japan, India, and the UAE. Researchers found the flaw before the planned integration of BioStar 2 into a software-based security management platform called AEOS. Governments and financial institutions in eighty-three countries use AEOS to control facility access. So does the Metropolitan Police Service in Great Britain. Vulnerability of critical facilities and infrastructure could have been life-threatening.

In 2014, hackers for the Chinese government broke into the US Office of Personnel Management systems.[26] They stole personal identifying data of more than twenty-two million Americans—including the fingerprints of 5.6 million people. As of 2020, that data doesn't appear to have surfaced for sale on the dark web. Just like the San Diego researchers who donned masks, a pair of researchers at Michigan State University used only an inkjet printer and special paper to convert—for less than $500—high-quality fingerprint scans into fake 3D prints that fooled smartphone fingerprint readers.[27] Absent a state-sponsored cyberattack, however, there are other ways to glean someone's fingerprint. Researchers at Tokyo's National Institute of Informatics could reconstruct a fingerprint based on a photo of a person flashing a peace sign taken from nine feet away.[28]

"Once you share them on social media, then they're gone," Isao Echizen told the *Financial Times*, explaining how they are up for grabs by the public.[29]

Face-shape data is also susceptible to hacking. A Georgetown University study found that images of 50 percent of Americans are in at least one police facial recognition database, from drivers' license photos to mugshots. Anyone can download photos from Facebook or Google Images, or can capture them in public. File sharing sites can be hacked. Visual data can be weaponized, just like fingerprints. Researchers from the University of North Carolina constructed a three-dimensional model of a person's head using his Facebook photos. The moving, lifelike animation was convincing enough to trick four of the five facial recognition tools tested.[30]

Few people know enough about biometrics to even consider this type of fraud and caution users accordingly. But experts on LinkedIn have considered it. They recommend that profile photos not have both ears showing to prevent the photo being used in identity theft.

Another limitation to relying on biometrics as personal identifiers is that they cannot be reset. If hackers compromise one fingerprint, backups exist in the form of other fingerprints. But if hackers compromise all fingerprints—some law-enforcement databases contain images of all fingers—there are no backups. The same for eyes, used for iris or retina scans, and the face. Unlike compromised passwords, it's impossible to "reset" fingerprints without surgery or mutilation.

"If Border Patrol and your bank and your phone all are collecting your fingerprint data, all it takes is one actor who figures out how to manipulate that and you've basically wiped out the usefulness of that information," said Betsy Cooper, the Director of the Center for Long-Term

Cybersecurity at the University of California, Berkeley. You have lost your key identifier and perhaps your identity.[31]

BIOMETRICS ARE NOT PRIVATE

Biometrics, compared with passwords, are not private. An individual's features—face, eyes, ears, and fingers—are public. Anyone can record, photograph, or trace them. Stores, financial institutions, many corporate offices, speed cameras, the media, Facebook, and other social media platforms all store images.

Yet some courts hold that before gathering facial imprints, collectors must give notice. Biometric Information Privacy, or BIP, statutes are under consideration in several states. The laws would regulate collection, use, and retention of biometric data. Illinois, Texas, and Washington had biometric privacy laws in place as of 2021, and several states have passed consumer protection legislation that has increased the scope of biometric data protections in 2020—including the California Consumer Privacy Act (CCPA), the Oregon Consumer Information Protection Act (OCIPA), and the New York SHIELD Act. Arizona, Hawaii, and Massachusetts have proposed BIP legislation, and others are considering laws regulating the collection, retention, and use of biometric data.

Harrah's Casino in Joliet, Illinois, scans facial biometrics for security and marketing purposes. The casino is the subject of a lawsuit alleging its Biometrica Systems software does not meet BIPA's informed consent requirements. "Defendants use facial recognition technology with their video security cameras at their Illinois casinos," the filing states. "Defendants' facial recognition technology identifies a person by scanning the geometry of a person's facial features and comparing that scan against databases of stored facial geometry templates."[32]

Also in Illinois, Facebook will pay a $650 million settlement under a law allowing people to sue technology companies that don't obtain users' consent before amassing data. The settlement came in a challenge under the state's Biometric Information Privacy Act, one of the strongest in the nation. Users' photos had been tagged by Facebook, at times prompted by an automated feature run by facial recognition technology. Class members will only receive about $150–$200 each. Presiding US District Judge James Donato of California noted how cheaply Facebook was getting off in the settlement given what the state legislature said might be due if the litigants proved their case. "They are taking what is effectively a 98.75 percent discount," he said.[33]

THEY CAN'T STAND ALONE

Do standalone biometrics schemes have the integrity needed for sensitive security purposes? It may be advisable to pair biometrics with traditional measures such as passwords or PINs.

Once a hacker has a photo of someone's ear, eye, or finger, they can access or falsify new legal documents or accounts. Many heralded Apple's TouchID as an advancement. Yet hacker Jan Krissler beat the system just one day after the iPhone's release. Hackers from Germany's Chaos Computer Club created fake fingers with which to unlock iPhones. Krissler used VeriFinger software to recreate German Minister of Defense Ursula von der Leyen's thumbprint after obtaining high-resolution photos of it from press conferences.[34]

Other hackers duped the Samsung S8's iris recognition system. They placed a contact lens over a photo of a user's eye. The S8 phone was the most expensive purchase of their exploit, showing how inexpensively perpetrators can effect biometrics fraud.[35]

There are ways to deter inherent vulnerabilities of biometrics. Requiring more than one fingerprint scan is one. Bank of America said its iris scan will be a part of multi-factor authentication instead of relying on it as the sole way to access accounts.

THE END OF OBSCURITY

The end of obscurity that comes with facial recognition is troubling, according to Georgetown Law Center expert Clare Garvie. "One of the elements of the First Amendment, recognized by the Supreme Court, is the right to anonymity." It's not always easy for tech literate users to visualize the erosion of anonymity. "Even though we present ourselves in public when we participate in a public forum or a protest, and yes, law enforcement officers are allowed to take photos—we'd be shocked, and it probably would be seen as a violation of our rights if police officers were able to walk through a political demonstration and demand everyone show our papers. Facial recognition is more closely analogous to that situation," she says. "It's a way of identifying people. It's not just photography."

And it's not entirely scientific. It is common practice, by many, to modify images of negligible quality prior to submitting them to recognition algorithms. That increases the system's chance of finding possible matches. Edits may exceed basic adjustments to lighting and color and may include fabricating new identity points absent in the original photo.

The lawyer whose vocation is facial recognition technology cautions says, "We have to think very carefully about how this may begin changing public faces, how it may chill free speech and free association particularly on issues that are contentious, in public forums that are so vital to these conversations taking place."

MYTH 11

"METADATA DOESN'T REVEAL MUCH ABOUT ME"

We kill people based on metadata.

—MICHAEL HAYDEN, former NSA and CIA director[1]

In the popular Terminator franchise, Skynet is an artificial intelligence system with machine-based military capability. In the movie, Skynet kills off most of humanity, then annihilates the few survivors. In real life, SKYNET is an NSA program, launched in 1997, that collects metadata and uses algorithms to identify suspicious patterns, such as al-Qaeda couriers communicating messages to plan terrorist activity.

NSA officials put many of the foreigners identified on so-called NSA kill lists without their knowledge or any legal recourse. Hellfire missiles, deployed by drones, pinpoint targets from these lists. More than 2,400 people in Pakistan, Yemen, and Somalia were victims of such extrajudicial killings by the US from 2010 to 2014, according to the London-based Bureau of Investigative Journalism.[2]

What is metadata, and why is it so valuable that it's used to kill people?

Metadata is data about data. One writer likens metadata to provenance, or an object's nature and origins. That way, if it's taken out of its context—as when one removes an artifact from an archaeological dig—it maintains its meaning and scientific value. Metadata summarizes information about data so it's easier to find and work within the future. And we can manually create metadata to include additional information and improve its accuracy.

The footprints of every digital transaction—its metadata—are an indelible part of its DNA. Think of creating a document and sharing it with one or more people who edit it using the Track Changes feature in Microsoft Word. You can hide or reveal the history of edits to the document, showing who added or deleted words, at what time, if they inserted comments, and what they said. Some metadata is easy to view, and other metadata requires extraordinary methods, such as special retrieval software, to access.

In the information age, metadata has cultural value. It lets us locate, preserve, and reuse data for multiple purposes in the future. Archivists can use metadata to remedy normally occurring inconsistencies in documentation. Archivist and scholar Anne Gilliland writes that the existence of different kinds of metadata is essential to "continued online and intellectual accessibility and utility of digital resources and the information objects that they contain."[3] Gilliland is associate dean for information studies at the University of California, Los Angeles, Graduate School of Education and Information Studies. She praises metadata for providing us with "the Rosetta stone that will make it possible to decode information objects and their transformation into knowledge in the cultural heritage information systems of the future."

That's lofty stuff. The future integrity of information systems aside, anyone interested in surveillance and privacy should understand the basics of metadata. A good place to begin is by dispelling the myth that "metadata doesn't reveal much about me."

DATA ABOUT RELATIONSHIPS AND MORE

In human terms, metadata is about relationships and connections. Digital forensics professionals at the International Institute of Cyber Security say that metadata answers the who, what, why, when, and where questions surrounding just about any digitally stored record: photographs, video, telecommunications, and geospatial information.

In social networks, metadata is used to group posts, track user interests, and help create a context around user data. Metadata in a posted photo, for example, can contain location data, time, and how long the person posed for the shot.

The US government does not just use metadata to pinpoint enemies on foreign soil, as in the drone hit list example. The NSA and other government agencies capture and analyze a vast swath of information about Americans' connections with international terrorists. In doing so, federal agencies can find out a lot about persons who have no links to criminal activities. Did you have an extramarital affair, or call a suicide hotline? Are you addicted to gambling, drugs, or alcohol, and do you have serious financial debt? From its trove of data, the government can usually answer these questions.

Metadata is as intrusive as the proverbial town gossip. It can reveal our innermost personal details, such as political inclinations, health status, financial situation, and family relationships.

Researchers Deepak Jagdish and Daniel Smilkov created a tool to contextualize email metadata. Analyzing emails, and only looking at the *From*, *To*, and *CC* information fields, as well as time stamps, researchers were able to make amazing discoveries about their senders' social interactions, relationships, social circles, and even their sleep cycles. They could calculate, for example, how many people they knew in a certain time period or which were the more productive moments of their day.[4]

The success in determining the identity of an individual from phone metadata was also demonstrated by Stanford University researchers. They found that the NSA's massive collection of telephone records can provide a lot more insight into the private lives of people than the government is willing to admit. By getting just the phone numbers of two people participating in a call, the serial numbers of the phones involved, the time and duration of the calls, and possibly the location of each person during the call, the investigators managed to isolate data identified with a specific individual.

As former NSA general counsel Stewart Baker said, "Metadata absolutely tells you everything about somebody's life. If you have enough metadata, you don't really need content."[5] That's because it's easier for computer algorithms to search through bulk collections of metadata than for a person or a computer program to listen to the content of phone calls or search through emails for keywords.

Edward W. Felten is a Princeton University professor of computer science and public affairs. The former consultant and tech advisor to such companies as Bell Communications Research and Sun Microsystems explains the appeal of metadata:

> Telephony metadata is easy to aggregate and analyze. Telephony metadata is, by its nature, structured data. Telephone numbers are standardized and are expressed in a predictable format: In the United States, a three digit area code, followed by a three digit central office exchange code, and then a four-digit subscriber number. Likewise, the time and data information associated with the beginning and end of each call will be stored in a predictable, standardized format.[6]

That stands in contrast to the content of phone calls, which Felten notes are not at all structured. People speak different languages, use street slang, and have stutters and accents. "Conversations also lack a common structure: Some people get straight to the point; others engage in lengthy small talk."

COLLECTION EN MASSE

After the attacks of September 11, 2001, the USA PATRIOT Act authorized the NSA to begin scooping up vast amounts of metadata about US citizens from telecommunications companies in its quest to root out terrorists.

In 2015, the USA Freedom Act, passed after Edward Snowden's 2013 revelations of mass surveillance, limited collection of phone metadata and other "business records." The newer law provides that records must remain with the telephone and internet companies, and the NSA can approach companies for access only on a case-by-case basis. NSA agents must show that reasonable suspicion exists that a person or account has links to an international terrorist or a representative of a foreign government or political organization connected to unlawful activity. The court can then mandate telecoms to produce phone call records of all numbers that communicated with the suspect number—the first "hop"—and up to all numbers with which those numbers communicated, or two "hops" out. A hop is the number of intermediate network devices through which data must pass between a source and its destination.

But the Freedom Act makes just a small dent in reforming bulk collection. The program still collected 151 million records in 2016. That number increased significantly in 2017 to 534 million, according to the report Call Details Logs.[7] Despite this increase, there were only forty terrorism suspects in 2017. This increase came despite the 2014 finding by the Privacy and Civil Liberties Oversight Board that metadata collection did not yield new investigative leads.

This board is a congressionally created independent agency within the executive branch. It advises the president and senior officials on privacy and civil liberties considerations when planning laws and policies pertaining to terrorism. The board analyzed bulk telephone record collection initiatives to gauge its value-to-detriment ratio with respect to national security and individual rights, respectively. It found that metadata-gathering affords some benefits. These include speed in meeting the legal standard for surveillance, historical depth in searching records, and breadth of searching through contacts of a particular phone number.

In balancing the investigative program's value with its infringement on individual freedoms, the board members concluded:

> We have not identified a single instance involving a threat to the United States in which the telephone records program made a concrete difference in the outcome of a counterterrorism investigation. Moreover, we are aware of no instance in which the program directly contributed to the discovery of a previously unknown terrorist plot or the disruption of a terrorist attack. And we believe that in only

one instance over the past seven years has the program arguably contributed to the identification of an unknown terrorism suspect. In that case, moreover, the suspect was not involved in planning a terrorist attack and there is reason to believe that the FBI may have discovered him without the contribution of the NSA's program.[8]

Patrick Ball, Director of Research at the Human Rights Data Analysis Group, which produces scientifically defensible statistics about human rights abuses, is more critical of the NSA's methods. The data scientist called the agency "ridiculously optimistic," saying the results of their metadata analysis are unsound. That's due to a flaw in how the NSA programs the algorithm to analyze cellular metadata. Most of the 2,500 to 4,000 people killed by drone strikes from 2004 to 2016 were classified—possibly erroneously—as "extremists."[9]

That's right. A flawed algorithm caused the US government to murder up to four thousand people who may have been innocent.

Reliance on a faulty formula speaks volumes about the integrity of America's highly publicized war on terror. Traditional methods of law enforcement investigation relying on human observation and instinct are still essential in rooting out criminal activities. While tried and true methods of criminal investigation can benefit from technology, algorithms alone may be too risky.

In 2018, the NSA began a process of erasing these records. Agency officials had discovered technical irregularities, the details of which it did not reveal. Because the NSA could not resolve the technology issues, in May 2018 the agency began deleting all Call Detail Records (CDR) data since 2015. According to 2019 testimony from the FBI and NSA, "After balancing the program's intelligence value, associated costs, and compliance and data integrity concerns caused by the unique complexities of using these company-generated business records for intelligence purposes, NSA suspended the CDR program."[10]

Over time, intelligence officials may come to realize the ways in which metadata can complement, rather than lead, their investigative efforts. As in any endeavor, a patchwork of intellect, experience, and creativity produces a more nuanced work product. When we're talking about human lives, the more robust the collaboration, the better the result for all.

METADATA ALSO MEANS PROFIT

Corporations collect metadata as part of their profit imperative.

They use it to analyze consumer habits and to fine-tune marketing strategies. The more data they have, the more businesses can save money by targeting their advertising. This also helps manage inventory and thus improve efficiency. Some companies also sell such data to other companies, working with data brokers. It's an estimated $200 billion industry.[11]

Data brokers specialize in culling information from public and private sources. Some are subsidiaries of the major credit rating agencies, who collect information about consumer habits across a wide range of platforms, from credit card companies, online vendors, and automotive dealers.

"The average consumer has no idea these companies even exist, let alone what their names might be." Dylan Gilbert is policy counsel for the advocacy group Public Knowledge. He says that the data-collection and data-sharing industry operates in the shadows. "If people have no idea what's happening with their data they have no way of truly protecting their privacy."

California and Vermont have laws requiring data brokers to register with the state's attorney general so the public can access their names and contact information.[12]

While many big tech companies don't sell their data, they often do share access to it. PayPal, for example, shares customer information with hundreds of entities globally, from credit agencies, to marketers, to financial service providers. The data shared includes name, birthdate, address, phone number, IP address, bank account information, and recent purchases.

Treatment of metadata is, like anything involving money and power, political.

Personal data, especially data that reveals opinions, attitudes, and beliefs, can advance both ends. In the process, users can suffer. Service providers and other third parties can expose users to harassment from internet trolls or identity theft fraud if data is not securely stored or transmitted, or if apps don't have strong security settings.

Metadata analysis can target entire communities, including activists, and can censor online activities. Individuals can misuse metadata to harass others, or "doxx" them by publishing private or identifying information about an individual on the internet, typically with malicious intent.

Geolocation data embedded in photographs is an efficient tracker. One South African game reserve posted a conspicuous warning urging visitors to turn off their phones' and social media accounts' geotag functions. That was to prevent poachers from using such information to locate endangered species. Many digital advertisers would say that, because data is aggregated, it's impossible to identify individuals. As we've seen, researchers have shown how easy it is to identify individuals based on metadata.[13]

As David Haynes, author of Metadata for Information Management and Retrieval, writes, "Good [data] governance also depends on a good understanding of metadata and accountability for past actions."[14] In the context of surveillance, good governance relies on taking privacy into consideration when enacting laws and practices related to metadata. That means dispensing with a false distinction between content data and metadata.

The public's lack of knowledge about metadata puts it at a disadvantage. Corporations and government agencies have taken advantage of this lack of understanding by collecting vast swathes of metadata without owners' knowledge or permission. Until metadata is afforded the same privacy protections as content data, harvesting metadata will serve the specialized interests of those who commodify personal data for profit and for politics and put ordinary people's data at risk.

MYTH 12

"THE CONSTITUTION
PROTECTS REPORTERS
AND THEIR SOURCES"

Despite the vaunted position a free press holds in the minds of many, it's a myth that the US Constitution protects reporters and their sources. The First Amendment's freedom of the press and the Fourth Amendment's right of the people to be secure from unreasonable government searches and seizures are revered in principle.

To three-letter agencies, however, they're often not worth the paper they're printed on.

Spain's Supreme Court investigated David Morales, a former military official who owns the security firm Undercover Global SL, for spying on Wikileaks founder and editor Julian Assange during his asylum stay at the Ecuadorian embassy in London. Morales allegedly recorded Assange's meetings with his attorneys and then handed over information to the CIA. Assange was indicted on eighteen counts of violating the Espionage Act for publishing, in 2010, military and diplomatic secrets received from US Army intelligence officer Chelsea Manning.

While government sources have said Assange is not a journalist, Bruce Brown from the Reporters Committee for Freedom of the Press observes: "Any government use of the Espionage Act to criminalize the receipt and publication of classified information poses a dire threat to journalists seeking to publish such information in the public interest, irrespective of the Justice Department's assertion that Assange is not a journalist."[1]

Government surveillance of journalists—often shading into harass-ment—threatens to dismantle a free press. When journalists are investi-gated for, and discouraged from, reporting on incidents that embarrass the government or uncover its covert activity, the public loses out on its right to know.

In 2006, James Risen and Eric Lichtblau of the *New York Times* received the Pulitzer Prize for national reporting "for their carefully sourced stories on secret domestic eavesdropping that stirred a national debate on the boundary line between fighting terrorism and protecting civil liberty."

Ironically, Risen was not just a reporter of government eavesdrop-ping. He was also a target.

It was a great year for Risen. His book *State of War: The Secret His-tory of the CIA and the Bush Administration* hit the national bestseller list. After its release, the Department of Justice (DOJ) opened an in-vestigation into some of the book's disclosures about a failed initiative called Operation Merlin. According to Risen they obtained his "credit card records, my credit reports, my travel records, probably my phone records, just about everything—just about all of my—any kind of com-mercial transaction record that they can get a hold of." Risen later told National Public Radio (NPR) that Merlin was "a mismanaged operation by the CIA, and I believe—I believe they got angry because I embar-rassed them."[2]

The DOJ tried to pressure Risen to testify against his suspected source, attorney and former CIA employee Jeffrey Alexander Sterling. Merlin was a covert operation under President Clinton to provide Iran with flawed blueprints for a nuclear weapon component to disrupt Iran's nuclear weapons program. Sterling was arrested, charged, and convicted of violating the Espionage Act of 1918 for leaking details of the operation to Risen. Officials then leaked information that they were secretly monitoring reporters' telephone calls, raising the specter of fear among journalists reporting on government activities.

DOJ efforts to pressure Risen to testify at Sterling's trial went on for seven years, and Risen lived with the possibility of facing prison

for shielding his source. In 2015, the pressure ended without his being forced to testify. Risen told NPR, "I know for a fact that the FBI
questioned people about a lot of other things in my book in addition
to Merlin. I think they were scouring my book, looking for something
to conduct a leak investigation on against me in isolation from the *New
York Times*."[3]

SEIZURES OF REPORTERS' RECORDS

In the United States, many jurisdictions protect a journalist from revealing their confidential sources in the discovery phase of a state lawsuit. That's often referred to as the reporter's privilege. The District of
Columbia and forty-nine states (Wyoming being the exception) have
enacted shield laws that protect anonymous sources. However, there is
no equivalent in federal law.

The US Department of Justice created guidelines governing when
it can launch a criminal investigation against a reporter. In response to
criticism of how the DOJ pursued and obtained phone records of AP
journalists in 2013, President Barack Obama ordered a review of the
guidelines. Two months later, new rules stipulated that the AG must
personally authorize any application for a court order involving a member of the press, albeit with two exceptions. One is if the journalist is
subpoenaed and agrees to turn over information; the other is in cases
involving exigent circumstances and national security or harm to a
person.

National Security Letters (NSL), however, are exempt from the media guidelines. NSLs can compel third parties to turn over customer
records, such as a journalist's call log. They carry a gag order, so no one
is allowed to talk about them. Trevor Timm, executive director of the
Freedom of the Press Foundation, has called them "an affront to press
freedom."[4]

We do know of several cases of government spying on journalists.

In 2014, it was reported that the DOJ had seized records as part of
leaks investigations for more than twenty Associated Press phone lines,
and obtained, with a warrant, emails sent by James Rosen (not to be

confused with James Risen), chief Washington correspondent for Fox News. The Justice Department was frustrated with Rosen's reporting on US intelligence about North Korea. After public outcry, that year the attorney general updated the federal guidelines for media subpoenas. The Reporters Committee for Freedom of the Press convened a group of more than fifty media companies and journalism organizations to propose revisions to strengthen protections for journalists in the guidelines.

ALI WATKINS

In 2018, it surfaced that the DOJ had covertly seized years of email and telephone records of Ali Watkins, a reporter for the *New York Times*. Watkins was a finalist for the 2015 Pulitzer Prize in national reporting for coverage of the Senate's report on the CIA's post–9/11 torture program.

The DOJ told Watkins it was investigating leaks, specifically how Watkins had learned that, in 2013, Russian spies attempted to recruit former Trump foreign policy advisor Carter Page. Watkins had published an April 3, 2017, piece in *BuzzFeed* about efforts to recruit Page.

The DOJ obtained years of her customer records and subscriber information from such providers as Google and Verizon. The Justice Department also obtained records from when she reported on national security for outlets including *BuzzFeed* and *Politico*.

Jameel Jaffer, executive director of the nonprofit Knight First Amendment Institute at Columbia University, said of the Watkins monitoring:

> Government surveillance of a reporter's communications would be concerning under any circumstances, but it is especially so here. It is unclear whether the government exhausted other options before seizing Watkins's phone and email records. It's also not apparent why it was necessary to collect years' worth of sensitive information. Finally, there is a question whether Watkins was notified in a timely way of the surveillance. It is thus unclear whether the search complied even with the Justice Department's own guidelines.[5]

FAST AND FURIOUS

In addition to James Risen, six-time Emmy winner Sharyl Attkisson was a target of eavesdropping.

The former CBS investigator and news host investigated a story that stained the administration: Operation Fast and Furious. It played out from 2010 to 2012 and was a sting operation. The Bureau of Alcohol, Tobacco, Firearms, and Explosives (ATF) let illegal straw buyers purchase guns, hoping they would smuggle them into Mexico and lead investigators to drug cartel leaders. They call the practice "gun walking." But more than two thousand firearms were left unaccounted for by the operation's end. Two were linked to the 2010 murder of a Border Patrol agent, Brian Terry, north of the Mexican border in Arizona. Suspects shot him using guns bought during the operation.

The public was not made aware of the link between Operation Fast and Furious, the gun walking, and Terry's murder. But ATF insiders shared concerns on the site CleanupATF.org. Gun rights supporters wrote about the rumors surrounding Terry's killing, and several ATF agents became whistleblowers, contacting Senator Chuck Grassley of Iowa. He began investigating the incident in January 2011. CBS News interviewed several ATF sources and reported on it a month later.

Although Attkisson received an Emmy for her Fast and Furious reporting, it came at a steep price. In her bestseller, *Stonewalled: My Fight for Truth Against the Forces of Obstruction, Intimidation, and Harassment in Obama's Washington*, she claimed CBS discouraged her reporting on several stories—including Fast and Furious and the 2012 Benghazi attack—and that evidence points toward the White House's having "an identified list of reporters who may be troublesome ... to the administration, who they may have targeted."[6]

Soon after Fast and Furious broke, someone hacked Attkisson's work and home computers. In 2011, her family's home and work devices turned on and off during the night. The television had interference and an alarm emitted random chirping sounds. In 2012, her Virginia home's FiOS line turned on and off. The interference grew to where ongoing interruptions made telephone calls unpredictable and sometimes impossible.

In early 2012, a forensic analyst determined that both computers were being monitored. When connected to the family computer, Attkisson's cell phone was tapped by an IP address at the United States Postal Service. Experts said the hacking "appeared to be connected to proprietary software used exclusively by government agencies" including the CIA, NSA, and FBI.[7]

Attkisson sued the Justice Department. The presiding judge described the salient facts: "An independent forensic computer analyst hired by CBS reported finding evidence on both Ms. Attkisson's work-issued laptop computer and her family's desktop computer of a coordinated, highly skilled series of actions and attacks directed at the operation of the computers." Further analysis revealed that in December 2012 someone tried to remotely remove evidence of the spying. An inspection of the exterior of the Attkissons' home revealed an extra Verizon FiOS fiber optics line. Attkisson asked a Verizon technician to leave the extra cable at the home, but it disappeared, and the family never found it.

Surveillance continued after it was detected. In March 2013, the family's desktop computer malfunctioned. That September, while working on a story, Attkisson noticed that someone was remotely accessing and controlling her personal laptop. They deleted data. The next month she filed a complaint with the Inspector General of the DOJ. The IG investigation was limited to an analysis of the compromised desktop computer. The partially released investigation report reported "no evidence of intrusion," but acknowledged much advanced mode computer activity not attributable to Attkisson or anyone in the house.

Proof would surface.

In late 2014, a trove of documents posted on the Judicial Watch website contained an email conversation between White House Deputy Press Secretary Eric Schultz and Attorney General Eric Holder's top press aide, Tracy Schmaler. The two discussed a plan to pressure the

CBS News network into silencing Attkisson. The email was a vindication for Attkisson, one of the few journalists covering Fast and Furious.[8]

When the government hacks, it threatens to undermine individual privacy and subvert protections of individual liberties that guide law enforcement. It also thwarts the media's ability to gather and report effectively. When journalists know the government may monitor their communications, it changes the way they relate to confidential sources. Government programs, notably the Department of State's Insider Threat Program, discourage government officials from sharing information with journalists even if the information isn't classified.

STEALTH STRINGERS, STEALTH SOURCES

Journalists must often operate like intelligence agents, according to the Committee to Protect Journalists. This especially impacts reporters on the police and national security beats. Implementing advanced security measures to protect sources and communications from monitoring is time-consuming and requires consistency. It cuts down on the number of stories that get written. It's also a factor in choosing which stories to cover.

Knowledge of potential surveillance can intimidate sources and discourage them from sharing information. If they know about monitoring, they may be less forthcoming in electronic communications and favor in-person contact. Such meetings require additional time and financial resources, especially if traveling is involved.

Sources don't talk about sensitive matters as they might have before surveillance was on everyone's minds. Confusion over what is sensitive further intimidates them in their communications.

As for the journalists who were spied on, Ali Watkins continues to write for the *New York Times*, covering New York City crime and law enforcement.

James Rosen's eighteen-year career at Fox News ended in December 2017 after several colleagues raised allegations of sexual harassment. As of 2021, Rosen was the National Investigative Reporter for Sinclair Broadcast Group in Washington, DC.

In August 2020, the Department of Justice brought a new indictment against Julian Assange, broadening the scope of his alleged conspiracy.

Sharyl Attkisson has her own podcast. She continues to cover issues of national security, just not with her previous corporate media affiliations.

James Risen left the *New York Times* in 2018 and began working with *The Intercept*, cofounded by Glenn Greenwald, one of the reporters Edward Snowden contacted initially. Risen emphasized the importance of protecting reporters in his interview with NPR:

> In order to talk about almost anything important to national security or the War on Terror, people have to take risks in order to tell the truth about what's going on. And we as reporters have to be willing to provide confidentiality in order to receive that information and report on that information and tell the American people what's really happening. If we don't have the ability to maintain confidential sources and protect our sources, then people won't be willing to talk to us, and we won't be able to find out what the government is doing.[9]

This irony is that this statement is coming from one of the leaders of *The Intercept*, which did not protect one of their sources, intelligence contractor Reality Leigh Winner, and landed her in federal prison. It was the metadata that got her.[10]

MYTH 13

"THE ATTORNEY-CLIENT PRIVILEGE IS SACROSANCT"

Sheriff Andy Taylor on *The Andy Griffith Show* told his son, Opie, about the attorney–client privilege after Opie and a friend eavesdropped on a conversation at the Mayberry jail to help mount a case against the inmate. "Whether a man is guilty or innocent," the wise sheriff said, "we have to find that out by due process of law."[1]

The attorney–client privilege is a legal right that allows individuals to resist compulsory disclosure of documents and information. It's aimed at keeping confidential all communications between a lawyer and their client. Examples of when the privilege can be asserted include discovery requests before or during a trial, or a demand that the lawyer testify under oath. The American Bar Association, and each state, have rules of ethics governing the legal profession. They reflect the broader principle that a lawyer's duty to maintain client confidentiality extends to all information related to representation in the attorney's possession.

It's a myth, however, that this privilege is inviolate.

New technologies have made surveillance tactics easier and affordable for both local police and intelligence agencies. For example, the DEA's mass collection of telephone call records precedes 9/11 and the USA PATRIOT Act, so mass surveillance is not specific to the "war on terror." New York City attorney Jonathan Stribling-Uss says that one of the bigger myths of mass surveillance is that it was started as part of the "war on terror." In fact, it is a long-standing practice, and the "terror" concept was added later as justification and expansion.[2]

Mass surveillance programs do not isolate and protect attorney–client communications, and lawyers must take extra measures to preserve confidentiality such as encrypting all electronic communications and taking information offline where possible. However, because of programs like the postal mail monitoring program, where the FBI takes a photo of the outside of every letter sent through the US Postal Service, such measures may not come easily or be practicable.[3]

Lawyers in a small practice may find it burdensome to circumvent government spying, such as traveling to meet one-on-one in person with clients, especially those residing outside the United States. Clients may also lack the means either to travel, or to learn and install adequate electronic protections. Fortunately, due to advances in cryptography and open-source public computing it is now easier and often free to communicate in ways that no state intelligence agency can conduct mass surveillance on. As Edward Snowden has stated in a live 2013 Q&A with *The Guardian*, "Encryption works. Properly implemented strong crypto systems are one of the few things you can rely on."

Aside from the extra steps and cost needed to safeguard the integrity of communications, there are significant societal downsides to surveillance of lawyers. Attorneys who suspect their communications are being monitored may think twice about representing clients with unpopular views. Representing individuals charged with terrorism-related offenses exposes attorneys to heightened scrutiny.

THE USUAL SUSPECTS

The Center for Constitutional Rights (CCR) in New York represents many people whose rights have been violated by detention and intelligence gathering practices instituted after the September 11, 2001, attacks.

Most of their clients are people whom the government has at some time suspected of a link, however attenuated and unsubstantiated, to al-Qaeda, groups supportive of al-Qaeda, or to terrorist activity generally. They fall within the class of people the government describes as the targets of the warrantless NSA surveillance program.

That's why in 2006 CCR filed *CCR v. Bush* (later *CCR v. Obama*) against President George W. Bush and the heads of the other major security agencies.[4] It challenged warrantless NSA surveillance of people within the US, including CCR attorneys, as a violation of the Foreign Intelligence Surveillance Act (FISA) and as an impairment of lawyers' ability to communicate via telephone and email with their overseas clients, witnesses, and others.

The lawsuit explained that CCR lawyers are obligated by professional ethics to take reasonable and appropriate measures to reduce the risk of disclosure of certain client confidences, once they're aware of unlawful government electronic surveillance. Such measures include "not communicating with certain individuals at all by phone or email, and avoiding subjects central to the attorney–client relationship and work product in electronic communications with others." Attorneys were forced to travel internationally to avoid the risk of jeopardizing the confidentiality of privileged communications.

The NSA and the DOJ refused to confirm or deny whether they were surveilling lawyers, saying that disclosure would compromise US intelligence methods. In early 2011, a federal district court dismissed *CCR v. Obama*, finding that CCR lacked standing to sue because the center lacked evidence of actual monitoring (and could not obtain or use such evidence in the court proceedings because such evidence would be a "state secret"). The court acknowledged that even though they couldn't prove surveillance, CCR attorneys appeared to have established that their litigation activities became costlier because of concern related to monitoring.

In 2007, CCR urged a federal judge to invalidate the Protect America Act of 2007, the law President Bush signed making surveillance of anyone overseas possible without a warrant even if it happens on switches or networks within the United States. Michael Avery, a constitutional attorney on CCR's legal team who at the time was the president of the National Lawyers Guild, argued that the surveillance Congress authorized in the statute was even more unconstitutional than the original program Bush had initiated without congressional approval.

Avery explained the harm to attorneys: "We filed suit against the illegal NSA Surveillance Program because it seriously disrupted the ability of the lawyers at CCR to communicate with their clients, witnesses, and co-counsel without revealing information to the government that the attorney–client privilege had historically protected. The program dealt a crippling body blow to effective advocacy precisely at a time when unpopular clients needed lawyers the most."[5]

Other organizations filed similar lawsuits, with the same result. "The failure of the courts to protect the attorney–client privilege was a catastrophic default of their responsibilities under our system of checks and balances, theoretically guaranteed by the separation of powers," notes Avery. "That failure emboldened the spymasters to create even more technologically sophisticated techniques to access information the government has no right to see. We are now worse off than ever."

The negative impact of monitoring privileged communications is obvious to most lawyers and scholars. But do law students and young attorneys grasp the consequences?

Avery pauses. "I tried to convey these risks to my constitutional law students at Suffolk Law School. Unfortunately, such concerns are remote to the average law student, just as they are to the average citizen."

MONITORING LAWYERS IMPERILS DEMOCRACY

The expectation of privacy between lawyer and client has been a cornerstone of the common law justice system for hundreds of years. Related entitlements are the right of an accused to a zealous legal defense and the right of an attorney to decide whom to represent. These rights are perhaps most precious to individuals who have been accused of crimes against the US or who hold viewpoints that the government does not favor.

When lawyers know their communications may be monitored, the nature of their professional responsibility is impacted. Jonathan Stribling-Uss is devoting his legal practice to bringing secure communications to fellow practitioners. As necessary as digital proficiency is in the legal profession, many lawyers have barely made it past the analog age. "Our current system of Internet communication is not constitutional, especially regarding attorney–client communications," he says.[6]

Stribling-Uss formed the aptly named Constitutional Communications, with attorneys from CCR and the ACLU, to educate lawyers and others to use open-source encryption for all communication. They found interest in developing secure communication capacities among local bar associations and civil rights and human rights attorneys representing journalists, as well as social justice activists around the globe.

After unfurling Tibetan flags at the opening ceremony of the 2008 Olympics in Beijing, an act for which he was deported, Stribling-Uss noticed the lack of privacy in digital environments. Tibetans and activist students emphasized that China was monitoring their communications. They had no choice but to use encryption to effectively organize, due to this government scrutiny. When he returned to the US and worked with Iraq Veterans Against the War, Stribling-Uss concluded that domestic activists also needed to encrypt. He saw service members speaking out against the military policy get fired or otherwise impeded in their work.

"We realized that Google was not appropriate for communication since Google was colluding with military officials. So service men and women had to maintain a database on a separate computer for organizing activities. While we're aware of surveillance issues related to the Chinese government, which was monitoring all their networks, we don't have the same understanding of our own government," the Brooklynite explains.

Lawyers' failure to encrypt is largely due to governmental collusion with industry to confuse the issue and ensure that basic systems have been backdoored, he asserts. "Attorneys have not been given good information about this since the companies advertising are selling products that are actually broken." He continues, "Clients have also not been educated about this. Clients control attorney–client privilege so they can demand that their lawyers use open-source encryption for their communication."

The US government's Vulnerabilities Equities Process (VEP)[7] is a set of guidelines federal agencies use to determine when to inform the public about security vulnerabilities in software and hardware. The government asserts that it must maintain failures in key information technology products so that the government may gain access to many types of proprietary software and encryption systems (so-called "backdoors"). What this means for attorneys is that all private propriety software is a black box—and intentionally kept that way by the government—that could, and by design is likely to, include serious vulnerabilities that imperil the security of attorney–client communications. To avoid this, Stribling-Uss says, attorneys should seek open-source products whose source code can be publicly accessed and vetted to ensure there are no secret, government-prompted flaws that risk revealing client information.

THE PREVALENCE OF PARALLEL CONSTRUCTION

One of the most persistent myths about surveillance in the US is that it is only used as part of the war on terror, and not used in everyday criminal cases. But consider this: evidence used regularly in criminal cases often comes from a secret police practice called "parallel construction," in which police and prosecutors avoid warrant requirements and initiate intrusive investigations. Information gathered from the NSA's mass surveillance programs is presented as evidence by police agencies in routine criminal cases. The fact that such evidence originated from warrantless government spying is intentionally kept from defendants and their attorneys. This is one of the major ways that clients' Fourth Amendment warrant requirements and their Sixth Amendment right to counsel have been undermined in the digital age.

Federal agents can search massive government databases for information on someone that they hope may relate to a crime. When something of interest is found they will send local police a "BOLO" (or "Be On the Look Out") order for the targeted person, with specific instructions that local police must "develop your own probable cause for conducting a traffic stop."[8] When police encounter the person they detain them, looking for some evidence of a crime, evidence originally discovered through warrantless mass electronic surveillance. If police find such evidence and initiate a criminal process, they deny the evidence's origin by using a false witness or confidential informant.

When Nancy Gertner, a Harvard Law School professor and former federal judge, heard of the concept of parallel construction, she said: "It sounds like they are phonying up investigations."[9]

"Phonying up investigations" is a routine US government practice. The Special Operations Division, a $125 million unit of the Drug Enforcement Administration (DEA), trains federal agents on parallel construction, and it's a formal policy to hide NSA data by covering it with false statements and fake witnesses. Because nearly 94 percent of state-level felony convictions and 97 percent of federal convictions are the result of plea bargains, it's rare that defense attorneys have full access to the initiating evidence of many criminal cases.[10]

The government has taken privileged information from larger US law firms and used it against their clients. For example, the NSA illegally obtained privileged and confidential information from Mayer Brown, a Chicago-based law firm representing the government of Indonesia in trade negotiations with the US government. The NSA was able to access the negotiation posture of the Indonesian government, including what Indonesia would or wouldn't accept in the negotiations. The agency shared this critical information with US government negotiators who used it against Mayer Brown in those negotiations.[11]

GUARDING AGAINST CYBER ATTACKS

While the possibility of government surveillance can chill attorney–client communications, the reality of daily breaches of computer systems is preventable.

As custodians of confidential, privileged information that is stored electronically in their computer systems, lawyers have an obligation to safeguard it. Law firms that experienced cyber attacks have reported business downtime, loss of billable hours, hefty fees for correction, costs associated with having to replace hardware and software, and loss of important files and information. That doesn't include harm to reputation and an erosion of trust by current and prospective clients and the public. Stribling-Uss says that law firms must, as a requirement for doing business, enact more robust cybersecurity to preserve client confidentiality.

The Model Rules of Professional Conduct expect attorneys to "keep abreast of changes in the law and its practice, including the benefits and risks associated with relevant technology."[12] Failure to take these precautions and affirmative actions can have dire consequences, including claims for legal malpractice. Cybersecurity legal malpractice claims typically cite negligence in terms of failure to protect clients' confidential and personal data or supervise members of the firm, as well as fraud and misrepresentation.

For example, a malpractice suit was brought by the Millard family against their New York real estate attorney after that lawyer's email was hacked.[13] Hackers posed as the lawyer and directed the Millards to wire $1.9 million to them; the Millards thought they were wiring money to the seller of the Manhattan co-op they wanted to purchase. The couple alleged that their attorney breached her duty to keep their communications secure, including taking adequate cybersecurity precautions.

Stribling-Uss's believes that the concept of attorney–client privilege is a core American value and that when mass surveillance programs routinely violate that protection, it undermines one of the bedrock principles protecting our freedom.

New York City Legal Aid Society's Digital Forensics supervising attorney, Jerome D. Greco also understands these issues. He says, "The dual threats of government surveillance and private bad actors continue to increase. The legal community is not immune. In fact, we are targets. Attorneys and law offices have an obligation to protect their clients' information and adopt necessary changes to meet that responsibility."[14]

Professional societies, not just in the legal arena, are starting to take this ethical duty more seriously. And that is trickling up to state governments. While many states' security breach statutes require companies to enact and maintain "reasonable" security measures, at least two have gone a step further.

In Massachusetts and Nevada, explains Stribling-Uss, laws mandate encryption of personal data when it is transmitted over public networks or stored on portable devices. In Massachusetts, a set of regulations adopted by the Office of Consumer Affairs and Business Regulation requires encryption "to the extent technically feasible," and applies to Massachusetts residents. The Nevada law incorporates requirements of the Payment Card Industry Security Standards for all data collectors that accept credit cards conducting business in the state.

In 2020, New York State's Department of Financial Services enacted regulations governing cybersecurity. They require law firms or attorneys working under "Banking Law, the Insurance Law or the Financial Services Law" to have comprehensive cybersecurity programs. The entities are required, among other things, to perform a risk assessment of their cyber risks, implement a written cybersecurity policy, and maintain a comprehensive cybersecurity program which "shall implement controls, including encryption, to protect Nonpublic Information."[15] These regulations, says Stribling-Uss, should be expanded to include requiring end-to-end encryption for all attorney–client communications with New York State residents.

As Surveillance Technology Oversight Project executive director Albert Fox Cahn stated in relation to the new regulations and government monitoring, "It is wrong to force New Yorkers to use insecure digital platforms just to have their day in court. Encryption is indispensable to effective lawyering in the digital age. Without end-to-end encryption, lawyers expose our clients' secrets and undermine their case."[16]

In surveillance of attorneys, the core principles of privacy, legal representation, due process, and assumption of innocence—once cornerstones that have historically set the United States apart from totalitarian societies—are imperiled by the very institutions mandated to protect them.

"THEY CAN'T DESIGN DEVICES AND PLATFORMS FOR PRIVACY"

Bobbi Duncan and Taylor McCormick were raised in conservative families. Duncan was homeschooled in North Carolina; her family attended a fundamentalist church. As she grappled with her sexual identity, she carefully adjusted her Facebook privacy settings so her father could not see all her posts. "Once I had my Facebook settings set, I knew—or thought I knew—there wasn't any problem," she told the *Wall Street Journal*.[1]

Taylor McCormick, from Texas, had told his mother he was gay. But he hadn't told his father.

After both joined the Queer Chorus at the University of Texas, Austin, the choir president added Bobbi and Taylor to the choir's Facebook group. In doing so, he unwittingly outed them to their parents. Facebook's software automatically notified their online friends—without their approval—that they were now members of the chorus. That happened even though both students had set their own Facebook privacy settings to keep some of their activity private.

Some technology designers adhere to the myth that they can't build products to reliably protect privacy. Lax privacy settings sustain a booming corporate data aggregator industry by minimizing barriers for first- and third-party companies to collect and sell data. Personal and behavioral data unique to each person is harvested and traded much like the metal, energy, agriculture, and livestock industries. For data aggregators like Acxiom, Factual, Infogroup, and Localeze, the more data they can scoop up, the better.

As artificial intelligence informs disruptive technologies—game-changing products or ones that displace an established technology—product developers have great leverage as gatekeepers of user privacy. Two factors converge to render imperfect privacy design harmful to users: 1) information commodification and 2) the practice of captology, or using computers for persuasion. At their intersection lies the "Texas Tea" of the information age.

CAPITALIZING ON CAPTOLOGY

Captologist Nir Eyal is a master of behavior design and habit formation.

"The rise of Facebook and then Twitter and [the game developer] Zynga, which manage to get people to do things they never have done before, fascinated me. I've put together a useful framework for how products form addictions and how products form behaviors and habits," says the Israeli entrepreneur.

His "hook" model, he claims, underpins the world's most popular consumer apps and platforms. Eyal is unabashed about its goal: to "build products that create habit-forming behavior in users via a looping cycle that consists of trigger, an action, a variable reward, and continued investment." In his two bestselling books, Eyal explains how to hook consumers, and then explains how to minimize distractions and "control your attention" so we don't let technology get the best of us.[2]

Along with a legion of future product designers, Eyal attended lectures by Dr. B. J. Fogg at the Persuasive Technology Lab at Stanford University, which was founded in 1999. Fogg is a master architect of captology. *Fortune* magazine says Fogg's research motivates a worldwide legion of user experience (UX) designers who use and expand his models of seductive design.[3]

Coercion techniques that foster addiction to apps and social media platforms cannot be separated from the design of electronic gadgets, platforms, and software. Together, this potent partnership bores into users' privacy. Every time we search for a new pair of shoes, or stream a science fiction movie, we reveal a bit of our soul in the form of our likes, attitudes, and habits.

ETHICS IN DEVICE AND PLATFORM DESIGN

Nir Eyal posits that with willpower we can control our lives. But it takes more than willpower to disengage from the clutches of personal devices and social media, according to Tristan Harris, another Fogg laboratory graduate, and a former design ethicist at Google.

Harris joins, as written in *Wired*, "a generation of students who learned how to harness the magic of notifications, nudges, and streaks to convince people to keep using their products." *The Atlantic* has called Harris "the closest thing Silicon Valley has to a conscience."[4] Along with venture capitalist Roger McNamee, an early Facebook investor, he believes focusing on willpower is pointless in the face of tech's manipulative design practices.

As a young magician, Harris learned to search for weaknesses in people's perception in order to exploit and influence them. From that vantage point, he became an outspoken whistleblower in tech. In 2012, while still at Google, Harris created a 144-slide presentation that went viral: "A Call to Minimize Distraction and Respect Users' Attention." It outlined ways in which small design elements like push notifications can become massive distractions at scale.[5]

How do you build humane systems?

Harris urges a focus on users reclaiming agency. "Never before has a handful of people working at a handful of tech companies been able to steer the thoughts and feelings of a billion people," he told a Stanford University audience. Of what he calls "attention economy," he observes: "There are more users on Facebook than followers of Christianity. There are more people on YouTube than followers of Islam. I don't know a more urgent problem than this."[6]

In 2018, Harris founded the nonprofit Center for Humane Technology (CHT). Its aim is to change the public's mindset from which persuasive technology is built. Harris blames societal ills and human- ity's degradation on tech platforms' conveyor belt of "clicking, scrolling, and sharing." CHT has the hefty mission of aligning technology and related business models with human welfare. Harris argues for extend- ing to internet companies the fiduciary duty that professionals such as doctors, lawyers, and others owe to their clients, legally binding them to act exclusively in accordance with their clients' well-being.[7]

If you have trouble visualizing how technology can persuade, John Herrman of the *New York Times* boils it down to a helpful motif: little red dots. They may offer a jumping-off point for design reform, or at least awareness of problematic designs:

> Commonly seen at the corners of app icons, where they are known in the trade as badges, they are now proliferating across once- peaceful interfaces on a steep epidemic curve. They alert us to things that need to be checked: unread messages; new activities; pending software updates; announcements; unresolved problems. As they've spread, they've become a rare commonality in the products that we—and the remorseful technologists—are so worried about. If not the culprits, the dots are at least accessories to most of the supposed crimes of addictive app design.[8]

The red dot became popular around 2000 with Apple's Operating System X for the iMac. It could be seen on Apple's Mail app with the number of unread messages. Herman notes that with the iPhone, in 2007, dots "transformed from a simple utility into a way of life—from a solution into a cause unto themselves."

After the iPhone was available to outside developers, badge use ac- celerated on a wide range of platforms, in different shapes and colors. Badges present an omnipresent distraction and reminder of life tasks unfulfilled. Herrman says tech titans are mindful of the problem from a user-experience perspective. Google's guide for app developers cau- tions not to badge every notification, while Apple's guidelines urge the minimization of badging.

DESIGNING FOR PRIVACY

The physical design of information technologies could be a powerful dam to curb data aggregators' harmful reach. Design can encompass engineering, product design, and user interface design, both in hardware and software.

So why aren't devices built to honor robust privacy?

Attorney Woodrow Hartzog writes in *Privacy's Blueprint*: "The problem is that there are overwhelming incentives to design technologies in a way that maximizes the collection, use, and disclosure of personal information." The internet business model of gathering and selling vast amounts of data motivates companies to focus on harvesting data, then resolving privacy issues later. "Although there are many great examples of privacy-protective design, the market is awash in privacy-corrosive technologies."[9]

The tech industry opposes government regulation of products. Hartzog contends that while legislators have tried to create guidelines governing data collection, use, and sharing, they have ignored device design.

Corporations profit by not building privacy into the architecture of product and platform. What incentive do they have to put the consumer first, ahead of profit? The commodification of personal data for marketers and other third parties is a goliath industry. And developers seek data: personal, engagement, behavioral and attitudinal, to build more desirable products. Since 2000, and begun by Google, corporations have engaged in what Shoshana Zuboff calls surveillance capitalism. She writes that "this new economics covertly claims private human experience as free raw material for translation into behavioral data. Some data are used to improve services, but the rest are turned into computational products that predict your behavior."

Zuboff continues:

These predictions are traded in a new futures market, where surveillance capitalists sell certainty to businesses determined to know what we will do next. This logic was first applied to finding which ads online will attract our interest, but similar practices now reside in nearly every sector—insurance, retail, health, education, finance and more—where personal experience is secretly captured and computed for behavioral predictions. By now it is no exaggeration to say that the Internet is owned and operated by private surveillance capital.[10]

With such a precious commodity to be harvested, it's no wonder that designers have few incentives to change their practices. Tech companies continue to reap huge profits and face minor penalties for doing so. Fines imposed have not served as a deterrent.

PRIVACY'S FAIRY GODMOTHER

Dr. Ann Cavoukian is Canada's national privacy treasure.

The world-renowned expert leads the Privacy by Design Centre of Excellence. Appointed as the Information and Privacy Commissioner of Ontario in 1997, she served for an unprecedented three terms and created Privacy by Design. It's a framework and now a movement for embedding privacy into the design specifications of information technologies, networked infrastructure, and even business practices. In October 2010, regulators at the International Conference of Data Protection Authorities and Privacy Commissioners unanimously passed a resolution recognizing Privacy by Design as an international standard. The General Data Protection Regulation (GDPR) in Europe includes privacy by design as the default in the law.

Cavoukian has worked with engineers, software designers, and data scientists to impart how critical it is to "bake it into the code that you're developing." Everyone she spoke to said they were able to embed privacy into the code and into their systems. The problem was that they were rarely asked to embed privacy into the code when writing a program; instead, they were asked to deliver it and then "bolt on a privacy solution after the fact." Cavoukian then met with executives to discuss dispensing with the silos of engineering, policy, and marketing. "Get rid of the silos and have an integrated approach so that when you do go to your code writers, your tech people, and ask for something, privacy is embedded into the process."

Privacy by Design encompasses six tenets. Some critics claim it is too abstract. Still, as of 2018, the GDPR in the EU makes data protection by design and default legally enforceable under its Article 25.

The first tenet is to be proactive rather than reactive, or preventative not remedial, so privacy violations don't occur. The second is to have privacy as the default setting with no user action required. Integrating privacy into the design and architecture of IT systems and business practices is the third precept. "It is not bolted on as an add-on, after the fact. . . . Privacy is integral to the system, without diminishing functionality," says Cavoukian.[11]

Full functionality is the fourth maxim, avoiding the pretense of false dichotomies, such as privacy versus security. The fifth tenet is end-to-end security for the full lifecycle. All data are securely retained, then securely destroyed at the end of the process, in a timely fashion.

The sixth tenet is operational visibility and transparency of operations to users and providers, subject to independent verification. Respect for user privacy is the seventh credo. Architects and operators must keep foremost the interests of the individual user with strong privacy defaults, appropriate notice, and user-friendly options.

The Federal Trade Commission in 2012 adopted privacy by design as one of the three elements in a new framework that would "incorporate the full set of fair information practice principles, updated for the 21st century." It cited privacy by design as integral to engineers' or website developers' thought process when writing code or creating a new product. But in practice there has been little legislative commitment and follow up.

In 2016, the National Institute of Standards and Technology (NIST), a Department of Commerce agency, issued an internal report featuring an introduction to the concepts of privacy engineering and risk management for federal systems. The European Data Protection Supervisor called this development "an outstanding novelty in the panorama of guidance provided by governments or data protection authorities, as the document includes a privacy risk model and a methodology to implement privacy requirements when engineering systems processing personal data." NIST documents are seen as standard bearers for US federal information systems and agencies are expected to meet them.[12]

IT'S HOW IT WORKS

The practice of aggregating and selling data affects many issues, including free speech, public health, data security, and human rights. Woodrow Hartzog notes that the Federal Trade Commission's Fair Information Practices—personal electronic data rules enacted at the dawn of the internet—are not adequate to protect consumers in the twenty-first century.

Better protection, he posits, would derive from specific laws dealing with biometric surveillance, social media interfaces, and how Internet of Things devices ought to be constructed. Professor Hartzog suggests a design agenda in which law and policy makers support standards of design that mandate safe user experiences and support privacy.[13]

Cavoukian's and Hartzog's focus on design standards, while late in the game, might mitigate the sway of Big Tech on users' habits. Steve Jobs said, "Design is not just what it looks and feels like. Design is how it works." As the creator of the most prolific personal surveillance device, the iPhone, Jobs would know.[14]

It's past time for legislators and policymakers to smarten up privacy laws to keep pace with the construction of America's growing inventory of "smart" products. Only then will there be a chance to scale down corporate harvesters' rapacious appetites.

"CONGRESS AND COURTS PROTECT US FROM SURVEILLANCE"

Before Congress and the courts can protect the public from intrusive surveillance, they first must know the difference between a browser and a router.

Their learning curve is steep.

Lawmakers stumbled into enacting the first computer-related laws after a Hollywood movie ignited Cold War–type fears. Decades later, in the Senate chamber and in the courts, they are still floundering. A look back informs the present and shows how misguided the myth is that our leaders protect us from intrusive surveillance.

FROM THE SILVER SCREEN TO CAPITOL HILL

Ronald Reagan kicked back on weekend evenings to escape the pressures of the job. The seventy-two-year-old immersed himself in the familiar world of Hollywood motion pictures at Camp David's Aspen Lodge in Maryland's Catoctin Mountain Park. In 1983, heightened tensions with the Soviet Union weighed heavily on Reagan's mind.

That April, Reagan referred to the Soviet Union as the "evil empire" when he addressed the National Association of Evangelicals. That year saw heightened strains from the Cold War—some historians say this period was one of the worst in the history of US–Soviet relations.

The president's terminology was straight out of the 1977 film *Star Wars*, televised for the first time on HBO at the time of his speech. His choice of words rejected nuances or ambiguities, as did the George Lucas film, reflecting a fantasy galaxy of moral absolutes. Released on the heels of the Vietnam War, *Star Wars* drew on the iconography of American westerns to provide a vision of moral clarity and breathe new life into a wearied national mythos.

Struggle with the Soviets was likely still haunting the fortieth president when he saw *WarGames* on June 4, 1983, a day after its commercial release. A few aides, the president's physician, the Camp David commander, and the senior Secret Service agent in charge—the regulars—were in their seats. Reagan, the twice-elected president of the Screen Actors Guild (SAG), who had worked to uncover Communists in Hollywood, sat on the couch in front of their guests with his wife, Nancy. Even their courtship was imbued with the fever of the times: the two met in 1951 during his SAG presidency, while Nancy was trying to get her name removed from the McCarthy-era Hollywood blacklist of suspected Communist sympathizers.

As the lights dimmed that Saturday, the president nestled next to Nancy to watch what was billed as a science fiction thriller. On screen, a young Matthew Broderick prepared to impress his girlfriend. For fun, his likable character, David Lightman, showed her how he could change her school grades online. But the real surprise was a new, unreleased computer video game he'd accessed from what he thought was the game's manufacturing site. He slid a floppy disk into his IMSAI 8080 computer.

A robotic voice asked, "Shall we play a game?" The wide-eyed teen agreed by hitting the enter button to launch the game "Global Thermonuclear War." He picked Seattle and Las Vegas as targets for Soviet missile strikes.

The site he hacks, however, is a real nuclear missile-command supercomputer at a top-secret US military installation. War Operation Plan Response, which when abbreviated became a droll nod to the Burger King hamburger ("WOPR"), was a computer programmed to predict different outcomes of a nuclear war. Lightman unwittingly started a simulation that convinced NORAD military personnel that real Soviet nuclear missiles were inbound.

Unable to distinguish between game and reality, WOPR kept feeding false data, such as Russian bomber incursions and submarine deployments, to NORAD. It pushed them to raise the DEFCON level toward a counterattack that would trigger World War III. The tech-savvy teen raced against the clock to stop the strike, all while being chased, arrested, and chased again by authorities who suspected him of being a KGB spy.

By the time of the closing credits, the clever teenager who averted a nuclear holocaust is the hero. In contrast, adults were hapless in the face of their own technological inventions. President Reagan had no way to know that despite his best efforts, over the next several decades this dynamic would play out in real life. Computer experts fluent in the emerging language of the digital would try to advise clueless government officials about the threats posed by a corporate-powered, digitally interconnected world. And those in charge would use the specter of cyberattacks to take control of and ultimately commercialize the internet. Mega industries vying for the larger control share of this new virtual domain would commodify the personal data of Americans, then use complex algorithms and social media platforms to influence public opinion. Through the same mechanisms, propaganda would reach new heights unforeseeable in the Cold War days.

Mark Weinberg, the president's special advisor, attended the movie screening. He described the mood when the lights came up after *WarGames*.

"The entire Aspen cabin was uncharacteristically quiet."[1]

WarGames was a box office hit, bringing in $80 million, the fifth-highest movie earner of 1983. What's not to love in a story of brash and innocent youth solving problems their elders created in the quests for power, annihilation of enemies, and profit? The film was more than just a popular success: after its debut, lawmakers and the public awoke to the dangers of war in a digital age.

And that is how it all began. Responding to the alarm coming out of Camp David, the FBI asked Congress to enact computer crime–related laws to protect the nation. But the result would be a crazy quilt of hasty, ill-informed laws that ushered in the surveillance state.

LAWS MISS THE MARK

The first federal computer crime statute was contained in the Comprehensive Crime Control Act (CCCA) of 1984, enacted on the cusp of the personal computing age.

As internet activity increased, federal cybersecurity lagged, resulting in repeated breaches of government computer systems. Meanwhile, corporations raced to market personal computers. With the advent of the World Wide Web and the internet, the same corporations looked for ways to collect personal data of users.

After tinkering with the 1984 act, in 1986 Congress finally passed the Computer Fraud and Abuse Act (CFAA). This vaguely written legislation, which remains in full force as of 2021, enables prosecutors to ensnare virtually anyone they wish to punish for computer-related offenses. Investigative reporters, for example, may face criminal or civil penalties if, while researching a story, they extract data from a website in an automated process called "scraping." Data scraping has yielded several stories of public interest. One was ProPublica's 2016 investigation of Amazon's pricing algorithm favoring its own products while hiding better deals from consumers.[2] While no journalists except for Wikileaks founder Julian Assange had been prosecuted under the CFAA at the timing of this writing, threats of litigation have allegedly delayed or withheld some stories from publication.

Even security professionals risk running afoul of the CFAA. Prosecutors issue indictments for "good guy" efforts, which identify risks in computer systems through a process called penetration, or pen, testing. IT security contractors have been prosecuted for penetrating networks they were hired to test. In 2019, the state of Iowa hired the well-known cybersecurity company Coalfire to conduct pen tests of municipal buildings. While testing the Dallas County courthouse and finding an open door, Coalfire employees Gary DeMercurio and Justin Wynn closed it, opened it, and triggered an alarm. They waited for authorities to arrive, as is standard protocol, and showed their paperwork. They spent a night in jail, only to be released when their state contractor went to bat for them.[3]

Conservatives and liberals alike criticize the CFAA. The conservative Federalist Society said in 2015 that the law has an over-criminalization problem. In 2005, Columbia Law School professor Tim Wu, who coined the term "net neutrality," called it an anomaly in a democracy: "The Computer Fraud and Abuse Act is the most outrageous criminal law you've never heard of. It bans "unauthorized access" of computers, but no one really knows what those words mean. . . . Over the years, the punishments for breaking the law have grown increasingly severe—it can now put people in prison for decades for actions that cause no real economic or physical harm. It is, in short, a nightmare for a country that calls itself free."[4]

Lawmakers still do not understand how the public uses computers. That ignorance engenders ineffective laws like the CFAA.

High-profile congressional hearings in 2019, notably with Facebook leadership, illustrated lawmakers' ignorance of internet platforms. Senator Orrin Hatch, an octogenarian, asked: "If [a version of Facebook will always be free], how do you sustain a business model in which users don't pay for your service?"

Facebook CEO Mark Zuckerberg paused, then answered: "Senator, we run ads." Zuckerberg and his staffers behind him smiled at the exchange.[5]

Journalist Garrett M. Graff writes, "Whether it's high-level physics research or the technology of our daily lives, the government's lawyers are struggling to grasp the increasingly technical cases that come before them. Both federal prosecutors and the attorneys who represent executive agencies in court are bungling lawsuits across the country because they don't understand what they're talking about. Too few lawyers have the skill set or the specialized knowledge to make sense of code, networks and the people who use them, and too few law schools are telling them what they need to know."[6] That's despite an Obama administration initiative, the US Digital Service (USDS). The USDS provides technical assistance—engineers, product managers, and designers—to federal agencies so they can use information technology to modernize their work, simplify digital service, and improve federal websites.

For twenty years, two former physicists who became Democratic congressmen have pushed to resurrect the Office of Technology Assessment (OTA). That congressional office, in existence from 1972 to 1995, gave representatives an analysis of science and technical issues. It was a leader in practicing and encouraging innovative and affordable delivery of public services, such as electronic publishing to distribute government documents. It was widely replicated around the globe. The OTA was eliminated after the 1994 midterm elections, which led to Republican control of the Senate and the House. Republican legislators characterized the OTA as wasteful and hostile to GOP interests.

Former chief technologist to the FTC, Ashkan Soltani, laments the OTA cut. He told *Wired* that legislators need expert advisors with no conflicts of interest—corporate ties that may lead to profit, or agendas to push—in the outcome. Instead, government-employed technology geeks can "basically be an encyclopedia for how things work, and can really help policymakers get to a good outcome," he said. "We had that in the OTA and that went away, and I think that was a huge mistake."[7] Physicist and Representative Bill Foster (D-IL) has observed that only about four percent of federal legislators have technical backgrounds. Instead of addressing this, it's been used as an excuse to avoid taking stands on controversial technology-related issues.

This lack of knowledge was obvious after the 2013 Snowden leaks. No legislator asked an intelligent question about the NSA's bulk metadata collection program, even though each member of Congress had been briefed on it, and have staff who can do research and prepare questions. In what may constitute legislative malfeasance, Congress has approved continuing legislation that empowers US spy agencies to collect data from US citizens and foreign nationals alike. They justify it by citing the war on terror.

The war on terror campaign—just like the war on drugs—has so-lidified the American spy state and elevated politics and power over individual privacy. Investigatory agencies, however, are not the only— perhaps not even the primary—factor in the trade-off of privacy and liberty for the promise of security. As technological illiteracy has per-sisted in Congress, it has abetted corporate as well as government efforts to amass huge troves of Americans' data. Both sectors have converged to usher in a high-tech surveillance state.

Digital corporate business models have created a market for data collection on the grandest possible scale, under the noses of the govern-ment that should regulate activities that encroach on our rights.

5G MAXIMUM OVERDRIVE

It will only get worse for Americans who put their faith in the courts or the federal legislature to protect their privacy. Advocates say the fifth-generation mobile network, or 5G, will be 4G on steroids—up to one hundred times faster. Everything will be connected and awak-ened, from vacuum cleaners to toothbrushes, like the Stephen King film *Maximum Overdrive*, in which inanimate machines pop to life. In the movie, lawn mowers, hair dryers, radios, and even an ATM wreak havoc. A gas dispenser spurts diesel into an employee's eyes and a vending machine kills a Little League coach by firing a can of soda into his head. With 5G, the casualties inflicted, of course, will be the vestiges of our privacy.

In the United Kingdom in 2019, Simon McDougall, the executive director for technology policy and innovation at the Information Com-missioner's Office, cautioned that 5G mobile data networks could pose a great threat to personal data and privacy.

"The potential for large volumes of data to be transferred at high speed over constantly connected networks, which can communicate with personal devices such as smartphones, opens up a variety of mar-keting uses that could be 'creepy' and 'intrusive" and poses 'dramatic challenges,'" noted McDougall at the Data and Marketing Association's 2019 Data Protection conference in London.

Smart and wearable devices are vulnerable to breaches. Location data privacy is potentially troublesome with 5G internet. It has a smaller coverage area and requires more cellular towers located in closer proximity to devices and to each other. Mobile operators can readily pinpoint users' location and movements and can sell this data to third parties.

Tom Wheeler, FCC chairman during the Obama administration, initiated security talks on 5G that were dropped when Donald Trump took office. In negotiations about international standards, the US got rid of requirements that technical specifications of 5G—building security into new networks—include cyber defense. The Trump FCC eschewed holding the companies that build and manage American digital networks responsible for building in security measures. Regulators and Republican lawmakers saw that as overly intrusive regulation.

In early 2018, a leaked National Security Council memo proposed that the government build a single 5G network to compete with China and protect from cyber attacks.[8] In March 2019, Trump 2020 campaign officials supported a proposal—which reportedly "spark[ed] wireless industry fears of nationalization"—under which the government would take over the spectrum designated for 5G and develop a system to share the spectrum with wireless providers on a wholesale basis.

Congressional pushback to nationalizing was swift. So was opposition from telecommunications providers. Bipartisan efforts encourage the government to support 5G but not intrude on businesses' activities. The twice-introduced Eliminate From Regulators Opportunities to Nationalize The Internet in Every Respect (EFRONTIER) Act prohibits the president and federal agencies from building, operating, or offering wholesale or retail service on a broadband network "unless a duly enacted Act of Congress signed into law by the President provides the President or the agency . . . with that authority."[9]

In April 2019, Donald Trump backed down, announcing that the nation's approach is private-sector led and private-sector driven. He called the alternative—government led—not as good or as fast.

Issues related to 5G are not just about personal security. They are also about national security. That same month, four former high-level military officials issued a statement expressing "grave concerns about a future where a Chinese-developed 5G network is widely adopted among our allies and partners." Espionage, security of future military operations, and the vulnerability of democracy and human rights globally were mentioned as concerns.[10]

THE STATE OF PRIVACY LAWS, GENERALLY

The US patchwork of laws, policies, and practices and increasingly biased judicial review allow unbridled government and corporate monitoring with impunity.

Over the years, there have been efforts to put legislative limits on civilian spying, but these efforts lack strong enforcement capabilities and do not reflect agreement on the issue. An increasingly Republican-leaning federal judiciary is inclined to favor government and corporate intrusions over the privacy, or rights to privacy, they invade.

The Constitution does not specifically recognize a right to privacy. Instead, it enshrines protections in the Fourth Amendment against unreasonable state searches and seizures. With the advent of mass electronic communication, statutes such as the Electronic Communications Privacy Act of 1986 attempted but failed to carve out protections for the digital age. And for years we've had common law torts such as intrusion or disclosure of private information.

The problem is that technology changes so quickly, augmented by artificial intelligence, that lawmakers and enforcers have no clue what laws are sensible. Nor do they seem interested in learning about the subject or staying on top of changes so laws can keep up with the times.

Privacy expert and author Anthony Gregory shows what lawyers are up against in the courts, fighting corporate and government goliaths. In *American Surveillance* he writes, "To advocate privacy is to step into a complicated cultural question, one without easy answers. The surveillance state's relationship with public opinion, tracked in arts and literature, often reflects government's boldness in surveillance technique and scope."[11] He writes what countless lawyers have learned in the late twentieth and early twenty-first century: "But to question surveillance power is to question power itself."

Harms from surveillance include different forms of discrimination, from denying people health insurance, to denying them jobs, to hurting their reputations and livelihoods.

The nature of covert spying presents a catch-22. It's difficult, if not impossible, to prevail in court when litigating challenges to mass surveillance. Courts have consistently claimed that litigants lack standing because the harms were intangible, or national security concerns outweighed any smaller harms, or because they cannot prove they were monitored.

In *Al-Haramain Islamic Foundation, Inc. v. Bush*, for example, the state secrets doctrine was invoked to preclude the plaintiffs from learning if they were subjects of covert surveillance under the program. A host of similar lawsuits, such as the 2013 Supreme Court case *Clapper v. Amnesty International*, have held that, absent concrete proof that their calls had been monitored, plaintiffs lacked standing to sue for violation of civil liberties. Other challenges to the NSA's wiretapping program have failed because plaintiffs were unable to convince federal courts that covert monitoring caused harm. In *ACLU v. NSA*, the Sixth Circuit dismissed any suggestion that First Amendment values were threatened when the government listened to private conversations.[12]

Our default legal setting seems to be that surveillance of Americans who are not suspected of engaging in criminal activity is legal unless specifically forbidden. And even then, there are many ways to get around the strictures of the law.

For example, National Security Letters (NSL) authorize government officials to seek information relevant to national security investigations. These administrative subpoenas allow the FBI to obtain information about people from their phone companies, internet service providers, banks, credit agencies, and other entities. No prior judicial approval is needed. NSLs come with a nondisclosure requirement, or "gag order," prohibiting recipients from disclosing their existence, even to the person whose secrets have been shared with the government. Five statutes authorize NSLs: the Right to Financial Privacy Act, the ECPA, the Fair Credit Reporting Act, the National Security Act of 1947, and the Stored Communications Act.

Wielding these laws, the FBI can access a wide range of information about people, including historical and transactional information about phone calls and emails, financial information, and consumer credit information.

Anthony Gregory notes that the role of the courts and Congress is limited. "Legal arguments and congressional reforms can stem the tide or temporarily reverse the trajectory, but they alone cannot sustainably create a future of privacy."[13]

PART THREE

IMPACT ON AUTONOMY, COMMUNITY, AND SOCIETY

MYTH 16

"SURVEILLANCE DOESN'T INFLUENCE HOW I ACT"

We are free only when it is we ourselves who draw the line between when we are seen and when we are not seen.

—TIMOTHY SNYDER, *On Tyranny*[1]

If surveillance doesn't make us act differently, explain this:

The psychology department's coffee room at Newcastle University in the United Kingdom offers coffee and tea on the honor system: users put their money in a box. The department decided to rotate different price list signs as part of a research study. One week a picture of flowers was featured at the top of the list; the next week a photocopied picture of human eyes aimed directly at patrons reading the sign.

On the weeks in which the eyes were displayed, people paid nearly three times as much for their caffeine fix as weeks when the flowers were shown.[2]

According to researchers in this and several other studies, the gaze of staring eyes—even a drawing or photograph—changes people's behavior.

Feeling watched is a powerful tool for social control, causing people to censor their behavior and conform to what they take to be the desired outcome. Security expert Bruce Schneier says the function of omnipresent surveillance is to control a population. "The fact that you *won't* do things, that you will self-censor, are the worst effects of pervasive surveillance."[3]

What's the purpose of a myth that surveillance doesn't change how we act? It's yet another way to normalize ongoing violations of personal privacy. Acceptance of a surveillance state numbs the desire to want to change it.

KNOWINGLY CHANGING ONLINE BEHAVIOR

Jonathan Penney of Oxford University offers empirical evidence supporting the premise that the existence of a surveillance state results in self-censorship, fostering fear and conformity, so that we refrain from acting in ways or saying things that may arouse suspicion.

His 2016 study shows that after Edward Snowden's 2013 revelations (about NSA mass surveillance) there was "a 20 percent decline in page views on Wikipedia articles related to terrorism, including those that mentioned 'al Qaeda,' 'car bomb,' or 'Taliban.'"[4] In addition to a statistically significant immediate decline in traffic for such articles, Penney found a change in the overall long-term trend in the view count traffic. That indicates not only immediate but also a long-term chilling effect of knowing the government is watching online activities.

PEN America surveyed nearly eight hundred writers around the globe on the impact of surveillance. Its 2013 report found that concern about surveillance is nearly as high among writers in liberal democracies (75 percent) as in nondemocratic nations (80 percent). More than one-third of writers from democracies self-censor. More than half (53 percent) surveyed said mass surveillance has damaged US credibility as a worldwide advocate of free expression.

"Fear of government surveillance is prompting many writers living in democratic countries to engage in the kind of self-censorship associated with police states," said Suzanne Nossel, PEN America's executive director. "We're all well aware of writers in places like China and Russia who must live life knowing they are always being watched—it's disturbing to recognize that those in the US, Canada, and Australia are now coming to adopt similar behavior."[5]

Two years after Snowden's revelations, Pew Research asked the 87 percent of respondents who say they had heard at least a little about the government's surveillance programs whether they had changed some of the ways they used email, search engines, social media, mobile apps, cell phones, text messages and landlines.[6] In total, 12 percent of those aware of the NSA surveillance said they changed their behavior a "great deal" in at least one of the formats, and 25 percent had changed their behavior either "a great deal" or "somewhat" in at least one format. The reasons respondents gave Pew for altering how they use communications technology since 2013 included these:

> "Somewhat concerned to look up certain information on search engines, since it may appear suspicious, even if my reason is pure curiosity."

> "I used to be more open to discussing my private life online with my select friends. Now I don't know who might be listening."

> "Can't joke about stuff that could be taken as a threat."

THE SPIRAL OF SILENCE

People steer away from talking about policy issues publicly or even among family and friends when they think their attitudes aren't widely shared. This inclination is known as the spiral of silence.

Knowledge of government monitoring influences online expression, especially if users think their opinions conflict with that of the majority, according to a study by journalism professor Elizabeth Stoycheff at Wayne State University in Detroit.[7]

Stoycheff asked 225 participants to fill out a survey about how they get their news, and about their views on surveillance. She showed them a fake Facebook page that reported on renewed US airstrikes against ISIS terrorists in Iraq. Its tone was neutral. Participants were asked if they'd be willing to express their opinion on the airstrikes, by liking, forwarding, or commenting on the page. Half received several reminders that although the answers were confidential, there was no guarantee that the NSA would not be monitoring them. Afterward, participants were questioned about their opinions of airstrikes and what they believed most Americans thought about them. They were also asked questions about the legitimacy of online surveillance by government agencies.

Their answers were consistent with the spiral-of-silence effect. The more their personal opinions diverged from perceived mainstream opinion, the less participants were willing to express their views. The effect was strongest in participants who believed that they might be monitored and that online surveillance was taking place: they answered in a more conformist way and engaged in self-censorship.

In another study, from the Pew Research Center, Americans were asked about their opinions on Snowden's leaks, their comfort level in discussing the revelations in online and in-person settings, and their perceptions of the opinions of others in both settings. They found that the spiral of silence was greater online. Eighty-six percent of the respondents were willing to discuss the topic in person, but fewer than half were willing to engage on Facebook and Twitter. And in both online and in-person environments, people were more likely to join in conversations when they thought others agreed with them.

Social media did not provide, or operate as, an alternative forum for those unwilling to discuss the issue in person, and respondents who thought social media friends and followers disagreed with them were more reticent to express their views in in-person settings.[8]

While Pew did not seek the reasons why people stay silent if they think their views are not widely held, the study's report indicated that the spiral of silence is related to a fear of isolation. A fear of ostracization, whether by disappointing friends or by having to be mindful of current or prospective employers, strengthens the spiral of silence. The authors of the study speculate, similarly, that this fear or experience of isolation and ridicule online makes its way into opinion sharing in other, nonvirtual settings as well.

LIVING UNDER THE CONSTANT LENS

Creeping surveillance is dangerous; first it comes in the guise of protecting the populace from crime. The UK and other countries have virtually blanketed their cities with cameras to capture criminal activity, calling them "rings of steel." With increasing face recognition capacity, those cameras can quickly help identify specific individuals. Then it leads to self-censorship and conformity with mainstream attitudes.

Many communities around the globe live under omnipresent surveillance. Journalists and human rights activists in nations with authoritarian regimes habitually self-censor. Joshua Franco, a senior research advisor and the deputy director of Amnesty Tech at Amnesty International, wrote on *Medium*: "The fear and uncertainty generated by surveillance inhibit activity more than any action by the police. . . . If that threat is there, if you feel you're being watched, you self-police, and this pushes people out of the public space. It is so hard to operate under those types of conditions."[9]

What if certain behavior was deemed unacceptable, even if not illegal? For example, during the Black Lives Matters protests following the murder of George Floyd, surveillance drones were used by the National Guard. Congress requested an investigation by the Department of Defense as to whether demonstrators' civil rights were violated by this. The Pentagon, of course, found that those rights were not violated. But if we remember East Germany's Stasi and look at what is happening in China today, it isn't hard to imagine what use could be made of "rings of steel," and of surveillance drones, in the US.

The 2014 implementation of a Chinese social credit system has been widely criticized by Western media. Local governments across China have developed a patchwork of social credit systems, some of which are run by private companies—like Alibaba affiliate Ant Financial's Shima Credit system (also known as Sesame Credit). A prominent article in *Time*, "What the Chinese Surveillance State Means for the Rest of the World," depicts the social credit system as Orwellian with respect to free speech and human rights.

In response, a 2020 report by the Chinese consulting firm Trivium argues that the social credit system seems more experimental and banal than Western critics describe. The system is "a disjointed mix of national and sector-specific policies, municipal pilot projects, and hybrid public-private sector cooperative agreements, loosely centered around the goal of enhancing market 'trustworthiness.'"[10]

Still, there's no denying that the level of surveillance in China's rapidly developing metropolises is expansive. Rongcheng is a coastal town in China of 670,000 people where one thousand social credit points are given to each person as a default. Behavior the authorities want to deter, such as jaywalking, will cost you points, and praiseworthy behavior is rewarded with points. Fighting with neighbors detracts five points; failure to clean up after a dog detracts ten. Donating blood earns five. Punishment comes when one falls below a threshold: bank loans or high-speed train tickets become unattainable. Rewards come in such forms such as discounted utility bills, faster internet service, or improved health care services.[11]

In the city of Chongqing, population 15.35 million, the ratio of surveillance cameras to residents is 1 to 5.9. *Time* calls it the world's most surveilled city. In the region of Xinjiang, home of the Muslim Uighur minority, rampant use of CCTV, facial recognition software, cellular apps, and electronic checkpoints led to the detention of an estimated one million individuals in re-education centers, according to UN reports. Algorithms applied to camera data resulted in their arrest, trial, and conviction, followed by forced indoctrination, according to Human Rights Watch.[12]

Chinese jails are an extreme example of the harm that can result from total surveillance. The *Time* article cites the testimony of Bakitali Nur, age forty-seven, who often travels abroad for his fruit and vegetable export business. Nur was arrested after authorities grew suspicious of his frequent trips. He recounts being held for a year in a room with seven other prisoners, and forced to sit on plastic stools for seventeen hours without moving. Four HikVision cameras recorded their every move. As Nur told *Time*, "Anyone caught talking or moving was forced into stress positions for hours at a time."[13]

For those who believe that surveillance doesn't change our behavior, let these be cautionary examples of the extremes that may attend knowledge of being monitored.

In his book *On Tyranny*, Timothy Snyder reminds us that loss of personal autonomy, whether taken from us or relinquished, quickly ushers in despotism. He writes: "What the great political thinker Hannah Arendt meant by 'totalitarianism' was not an all-powerful state, but the erasure of the difference between private and public life. We are free only insofar as we exercise control over what people know about us, and in what circumstances they come to know it."[14]

MYTH 17

"TEENAGERS DON'T CARE ABOUT PRIVACY"

"Do Not Disturb—Genius at Work"
"tips on how to enter my room properly: 1. do not"
—SIGNS ON TEENAGERS' BEDROOM DOORS

Preteens and teenagers are hardwired to guard their privacy from prying parents and siblings.

Do Not Enter signs for bedroom doors—its own cottage industry—journal-keeping, and creating private clubhouses or retreats are some of the normal ways teens feel out their personal boundaries and establish autonomy.

Diaries are such a fixture in the American coming-of-age experience that many come outfitted with locks and keys to keep curious parents or siblings from reading them. These repositories of young people's dreams, worries, and crushes help them differentiate what they can keep to themselves and what parents ought to know. In addition to establishing private turf, teens are also seeing their bodies change, and are reckoning with the ups and downs of psychological growth.

Signs, diaries, and clubhouses remind us that it's a myth that teenagers don't care about privacy.

How did this myth come about?

Many people assume that because 95 percent of teens are connected to the internet and 85 percent used social media as of 2018, according to Pew Research polls, "iGen" teens don't mind sharing their personal lives with the public.[1] Used to described people born after 1995, iGen is the first generation to spend their adolescent years in the smartphone age. Social media activity and texting others often takes precedence over in-person activities.

It's more likely that teens don't always appreciate the long-term consequences of posting certain material on social media. And why should they? A majority of Americans, as we've seen, are confused about how their personal data is collected and used by corporations and government agencies. Unless young people are educated about surveillance techniques from the day they type their first keystrokes, it's understandable that they may post first, then think later. Furthermore, these apps are carefully designed to draw users in and encourage more and more engagement with the platform. Constant, small interactions with apps and online sites release dopamine, suggesting it's also a chemical response (not unlike addiction).

Dr. Dimitri Christakis, director of the Center for Child Health, Behavior and Development at Seattle Children's Research Institute explained that touching a screen to cause something to happen "is intensely gratifying." He also noted that apps and video games frequently offer rewards such as points or virtual stickers. "The purveyors of games and apps are very well aware they are monetizing our children's attention," Dr. Christakis said. "They build in design features that make them difficult to put away."[2]

PEERS: ONLINE CLIQUES

While teens may share intimate details with their closest peers, they differentiate between inner and outer circles. Keeping information from other adolescents is one way of establishing their "cliques" so prevalent in high school.

An MIT study suggested that social networks fosters cliques. The trend began in 1980 with Usenet and continues with Facebook and other platforms.[3] People tend to join online groups that share similar interests such as music, animals, and politics. The website Netsanity summed it up: "In effect, social media is just one, big high school." Most people will likely recognize these stereotypical behaviors from their own childhood rites of passage, described by *TeenLife* in three teen archetypes:

The Garbage In, Garbage Out Teen posts every thought as it enters their head. They post tacky photos, swear, and snap at anyone who challenges them. They try to provoke responses from followers.

The Teen Braggart brags about their conquests, hook ups, and everything else. They are full of themselves ("hot air") and everyone knows it. Nobody believes anything they say and everyone ignores most of what they post.

The Teen Seeking Popularity posts pictures of all kinds of questionable behavior. They comment on other posts and pictures just to boost their popularity. They'll find over-the-top stuff to upload to Instagram and their YouTube videos to gain popularity among their peer group.[4]

UNFORMED BRAINS

It may be that adults who see these kinds of posts by teenagers jump to the conclusion that they do not value privacy. But their youthful brains are not equipped to calculate the future implications of acting like teens. While parents think ahead to how a pubescent post may impact college applications or job prospects, to a high school sophomore, university applications seem light-years away.

Frances Jensen, author of *The Teenage Brain* and chair of the neurology department at the Perelman School of Medicine at the University of Pennsylvania, explains how teenagers' minds grow. Once dismissed as slavishly subject to hormonal fluctuations, the teen brain, it turns out, is quite plastic. It changes and adapts to the external environment, developing well into an individual's twenties. Brain growth occurs through increased connectivity between regions. "As the brain develops," she writes, myelin wraps itself around nerve cells' axons—long, thin tendrils that extend from the cell and transmit information—like insulation on an electrical wire."[5]

Myelination, as it's called, speeds up and solidifies communication between brain regions. The process begins from the back of the brain and works its way to the front, leaving the prefrontal cortex—think decision-making, self-control, planning—as the last part to mature. Teenagers do have frontal-lobe capabilities, but it takes longer for inhibitory signals from the front of the brain to reach the back and regulate their emotions. Hence more impulsive behavior in teens and people in their twenties, along with fewer long-range planning skills.

Teens are often self-conscious, susceptible to peer pressure, or likelier to take risks. These aspects are influenced by the environment and are important when learning social information such as interpreting what others are thinking and feeling. That's why friends are necessary at this time, and also why peers have a greater chance of influencing friends to engage in behaviors like risk-taking. Sarah-Jayne Blakemore, a professor of cognitive neuroscience at University College London and author of the book *Inventing Ourselves: The Secret Life of the Teenage Brain*, says that "fear of being excluded by the peer group is a big driver of adolescent typical behavior."[6]

Inclusion by their social group and friends matters, and so they're likely to go along with what their friends think. Instagram, Snapchat, Facebook, and other social media platforms allow teenagers to exercise their desire to make social contact all the time.

The implications of this for social media use by teens are that they are likely to post without considering the long-term consequences. They lack the brain capacity to do so. This is why parents (continue to) exist, and why there are laws to protect young people from themselves. It's why the drinking age is twenty-one in the US, and why kids in many states have to take driving lessons before they can get a driver's license. All fifty states now have anti-bullying laws, because adults recognize the danger bullying poses to teenagers.[7]

Don't confuse teens' adeptness at using technology with not caring about the repercussions of technology on their lives. While teens might complain about or rail against laws or parental prohibitions, on some level most know that it *is* in fact "for their own good." Even if it is still developing, their prefrontal lobe recognizes that there are consequences for actions, even if they wish to reject the likelihood of those consequences affecting them.

CLASSROOM CONCEALMENTS

Liz Geisewite is a full-time public-school music teacher in Midwood, Brooklyn, who also has taught at the Brooklyn Youth Chorus. Her students range from fourteen to eighteen years in age. Like most music teachers, her tasks transcend typical book learning and are a balance of teaching and performing. She employs imagination, improvisation, interpretive creativity, listening, performing, and critical judgment.

Geisewite stresses: "Students definitely guard their privacy from their teachers."[8] She goes on to explain:

> Even as a music teacher, students see me as an authority figure, though it seems that students are more prone to sharing personal details with teachers in the arts than teachers of strictly academic subjects. Most teenagers I've taught will share specific personal information when they feel the classroom is a safe environment. As we cultivate relationships, students begin to open up more, but the depth of that sharing is usually limited. They are likely to share information about their past educational experiences, but less likely to speak about their home/family lives, and much less likely to discuss issues involving their relationships with peers.

She notes that many students are constantly engaged with social media. During the Covid-19 pandemic, remote teaching and learning has raised the issue of whether to allow students to keep their cameras turned off while participating in videoconference classes. "It's easy to assume that at least some of those 'invisible' students are using social media during online classes. For many students, their social media lives take precedence over their 'in-person' lives."

"In-person oversharing" happens rarely in school spaces where teachers are present. Geisewite says that it may be happening, but students are often keenly aware of when an adult may be listening. Oversharing seems more prevalent on social media platforms where teenagers curate their social images for the intended audience of their peers.

Are students aware that their personal information is captured and used by tech companies and third parties?

If they are, Geisewite suspects that awareness doesn't hinder their desire to engage with social media. "The immediate gratification of attention from peers outweighs considerations of future impact on education and employment opportunities." The same thing goes for awareness that personal data can be hacked. Adolescents are likely aware of the risk, but in the moment, the benefits of peer attention are more important to them than the dangers of a personal data breach.

By the time teenagers get to high school, they definitely have been warned, at least in school, that everything they share online is permanently available and traceable. But teens are impulsive and may not integrate that warning with their actions. Geisewite says they "generally care a lot more about next week than next year."

External factors contribute to their focus on the present. "This generation (iGen) is growing up in a world that is full of insecurity—economic, social, political, environmental—where their future is not guaranteed to be bright. Teenagers, now more than ever, live for the day because the future is so uncertain, and they don't want to miss out on any chance of immediate gratification," notes the teacher.

If we say young people—society's newest generations—who were raised in a digital world, don't care about privacy, we succumb to claims that there's nothing we can do to stave off the surveillance state. We're also abdicating our own responsibility to protect young people from corporate and government intrusions and profiteering.

Joel Bakan, author of the popular book and film *The Corporation*, observes how marketers of TeenTech (discussed in Myth 8—"No one wants to spy on kids") aggressively breach parent-child bonds that are critical to developing self-esteem and independence. "The real credo of kid marketers—the one that truly explains their ambitions and behavior—is not 'let kids be kids,' but rather 'let us get at your kids.' And the reasons for outrage only mount when we consider what kid marketers do with, and to, kids once they have them within their grasp."[9]

Teenagers grapple with managing their dual lives—online and "in real life"—in tandem with their brain maturation. That's a lot to juggle. The myth that teens don't care about privacy does a disservice to a sector of society while also feeding into mass complacency and ceding privacy to corporate power.

How did the myth come about, that "teens don't care about privacy"? Liz Geisewite shares her thoughts on the matter:

> To adults who remember a time before the internet held all our personal data, the boundaries of public and private information are concrete. For iGen teens, privacy is shielding parts of yourself from people you know or can identify. Tech companies and third parties who are using teenagers' online data are anonymous and, thus, invisible to teens.
>
> Like adolescents throughout time, teens today want some degree of control over their own not-yet-independent lives. Their curated online personae can be very different from the ones imposed on them at home, steeped in familial experience and closeness. On social media platforms, teens don't have a feeling of self-consciousness that comes from exposing their evolving thoughts and selves to people (e.g., parents) who have known them from infancy.

"SURVEILLANCE AFFECTS EVERYONE EQUALLY"

Syed Farhaj Hassan didn't grow up in a devout household, but after helping Haitian earthquake victims in 2010, he became curious about his family's religion. The sergeant in the 204th Civil Affairs Brigade and member of the US Army Reserve since September 2001 explains what changed: Hassan, who was raised in New Jersey, had been previously deployed to Qatar, Kuwait, and Iraq to support Operation Iraqi Freedom. But his humanitarian assignment awakened him in a different way. He says, "I knew how to pray and was a moral person, but something about hard-hit Haiti really sparked a deep interest in me to learn more about my religion."[1]

Hassan joined a recently opened mosque, Masjid e-Ali, in Somerset, New Jersey, and became an observant Shia Muslim. "I learned that the Friday prayers were especially powerful and beautiful, and was lucky to have my Army unit accommodate my regular attendance there." The comfort he found in practicing his religion was short lived.

The Associated Press broke the story in 2012, for which its reporters won the Pulitzer Prize,[2] that NYPD detectives in the Demographics Unit, a division of the Intelligence Bureau whose existence was denied, had eavesdropped on Muslim students and designated mosques as potential terrorist organizations. They listened in on private conversations in cafés and asked people what they thought about drone strikes.

Upon learning of the surveillance, Hassan says community members began sharing stories about odd sightings of strangers lingering around community centers and places of worship. One friend, attending an Iraqi mosque, saw a man with a camera parked outside. Surveillance of congregants caused Hassan to worry. *What if they took away his security clearance as a result?* Fellow soldiers and superiors, he feared, might lose trust in him. That could hurt his career prospects.

So he stopped attending the mosque.

Police surveillance had a chilling effect in unexpected and deeply impactful ways. Knowing that their house of worship—once a place of sanctitude—had been violated, Hassan felt forced to give up his constitutional right to practice his religion.

In 2012, Hassan and others sued on behalf of individuals, businesses, student associations, and New Jersey mosques. They claimed that New York detectives violated the Constitution by surveilling at least twenty mosques, fourteen restaurants, eleven retail stores, two grade schools, and two Muslim student organizations. The lawsuit alleged that the program operated on the unfounded premise that Muslim religious identity is a valid factor for identifying surveillance targets, or a benchmark for criminal activity.

Nationally, New Jersey ranks number one in percentage of Muslim residents. The suit also alleged that police created more than twenty maps of Newark marked with location of mosques and delineating Muslim neighborhoods.[3] As for the details of mosque monitoring, the complaint says: "NYPD officers snap pictures, take video, and collect license plate numbers of congregants as they arrive at mosques to pray, making records of those in attendance. . . . They also mount surveillance cameras on light poles and aim them at mosques." It adds, "Officers can control the cameras with their computers and use the footage to help identify worshippers."[4]

Hassan's case was one of three major lawsuits challenging this far-reaching program of surveillance. It settled in April 2018. Police agreed to make "reasonable and diligent efforts" to expunge certain information gathered on Muslim communities in New Jersey. For damages, the city paid ten businesses, mosques, student groups and individuals amounts ranging from $1,250 to $22,500.[5] In 2014, William J. Bratton, then NYPD police commissioner, disbanded the Demographics Unit. The department acknowledged that the unit had not generated a terrorism investigation in six years of monitoring.

The NYPD's blanket surveillance of Muslims, absent any credible leads that criminal activity was afoot, is one example of how state surveillance disproportionately affects stigmatized communities.

Surveillance and suspicion of criminal activity based on religion or on the color of one's skin is as old as the nation. The color of one's skin has its own significance in the United States, tied to the history of slavery. It is almost unimaginable that this bias wouldn't spill over to the surveillance state.

In *Black America's State of Surveillance*, Malkia Amala Cyril describes the damage surveillance causes to black people and their communities. Cyril is founder and executive director of Media Justice, a grassroots movement devoted to attaining a just and participatory media in the digital age. They describe targeted surveillance in America that "frequently includes the indiscriminate collection of the private data of people targeted by race but not involved in any crime." Advances in technology, they claim, have ushered in "predictive policing" designed to analyze trends and patterns in data to determine and preempt crime.[6]

Cyril notes how deceptive this model is, with its presumption that data inputs are neutral. They continue: "They aren't. In a racially discriminatory criminal justice system, surveillance technologies reproduce injustice. Instead of reducing discrimination, predictive policing is a face of what author Michelle Alexander calls the 'New Jim Crow'—a de facto system of separate and unequal application of laws, police practices, conviction rates, sentencing terms, and conditions of confinement that operate more as a system of social control by racial hierarchy than as crime prevention or punishment."[7]

NYPD's stop-and-frisk program is a stark example of failed blanket policing that operated in so-called "high crime" neighborhoods where authorities predicted more crime would occur. A court held the program unconstitutional after years of daily stops and searches of black and Latinx persons with a near-zero rate of rooting out crime.

The Century Foundation, a progressive policy think tank, notes the challenges in assessing algorithms' biases: "Prejudice embedded in computer code will be an exceptionally difficult question for lay policy makers to judge." The foundation quotes Hamid Khan, campaign coordinator of Stop LAPD Spying, in explaining the risk: inaccurate or poor-quality input will always produce faulty output, in computing and other fields.

Khan said, "It's racism in, racism out." While white people may not understand the breadth of surveillance of persons from stigmatized communities, it's something that people of color, of all ages, are all too familiar with.[8]

IN SEARCH OF EXTREMISM

On the other coast, in 2017, young people in Los Angeles gathered to learn about a Department of Homeland Security program that might put them at risk of surveillance. "Countering Violent Extremism," or CVE, refers to federal initiatives in three pilot cities to counter efforts by extremists to recruit, radicalize, and mobilize followers to violence. DHS launched the program in 2011. The group Stop LAPD Spying and a coalition of racial justice groups began developing a curriculum contextualizing CVE in the context of racial profiling.[9]

The CVE program extends the arm of the law by turning community members, workers and service-providers into snitches. Three municipal CVE pilot programs announced in 2014 enlisted mental health and social service providers as community partners to screen for potential violent actors. One was a mentoring program for Somali youth in Minneapolis, and another was an anti-bullying program in Boston. In Los Angeles, the third pilot city, the mayor's office accepted at least a quarter of a million dollars to fund CVE programs. One nonprofit, the Muslim Public Affairs Committee, received tens of thousands of dollars for a pilot program called Safe Spaces. The initiative usurped standard counseling by focusing on the sole mission of screening participants for "threats of public violence." Muslim community members engaged in individual, couples, and family counseling with one goal: preventing "ideological violence."[10]

An Illinois program, according to the *Chicago Reporter*, "explored enlisting mental health providers for interventions with those deemed at risk of radicalization, an approach that has alarmed some mental health providers who fear being deputized as a means of intelligence gathering for law enforcement and jeopardizing their relationship with patients." The program distributes training materials to help community members so they can identify warning signs of extremists, despite no evidence that such signs exist.[11]

The Brennan Center notes that CVE programs "are based on junk science, have proven to be ineffective, discriminatory, and divisive." The notion that predictive risk indicators exist has, according to the center, been long discredited by years of research. "They have been targeted almost exclusively at Muslims and employ spurious criteria, such as religiosity and political activism and vague feelings of alienation, as proxies for violent tendencies."[12]

Trump vowed to stop CVE funding after a deadly shooting at a Pittsburgh synagogue grabbed the nation's attention. It wasn't that he was defunding it because it targeted communities by color or religion. Rather, as Peter Beinart of *The Atlantic* suggests, he did so because he supports white supremacist and right-wing extremist groups whom he feared might be targeted. Trump's fear of losing votes from white nationalists flies in the face of acknowledged threat assessments by his own intelligence agencies.[13] The Department of Homeland Security has identified white supremacists as the most "persistent and lethal threat" in the US through 2021.[14] But the nation's long racist history indicates that such an allegiance to white supremacism is likely to endure, as we saw in the January 2021 Capitol insurrection.

Mike German from the Brennan Center for Justice's Liberty and National Security Program notes that even if DHS ends CVE funding, the Justice Department, US attorneys' offices, and the FBI each have their own programs. He told *In These Times* how they skirt accountability by reinventing themselves: "Another feature of CVE programs is that they often rebrand to escape scrutiny and accountability, so communities and local policy makers need to be cautious about new government

programs moving forward."[15] The Trump administration launched a
new ten million dollar domestic counter-extremism grant program that
many say is a rebranding of CVE.[16]

FACES OF DIFFERENT COLORS

Facial recognition surveillance technologies, increasingly employed by
police, pose unique threats to communities of color. A walk through black
and brown neighborhoods in large urban areas shows a great number
of surveillance cameras. Surveillance there, including monitoring social
media, often seeks to identify people suspected of drug or gang associations, or using political speech, which is too often conflated with "terrorism." CCTV cameras—without facial recognition—require someone to
look through hours of footage to find what they want. Facial recognition
software, however, turns cameras into constant, real-time monitors of individual behavior. The effect on targeted communities is chilling.

Facial recognition technology is far from error-free. The reason is
more insidious than just technological bugs in need of fixing. Research
by black scholars Joy Buolamwini, Deb Raji, and Timnit Gebru in 2018
found that some facial analysis algorithms misclassified black women
nearly 35 percent of the time, while nearly always being accurate for
white men. A later MIT study by Buolamwini and Raji found these
problems existed in Amazon's software as well as the systems studied
earlier.[17]

In 2019, the US government released a report on bias in face recognition algorithms. That report concluded that the systems perform
best on middle-aged white men's faces. They didn't function as well
for people of color, women, children, and the elderly. Error rates were
highest for black women. Because as many as 25 percent of police departments can access facial recognition to identify suspects and make
arrests, these biases can cause wrongful arrests, detention of innocent
people, and violence at the hands of police—putting people of color at
even greater risk.[18]

The problem is not accuracy, strictly—we cannot overlook the intersection of new technology and old racial biases. Law enforcement

departments often use mugshot databases to ID people with face recognition algorithms. The results, as the ACLU says, are that "recognition recycles racial bias from the past, supercharging that bias with 21st century surveillance technology."[19] And there's much to recycle. Black people are arrested for several crimes at greater rates than whites. For example, even though cannabis use is about the same for white and black people, blacks are nearly four times more likely to be arrested for possessing marijuana than whites. For each arrest, police take and store a mugshot in a database. It goes without saying that because black individuals are likelier to be arrested for minor infractions, their faces and data are likelier to be in the mugshot database. Using facial recognition technology in mugshot databases augments racism in a system that already disproportionately polices and criminalizes black people.

In June 2020, IBM, Amazon, and Microsoft said they would pause or end sales of facial recognition technology to US law enforcement.[20] They did so in the face of growing public pressure: when people flooded the streets to protest anti-black police violence and systemic racism, these tech goliaths were implicated for their role in perpetuating racism.

The Boston Police Department used social media surveillance technology to track the words "Black Lives Matter." Police in Memphis spied for years on black journalists and activists, violating a 1978 consent decree, using undercover operations on social media to target people engaged in First Amendment–protected activity. In New York, police also monitored Black Lives Matter protesters,[21] while in Chicago, activists suspect police used Stingray spying devices to eavesdrop on protesters criticizing police harassment of black people.[22] Stingrays, or "cell site simulators" mimic cell phone towers. They emit signals to trick cell phones in the area into transmitting locations and identifying information so authorities can conduct covert surveillance.

BRIGHT LIGHTS, BIASED CITY

In 2016, New York City conducted a five-million-dollar, six-month experiment. The police department partnered with the University of

Chicago's Crime Lab to bring public-housing residents mobile, diesel-powered flood lights blasting six hundred thousand lumens. Researchers placed an average of seven mobile light towers in each of forty developments. The powerful lights affected about forty thousand residents.[23]

Before the installations, from 2010 to 2016, outages in street lighting were the third most common complaint reported to city 311 operators.[24] The mega-watt experiment was cited as a response to streetlight outages. But the powerful floodlights evoke police presence. Katy Naples-Mitchell is a fellow at the Charles Hamilton Houston Institute for Race and Justice at Harvard Law School. She questions how calls for better lighting ended up with "the remedy of floodlights operating from sundown to sunrise in their neighborhood." That the experiment happened in public housing complexes—in New York City in 2015, 90 percent of residents in the public housing system were nonwhite—highlights racial disparities in the criminal justice system. "If there was a dearth of street lighting on the Upper West Side, would the mayor's office have dreamed up a response in consult[ation] with the NYPD and invited outside researchers to do a randomized controlled trial?" asks Naples-Mitchell.[25]

Richard Stevens from the University of Connecticut studies the effects of artificial light on human beings. Bright lights have several deleterious health effects. "Constant light is a torture. People used to use that to torture people," Stevens said. "Why do they subject poor people to that?"[26]

The answer is simple: social control.

In 2017, the experiment became permanent. A $210 million Mayor's Action Plan for Neighborhood Safety installed the high-powered "safety lights" in several NYC public housing complexes.[27] The crime decrease is negligible to nonexistent. Crime statistics for 2017 in four Brooklyn developments showed a 3 percent decrease from the prior year.[28] That was lower than the 10 percent drop in that borough's developments. The Center for Media Justice (now Media Justice) called for a ban on the government's use of this nightmarish technology, and ACLU advocates on both coasts are advocating the same.[29]

Even if the lights resulted in a crime decrease, the bold-faced deployment of social control is unacceptable.

"RACISM IN, RACISM OUT"

"Big Data techniques have already begun to amplify the disparate harms of surveillance in disfavored neighborhoods," according to the Century Foundation.[30] "Big Data" describes the intersection between sophisticated computational techniques and inexpensive storage and faster and more versatile hardware. Analyses of crime, for example, show that police officers continue to focus on neighborhoods traditionally deemed "high risk." Focusing on the same over-policed neighborhoods perpetuates a cycle of arrests for minor infractions and inflated crime statistics.

Such a concentration of law enforcement power in targeted communities reinforces the toxic effects of racial biases. It subjects all community members to ongoing monitoring and aggressive law enforcement interventions. The Century Foundation cautions: "Policy makers should give careful thought to that punitive impact on the blameless majority, which is exactly akin to the central grievance of the colonists against King George."[31]

MYTH 19

"'IF YOU SEE SOMETHING, SAY SOMETHING' IS A CIVIC DUTY"

The day after the Twin Towers fell, advertising executive Allen Steven Kay wrote the slogan "If you see something, say something." Kay had created Dominic, the popular Xerox monk commercial during Super Bowl XX in 1976. For a nation reeling in grief, he intended the new slogan to be positive and action oriented.[1]

New York's Metropolitan Transportation Authority (MTA) trademarked and implemented the six words as an anti-terrorism campaign. The MTA licensed it to the Department of Homeland Security for nationwide use in 2010. Local transit and law enforcement agencies also obtain licenses to use the slogan. In 2011, the campaign spread to the National Basketball Association to "help ensure the security of players, employees and fans," according to then secretary of homeland security Janet Napolitano.[2]

Authorities want people to become attuned to, and report, so-called "suspicious" activity. Examples are unattended packages or backpacks, or circumstances that appear out of the ordinary: an open door that's usually closed, a person asking for detailed information about a building's layout or purpose, and changes in security protocol or shifts. Also of concern, authorities assert, is a person loitering around a building, writing notes, sketches, or taking photographs or measurements. The DHS website is careful to note, "Factors such as race, ethnicity, and/or religious affiliation are not suspicious."[3]

But all those factors influence the "tips" that are called in.

Tips from "Say Something" calls are often used in Suspicious Activity Reports (SARs). Officials share those with federal fusion centers, which analyze them for leads on terror plots. SARs have "flooded fusion centers, law enforcement, and other security entities with white noise" that "complicates the intelligence process," according to a report from the Homeland Security Policy Institute at George Washington University, coauthored by Los Angeles Police Department Chief Michael Downing.[4]

That's in part due to the effectiveness of well-conceived marketing jingles that nag at the public's subconscious. Six singsong words—emblazoned on subway systems and other public places—have for many become confused with the ethos of patriotism. If citizens show allegiance to their government, many believe, that government will protect its citizens. Informing on your neighbors and ordinary folk, the thinking goes, is on a par with obeying the law, paying taxes, voting, and serving on a jury.

That's a myth.

REGULATING CITIZEN CONDUCT

No one likes a snitch.

Popular culture's lexicon of slang reflects disdain for informants. Derogatory terms such as *rat* or *cheese-eater, snitch, stool pigeon, mole, fink*, or *narc* are as old as the practice.

That helps explain why intelligence agencies employ a marketing campaign to nudge people out of cognitive dissonance. Equating spying with civic duty tips the scales from individual rights on one hand to national security priorities on the other.

In *Citizen Spies: The Long Rise of America's Surveillance Society*, Joshua Reeves documents how a convergence of politicians, experts, and state authorities encourage tattling on others.[5] The media and public relations campaigns bolster their efforts. As government intelligence agencies characterize dissidents as enemies, efforts to enlist citizen informants have assumed varying levels of urgency. No element of society is exempt from the dictate. Even children and librarians—innocents and guardians of information—are called on to adhere to authorities' notion of good citizens.

For decades, social institutions (schools, police departments, and youth programs) have regulated the conduct of American citizens by igniting their surveillance and communication skills. Authorities want us to believe we must keep tabs on one another to supplement policing as an institution. Reeves reminds us of periods of vigilance that were taken to heart at the time but that in retrospect seeming like a form of hysteria: "From its early displays in the witch hysterias and Puritan moral panics of colonial New England; to the vigilante posses of the Wild West and the Ku Klux Klan; to its Brown Scares, Green Scares, and Red Scares; and to the US's recurrent anxieties about immigrants, political dissidents, rebellious youth, criminals, and religious minorities, vigilance toward neighbors has long been aligned with American ideals of patriotic and moral duty."[6]

Children and students are prompted to join in the practice, much like a lab experiment. In the early twentieth century, New York enlisted junior cops, or "coppettes." Boys would focus on petty crime, and girls largely had duties regulating the moral behavior of family and neighborhood youth. "That included preventing children from watching movies unattended by parents, snitching on merchants who sold tobacco to minors, and tattling on underage girls who tried to enter dance halls," writes Reeves.

Police in Rochester, New York, enlisted twenty thousand Boy Scouts in Operation SAFE (Scout Awareness for Emergency) in the 1960s. Scouts received ID cards with their thumb prints printed on them, along with the phone numbers of local police and the FBI. The boys also got a list of suspicious activities to report if observed.

College students have also been go-to deputies. John Prados of the National Security Archive commented on the 2020 release of the Huston Plan, written more than half a decade earlier. The secret government plan encompassed several covert operations, from spying on domestic groups such as the Black Panthers, to office break-ins. The plan found, according to Prados, that "primary coverage of student groups came through 'live informants' whose increased manpower would 'facilitate more effective coverage.'"[7] Prados writes that in 1967, the FBI instituted a rule that undercover informants recruited to report on campus disorder must be at least twenty-one years old. On September 2, 1970, a new directive lowered the age for African Americans to just eighteen, claiming that "Black Student Unions (BSU) and similar groups . . . are targets for influence and control by the violence-prone Black Panther Party (BPP) and other extremists." Such racist and baseless thinking continues to inform law enforcement policies into the twenty-first century.

The "Say Something" campaign isn't the only civilian spying program around. Many jurisdictions have Neighborhood Watch programs. In 1972, the National Sheriffs' Association responded to an uptick in crime by creating the nationwide Neighborhood Watch program. Working with local law enforcement, communities create their own "block watch," "crime watch," or other entities focused on preventing crime through citizen participation.[8] After the attacks of September 11, 2001, these watch programs expanded to encompass emergency response and terrorism awareness. The Department of Justice's National Neighborhood Watch initiative enlists community members to assist crime prevention and prepare neighborhoods for disasters and emergency response. Enlisting residents as the long arm of the law is fraught with personal biases and thus rife for abuse, even if well-intentioned.

The DOJ has an Office of Community Oriented Policing Services (COPS Office) to advance and support community policing by the nation's state, local, territory, and tribal law enforcement agencies through information and grants. Its website describes community policing as a philosophy that supports partnerships and problem-solving techniques, to address conditions that result in public safety issues such as crime, social disorder, and fear of crime. It says, "Community policing concentrates on preventing crime and eliminating the atmosphere of fear it creates instead of responding to crimes once committed."[9]

The COPS Office awards grants to hire and train community policing professionals, obtain state-of-the-art crime fighting technologies, and develop and test new policing strategies. Funding provides training and technical assistance to residents and local government leaders and all levels of law enforcement.

Reeves explains how citizen watch programs work to program neighborhood detectives: "Regulating the conduct of citizen patrols become[s] a matter of cultivating the seeing/saying habits of the public while preventing their behavior from escalating into vigilism [sic] and other acts of direct physical engagement."[10]

Society's revered guardians of intellectual freedom—its librarians—aren't immune from government efforts to recruit turncoats. In 1987, FBI agents asked librarians in New York City to cooperate with a Library Awareness Program and keep their eyes open for and report on patrons who might be gathering information that could harm national security.[11] Library officials objected to the notion of turning librarians into informants. The outreach to librarians came on the heels of an espionage case in which Gennadi Zakharov, a Soviet employee of the United Nations, recruited a Queens College student as an agent. The contacts had been made at a city library. Zakharov was apprehended and traded for US reporter Nicholas Daniloff who had been seized in Moscow.[12]

"THOUSANDS OF CYBER DETECTIVES"

After the Boston Marathon bombing, on April 15, 2013, residents sent police more than 13,000 videos and 120,000 photos from the scene. [13]

Crowdsourcing is a term that Jeff Howe first used in a 2006 article in *Wired* to describe the act of enlisting a number of people to assist or work on a project.[14] As the name implies, crowdsourcing is outsourcing a task to a large group of people. The concept, however, is not new. Video game developers have let fans test out new games so they can catch bugs that testers in the development stage missed, recognizing that a large number of amateurs can sometimes be more effective than a small number of professionals.

But while crowdsourcing is often more affordable, and can cover much territory efficiently, it has disadvantages: mass testing and inexpensive labor can yield inferior results and have less credibility than the work of professionals. When the purpose is to solve crimes rather than improve video games, the trade-off is a much greater concern.

According to *Police Chief* magazine, while issues exist with some community-gathered evidence—accuracy, for one—the outpouring in the Boston Marathon incident gave law enforcement a "wake-up call" about the role such evidence can play in solving crimes. "Similar to the skepticism when DNA evidence was first introduced, crowdsourced evidence is experiencing an acceptance curve for law enforcement, the public, and the courts. The idea of thousands of 'cyber detectives' capturing and submitting evidence to law enforcement has the potential to transform the way crimes are investigated, solved, and prosecuted."[15] Still, this relatively new practice has wrinkles.

Police Chief cites three areas where they would like to see crowdsourcing improve: (1) police should create systems and protocols for sharing along with a national database for all jurisdictions to access; (2) law enforcement should educate the public about how they collect, store, and use crowdsourced evidence; and (3) law enforcement should work with prosecutors and the court system to help ensure that crowdsourced evidence will stand up to rigorous court standards in criminal trials.[16]

Corporations see the profit in crowdsourcing. They make apps to help collect and manage data provided to law enforcement by community members. One is Axon Citizen. Its marketing materials to law enforcement say, "You can invite individual witnesses—or an entire community—to submit photos and videos of an incident directly to your agency." It also has produced a law enforcement–facing app, Citizen for Officers, so police can issue invitations directly to witnesses and Citizen for Communities to create public evidence submission portals.[17] Law enforcement can then gather evidence from the public during events.

America's Most Wanted is another example of crowdsourcing, from the onset of the digital age. This TV program first aired in 1988 and was hosted by John Walsh after his son Adam was abducted and murdered. It aired for twenty-five years and reportedly helped apprehend over 1,200 offenders, including 17 on the FBI's Most Wanted list.[18]

Other than *America's Most Wanted*, however, do citizen spy programs have a good track record in preventing crime?

CORPORATE CROWDSOURCING

Policing priorities are often informed by corporate interests. While private–public partnerships have long existed, one emerging model suggests a new way of crowdsourcing that exceeds the traditional role of state-sanctioned law enforcement.

In 2006, a pioneering data intel gathering initiative was adopted by the Albuquerque Police Department (APD). The department hired the Web development firm Netsential, with funding from the retailer Target, to build CONNECT, a secure website to help the department merge data-gathering among several anti-crime programs, including retail, property, and anti-gang units. One is the Albuquerque Retail Assets Protection Association (ARAPA), a public–private partnership between APD and retailers such as Walmart and Target. Documents obtained and leaked in a hack called "BlueLeaks" by the group Distributed Denial of Secrets (DDOSecrets) in 2020 revealed the program's existence. Their veracity was confirmed by the National Fusion Center Association.[19] According to the leaked documents, ARAPA and its successor CONNECT are much larger than APD has claimed publicly, and the focus of the information-gathering operation exceeds retail and property crime. That opens up the possibility of increased errors in a covert operation not dissimilar to secret government monitoring.

Big Box retailers upload photos, video, descriptions, license plate numbers, and more to the website. Leaked files reveal a membership roster of thousands of Albuquerque residents, business organizations, neighborhood association block captains, apartment managers, hotel clerks, bank tellers, and pawnshop owners. The operation also focused on general data and intelligence gathering on anything members deemed "suspicious." BlueLeaks documents show CONNECT has included 2,666 users across more than a dozen different data-gathering operations. Nearly a third of all the names on the list are local, state, or federal law enforcement officers, but the list includes hundreds of officers from departments, including federal agencies, with no clear role in Albuquerque retail crime enforcement.[20]

It's a model that helps the APD avoid community oversight and judicial review in gathering the information, some of which would otherwise have needed a warrant. Private security forces and APD employees recruit retailers to join ARAPA. Members access a secure website where they can upload videos, images, descriptions, or other information related to possible retail or property crime. But there are no limits to the information retailers can upload. Uploads are available to all ARAPA members, including five APD investigators. ARAPA and CONNECT information has been stored on APD servers, managed by Netsential, in a searchable database. Police claim that only a small team of APD investigators assigned to ARAPA access the information, along with a few other local law enforcement agencies limited to the sheriff, postal inspectors, and the district attorney.[21]

APD, in short, has privatized information- and intelligence-gathering and shifted authority to determine policing priorities to the private sector. Most ARAPA or CONNECT representatives with the authority to approve business and law enforcement access requests have been private sector or non-police APD employees. An ARAPA founder, Karen Fischer, and others vetted and approved which law enforcement officers had access to it. In January 2020, Steven Roberts, an ARAPA member and security division executive with Smith's grocery stores, approved data access to a New Mexico Homeland Security Specialist. Fischer and Roberts, and other private industry representatives, approved access to local students, professors, religious leaders from two churches, and others. Private-sector ARAPA leaders encouraged neighborhood associations to join, suggesting that block captains persuade homeowners to link residential doorbells and security cameras to APD via CONNECT.

Target Corporation gave APD $100,000 to create CONNECT. Its executives, and executives from Walmart, have served in leadership positions at ARAPA and CONNECT. They determine who gets to join ARAPA, who collects information for APD via CONNECT, and which law enforcement agencies can access it. Though Walmart and Target are just two of the thousands of retailers involved with CONNECT since its inception, nearly 60 percent of all shoplifting criminal complaints filed with the court by APD came from Walmart or Target.

While most police agencies rely on information collected from corporate or private security firms, few have their own privatized operations like the APD's. But there are other corporate links that blur the line between law enforcement and private interests. Some police agencies buy from data-aggregating companies such as ChoicePoint, which maintains enormous databases of information that it tailors for clients, including police. The use of corporate data collection by law enforcement renders almost moot the protection offered by judicial oversight.

BUT DO CITIZEN SPY PROGRAMS WORK?

Person-to-person surveillance programs continue to proliferate, but officials have not demonstrated their intelligence value.

Reeves notes that "as citizens are encouraged to report innocuous everyday activities that under typical circumstances could never be considered threats, e.g., a college student walking through an apartment complex with a pressure cooker—these tips provide very little in the way of actionable intelligence."[22]

The ACLU of Northern California obtained documents showing that citizen tips resulted in government investigations of innocent people, including persons of Middle Eastern descent who purchased several pallets of bottled water, an artist taking photographs of industrial buildings, and a man in his twenties who was playing computer video games.[23]

When authorities condition the public to look for hints of terrorist activity, they're prone to see danger on every street corner.

Sixty-four interrupted terror plots against American and allied nations, from 1993 to 2013, were prevented in part by information from informers, and surveillance was significant in 66 percent of the cases, according to research by the National Consortium for the Study of Terrorism and Responses to Terrorism (START) at the University of

Maryland. Tips from family and community members accounted for just 13 percent of all foiled attacks. That might lead some people to say programs like "See Something, Say Something" are ineffective, noted START's director William Braniff.[24]

In a study of 303 legal cases involving charges of terrorism, Braniff found that the most common way to thwart a terror attack is simply listening to the words would-be criminals say. In 32 percent of the cases, the attackers implied or threatened a physical attack against future victims. People reported those threats in only half the cases.

As with other forms of surveillance, marginalized communities endure the shortfalls of unconscious personal biases of citizen spies.

William Staples, professor of surveillance at the University of Kansas and author of several books on the topic, calls the US a leader in fostering a culture of surveillance. He notes that it's "a culture that's generated by fear, and it's kind of spread by the media, and [it's] the kind of media that we have today that everyone is on edge because they think that they're going to be the next victim of something, even though it might be an incredibly rare thing."[25]

As discomfiting as this ethos may be, it makes it easier to understand how Americans are indoctrinated to be vigilant about, and suspicious of, their neighbors, and sometimes, even their family members.

"SURVEILLANCE CAN'T PREDICT FUTURE BEHAVIOR"

The American retail company Target found out about a teenager's pregnancy before her family did.

An angry father near Minneapolis got the news in the mail when Target sent coupons for baby clothes to the family home.[1] He confronted store management and learned about Target's pregnancy prediction score, designed to entice parents-to-be to become loyal consumers. As Charles Duhigg reported in the *New York Times*, shoppers receive a guest ID number linked to their credit card, name, or e-mail address. It retains their buying history along with demographic information that Target collects or buys from other sources. A Target statistician analyzes purchasing data for women who signed up for store baby registries for patterns such as unscented lotion purchases, which typically occur around the second trimester. After estimating delivery dates, Target sends coupons tailored to women's different stages.[2]

So much for keeping intimate details all in the family.

PREDICTIVE ANALYTICS

Much of the surveillance discussed thus far in this book involves gathering, analyzing, and selling personal data. The study of our habits is called *behavioral analytics*. Corporations gather so much data because the more information they have on hand, the more accurate the inferences marketers and others can make. Evidence about what you do can help fill in more details about your life.

Predictive analytics, on the other hand, is the science of collecting, or mining, data and creating a predictive model to assess the chances of a future event occurring. Begin with "data lakes," which are repositories of raw data gathered by a corporation or other entity. These nonrelational databases offer more flexibility for different kinds of analysis, and programs like NoSql and Hadoop enable users to decipher patterns in massive sets of somewhat heterogeneous data. These patterns, as they are confirmed on bigger sets of data, offer a reasonably clear prediction for behavior that aligns with the patterns over time.

These are the horizons of Big Data. In work and leisure, we generate huge amounts of data, as we log on to computers and websites, appear in security photos, walk around with our phones constantly reconnecting with a signal. The ability to reach across platforms and databases to draw this information together is providing an increasingly incisive look into our collective lives in the digital age.[3]

PREDICTIVE POLICING

Big data is used increasingly in law enforcement. Anticipating criminal activity has become big business—the interest of police in the data-gathering techniques perfected by tech companies and corporations creates new opportunities for data-mongers to profit at our expense.

Across the country, law enforcement agencies dabble in ways to conduct "predictive policing." Algorithms analyze data sets to inform where police departments focus their resources. One argument in favor of using computer-based analyses is that technology may remove bias in deciding where to focus police efforts, though as noted above, it is equally possible that existing racial biases will be baked into the analysis. It's also cost-effective, advocates say, and is allegedly more objective than the "gut" instincts of police.

It comes in two forms. *Place-based* predictive policing uses historic crime data to identify places and times that have a high risk of crime. *Person-based* predictive policing, on the other hand, attempts to identify individuals or groups likely to commit or be victimized by a crime. It analyzes such risk factors as past arrests or calls for emergency assistance.

Critics say that agencies are not transparent about their prediction programs. This raises concerns that algorithms will utilize unreliable data sets or reinforce racial biases that are already rampant in the criminal justice system. There is some evidence of this. Independent audits have resulted in departments such as Chicago and Los Angeles reducing or eliminating predictive initiatives.[4]

Predictive policing tools are mainly deployed by municipal police departments, though private vendors and federal agencies play major roles in their implementation. The Los Angeles Police Department (LAPD) began working with federal agencies on predictive policing in 2008. One initiative launched in 2011, operation LASER, focuses on data spanning two years to score information from individuals' rap sheets. Being in a gang, or being on probation or parole, carries a certain number of points. PredPol is software that anticipates property offenses. It analyzes different types of crimes in particular areas, along with time, to predict if another crime may occur there. It generates maps that indicate hotspots for officers to patrol. The federal Bureau of Justice Assistance funded both. LASER ceased operating in 2019 after an internal audit by LAPD's inspector general found several problems with the program. Among them were inconsistencies in how individuals were selected and kept in the system. Some police departments have also discontinued their PredPol programs.[5]

The New York Police Department (NYPD), the largest police force in the United States, started testing predictive policing software as early as 2012. The success of the NYPD's CompStat program (launched in January 1994 under Mayor Rudolph Giuliani) in using data to reduce crime led to a desire for more and more data. A series of documents released by the department in 2018, after the Brennan Center filed a lawsuit, identified three firms—Azavea, KeyStats, and PredPol—involved in an NYPD predictive policing trial.[6] Ultimately, the NYPD developed its own in-house predictive policing algorithms and started to use them in 2013. According to a 2017 paper by department staff, the NYPD created place-based predictive algorithms for several crime categories, including shootings, burglaries, felony assaults, grand larcenies, grand larcenies of motor vehicles, and robberies. Those algorithms are used to help assign officers to monitor specific areas.[7] While the NYPD has described the information that's fed into the algorithms—complaints for seven major crime categories, shooting incidents, and 911 calls for shots fired—it has failed to disclose the data sets in response to a public records request from the Brennan Center.

The Chicago Police Department piloted one of the largest person-based predictive policing programs; the "heat list" or "strategic subjects list" predicted who was most likely to engage in gun violence or be a victim of it. The algorithm, based on a study from Yale University,[8] argued that epidemiological models that track disease can be used to predict gun violence.[9]

Critics say that agencies are not transparent about their prediction programs. That raises concerns that algorithms will utilize unreliable data sets or reinforce racial biases that are already rampant in the criminal justice system. There is some evidence of this. Independent audits have resulted in departments such as Chicago and Los Angeles reducing or eliminating predictive initiatives.

Analysis of an early version of the Chicago program by the RAND Institute found it was ineffective, and a legal battle revealed that the list, far from being narrowly targeted, included every single person arrested or fingerprinted in Chicago since 2013.[10] Civil rights groups had criticized the program for targeting communities of color, and a report by Chicago's Office of the Inspector General found that it overly relied on arrest records to identify risk even in cases of people who were not convicted or arrested again. Headlines from local and national newspapers and broadcast media about record levels of shootings in the late 2010s told the tale of the program's failure. The program was shelved in January 2020.[11]

Some of the skepticism around predictive policing programs has less to do with specific technologies than with the lack of transparency from the agencies that administer them—both in terms of what kinds of data are analyzed and how the departments use the predictions. Major details about predictive policing in Los Angeles, for example, surfaced only after years of activism demanding more information from the LAPD about its programs.

The Los Angeles initiative began in 2015, but it wasn't until 2019 that the city's Inspector General issued a report to the Police Commission. The report cited inconsistent criteria used to identify and track people they deemed likeliest to commit violent crime. An editorial in the *Los Angeles Times* noted the potential for algorithms to enhance bias. Existing data shows arrests—for the same crimes—of black and Latinx people surpassing those of white persons: "If the algorithm crunches arrest, incarceration and probation or parole data and then spits out a risk assessment, it will signal to cops that the black or Latinx subjects—already subject to unequal criminal justice treatment—ought to be more closely watched."[12]

The editorial continued, "The cycle of inequity will be repeated, this time enhanced by the data 'science' that is supposed to erase bias."

Transparency concerns also taint the NYPD's predictive policing efforts. As part of the Brennan Center's efforts to obtain documents under the Freedom of Information Act, the organization was forced to file a lawsuit to obtain the materials it was requesting. Only after an expensive, multi-year legal battle did the department finally disclose some documentation about the agency's use of in-house algorithms and predictive policing software. Numerous concerns remain, however. The NYPD claims not to use enforcement data, such as arrest information, for predictive policing purposes. But as they remain reluctant to produce documentation to back up their claims, there is ultimately little transparency about the source of the data sets used as inputs for the NYPD's algorithms.[13]

There is also a dearth of information about how crime predictions are ultimately used—a problem exacerbated by the fact that the NYPD does not keep audit logs of who creates or accesses predictions, nor does it save the predictions it generates (or so it claims).[14] This limits the amount of available information on the department's use of predictive policing and would make it difficult for independent auditors or policymakers to properly evaluate these tools, including to assess whether predictive policing is reinforcing historical over-policing of communities of color and whether there is a meaningful correlation between police deployment to "hot spots" and crime reduction.

CONSTITUTIONAL CONCERNS

Some legal experts argue that predictive policing systems threaten rights protected by the Fourth Amendment, which requires "reasonable suspicion" for a police officer stop—a legal standard that helps protect individuals against "unreasonable searches and seizures" by the police. Predictive analytics tools may make it easier for police to claim that individuals meet the reasonable suspicion standard without concrete evidence of wrongdoing, ultimately justifying more invasive policing practices.[15]

Additionally, civil rights organizations, researchers, and advocates from overly policed communities have expressed concerns that using algorithmic techniques to forecast crime, particularly relying on historical police data, could perpetuate existing racial biases in the criminal justice system. A 2019 study by the AI Now Institute, for example, describes how some police departments rely on "dirty data"—or data that is "derived from or influenced by corrupt, biased, and unlawful practices," including both discriminatory policing and manipulation of crime statistics—to inform their predictive policing systems.[16] Relying on historical crime data can replicate biased police practices and reinforce over-policing of communities of color, while manipulating crime numbers to meet quotas or produce ambitious crime reduction results can give rise to more policing in the neighborhoods in which those statistics are concentrated.

Some critics have labeled predictive policing a form of "tech-washing" that gives racially biased policing methods the appearance of objectivity, simply because a computer or an algorithm seems to replace human judgment.[17]

Rachel Levinson-Waldman, a senior counsel in the Brennan Center's Liberty and National Security Program, is struck by the consistent lack of enthusiasm for predictive policing from community groups.

"What stands out for me in my interactions with the people most likely to actually interact with police," she says, "is that groups and community organizations are not actively pushing for predictive policing as a preferred way to serve their neighborhood or community."[18]

Instead, they often call for more training in conflict resolution and conflict mediation in order to enable the community itself to resolve issues and reduce conflict, so that violence is not the go-to method for handling disagreements. The Newark Community Street team, in Newark, New Jersey, for example, replicates a model used in Chicago and New York called Ceasefire. The model, which has reduced gun violence, treats violence like a disease and uses public health strategies to control the spread of violence. Outreach Workers and Violence Interrupters engage with community members at risk of perpetrating or being victimized by violence. Staff members are familiar with life on the streets and serve as peer counselors by offering advice and guidance on how to respond to conflicts without violence.[19] Camden, New Jersey, was one of the country's poorest and most dangerous cities, enduring police brutality-related riots in the 1960s and 1970s. In 2013, Camden dismantled its city police and replaced it with a county-run force. New officers were hired and trained in community policing and de-escalation techniques. As a result, violent crime in Camden has declined.[20]

Low-tech responses to violence can be highly effective in a world increasingly dominated by high-tech solutions in search of problems.

GARBAGE IN, GARBAGE OUT

Predictive analytics aren't necessarily accurate.

Anyone familiar with stupid, funny, or annoying autocorrect errors is familiar with the limitations of artificial intelligence. Databases contain errors, as we've seen in the corporate and government sectors. When analysis of data files is based on inaccurate information about individuals, the results will be flawed. The same holds true for using data models that are incorrect about certain individuals—accurate data can produce flawed models with the wrong assumptions. Algorithms can also be flawed. Such risks grow as data is continually added to databases.

George Fuechsel, an early IBM programmer and instructor, is credited with coining the term "garbage in, garbage out" (GIGO) to remind students that computers can only process the information we give them. GIGO is often used to refer to situations in the analog world, such as flawed decisions made from incomplete or incorrect information.

As we have seen, the glut of data generated and swept up every day by corporations and government agencies is rife with errors. A Pew Center report, *Code-Dependent: Pros and Cons of the Algorithm Age*, finds that while algorithms—"elegant and incredibly useful tools"—are intended to optimize our lives, experts find cause for concern. In addition to resulting in disparities in health care, criminal justice, employment, and education, algorithms "can also put too much control in the hands of corporations and governments, perpetuate bias, create filter bubbles, [and] cut choices, creativity, and serendipity."[21]

The consequence of imperfect data management and bias-informed analytics can range from mere annoyances to utter ruination of lives.

MYTH 21

"THERE'S NOTHING
I CAN DO TO STOP
SURVEILLANCE"

On June 19, 2002, the FBI agent was still reckoning with the 9/11 attacks on the World Trade Center. He needed information to lead his team to a suspected cache of explosives in a Florida storage unit.

The target was artist Hasan Elahi, fresh off the plane from the Netherlands. Elahi had landed in the Detroit Metropolitan Airport, and he was on a terrorist watch list. Agents pulled him into an interrogation room for questioning:

"Who paid for your trip?"

"When did you last visit a mosque?"

"Have you moved explosives out of a storage unit?"

The FBI let him go. But Elahi clocked seventy thousand air miles annually to exhibit his artwork. The FBI advised him to tell them of his comings and goings for his own good, or other agents relying on the Bureau's faulty watch list might subject him to another hellish experience.

Elahi, a Bangladeshi-born US citizen, complied.

Then he went further. . . .

He exposed everything he did to the FBI and the world, no matter how mundane. He uploaded his life evidence in a multimedia journal, with tens of thousands of photographs documenting street signs, parking lots, bedrooms, food consumed, financial transactions, communications, travel logs, and more.

"FBI, here I am!" proclaimed Elahi at his 2011 TED Talk audience.[1]

Elahi knows government agencies have their sights on something more permanent than money: social control. The US Aerospace Corporation, for example, is readying for "GEOINT (geospatial intelligence) Singularity." It will monitor, in real time, everything on the earth's surface, 24-7. Artificial intelligence systems will analyze the massive trove of data in the search for, well, what?

Elahi tells us what to do when everything is up for grabs in the digital orbit: "You have to take control over it. And if I give you this information directly, it's a very different type of identity than if you were to try to go through and try to get bits and pieces. . . . Intelligence agencies . . . all operate in an industry where their commodity is information, or restricted access to information. And the reason their information has any value is, well, because no one else has access to it."

His approach may not be for everyone, but the premise is something many desire: creating and then controlling your digital footprints.

One online commentator described Elahi's project as a "million lilliputian counterstrikes, each innocent in itself."[2] For such a project to have protective value, however, a critical mass of other individuals must participate.

TIME TO GALVANIZE

For now, many Americans are content to do nothing about controlling their own data. Others are eager to debunk this pernicious myth: "There's nothing I can do to stop surveillance."

Human tendencies toward inertia, rationalization, and fear of the unknown provide oxygen to this myth. It's the motherboard into which all other myths feed. Variations on this myth are: "I cannot control my digital data." Or, "I don't stand a chance against Big Data and the Big Five": Amazon, Apple, Google, Facebook, and Microsoft.

Privacy in the digital age is a matter of control over disclosure. While there's truth to the power inequities that exist between mighty corporations and individuals, mavericks like Elahi have confronted the forces of data aggregators and made promising dents in the commodification of personal data.

The three branches of government, as well as people—the so-called "fourth branch"—must galvanize. The legislative branch needs to become tech savvy, understand the needs of consumers and the threats they face, and pass laws that favor privacy over profit. The judicial branch must also modernize its knowledge of the digital age to rule more fairly in court. The executive branch has a duty to prioritize citizens' right to control their data.

But individuals need to take the lead. Without that, the other branches won't fall into order.

THE FOURTH BRANCH: SENTINELS OF SURVEILLANCE

How can individuals move the privacy compass? Because intelligence apparatus is covert, ordinary people need help from whistleblowers. Civilians with the wisdom and the will are already engaging in creative challenges to the surveillance state. In tandem with intelligence experts who have security clearances and a conscience, they can make seismic shifts in reclaiming individual autonomy over personal data.

As 5G and the Internet of Things speed up global connectivity, it's a critical time to get "smart" about reclaiming control of digital data. Individual actions have formed some of the most important advances for privacy.

"MY PRIVACY IS NONE OF YOUR BUSINESS"[3]

How much can an Austrian law student, bringing legal complaints in Ireland, impact privacy protections on a global level? It turns out, quite a lot. Max Schrems was studying law during a semester abroad at Santa Clara University when he took on tech conglomerate Facebook. At age twenty-three, while doing research for a paper, he asked Facebook for his personal data. It shocked him to receive 1,200 pages that included everything he'd ever "liked," and every private message he'd ever sent.

Schrems filed several complaints with the Irish Data Protection Commissioner, because Facebook's European headquarters is in Ireland, claiming that Facebook was breaking European data protection laws and undermining the right to privacy. In 2015, the Court of Justice of the European Union (CJEU) invalidated a prior "safe harbor" decision governing data transfers between the EU and the US, concluding that the US doesn't supply adequate protection for personal data being transferred there from Europe. In July 2020, the CJEU agreed, ruling that personal data from people in Europe was probably exposed to over-broad US government surveillance with insufficient avenues for redress.

The Electronic Privacy Information Center noted that the ruling has significant implications for US businesses and for Congress because it calls into question the adequacy of protection against surveillance of people's data in the United States.[4] The Electronic Frontier Foundation reiterated the value of the Schrems cases as being a critical indicator that the US must build more privacy protections into its surveillance apparatus.

THE WHISTLEBLOWERS

Surveillance by the US government is covert and carried out by a once well-hidden network of agencies and programs. Today, the public knows quite a bit about the NSA, the role of FISA courts, and other elements of the nation's intelligence apparatus. This is due to the courage of a few privacy patriots who have used their access to government programs to expose abuses of privacy. Whistleblowers have paid a serious price for coming forward.

In 1971, the first NSA whistleblower, NSA analyst Perry Fellwock, exposed ECHELON, the agency's covert global mass surveillance program. Fellwock's revelations, including that its budget was far larger than the CIA's and that it was conducting illegal wiretaps on Americans, ignited a national controversy.[5]

With the acceleration of counterterrorism work after September 11, whistleblowers have been a staple of our political diet.

Russell Tice is a former intelligence analyst for the Defense Intelligence Agency, the Office of Naval Intelligence, and the US Air Force. He was a source for the *New York Times*'s 2005 reporting on wiretap activity.[6] We've discussed the ThinThread NSA whistleblowers—Bill Binney,

Thomas Drake, Ed Loomis, and J. Kirk Wiebe—who, after 9/11, challenged the costly privacy-invading Trailblazer project.[7] Also mentioned earlier is former AT&T technician Mark Klein, who leaked information in 2006 about the telecommunications giant's cooperation with the NSA, which they had done by installing network hardware to monitor, capture, and process US telecommunications en masse.[8]

But Edward Snowden may go down in history as the most impactful surveillance leaker of the twenty-first century. His 2013 release of classified material revealed internet surveillance programs such as PRISM, XKeyscore, and Tempora, and the interception of US and European telephone metadata. Snowden's revelations brought a halt to at least some illegal surveillance.

Given the enormous personal risk that whistleblowers face, due to toothless legal protections, it's incumbent on other citizens and the other branches of government to do their jobs in helping to prevent illegal surveillance.

WHAT YOU CAN DO TO HELP STAVE OFF THE SURVEILLANCE STATE

Privacy is a process. Like the concept of health, it has elements that are individual and elements that must be group- and even society-wide. At times we make choices that we know aren't the best from a privacy perspective. But a few simple steps can improve our privacy hygiene and help others do the same.

1. *Conduct a privacy audit:* Start with an audit of your cell phone and computers and expand to review all the ways you create, store, transmit, and delete digital information. Many alternative software apps and programs exist that are far more secure than corporate ones. Privacy advocates like the Electronic Frontier Foundation have useful guides on their websites to assist in identifying better alternatives and practices, based on your needs and circumstances.
2. *Remember to FLOSS:* Free/Libre and Open Source (FLOSS) or Free and Open Source (FOSS) software are collaborative

projects that make the code they build publicly available to everyone free of charge, or "open source." It's nearly impossible to hide malicious code in a product that has so many privacy-minded developers continually looking under the hood and communicating about what they see there and how they can improve it.

3. *Show me the money:* The axiom, "If it's free, then you are the product," is a useful reminder that the proliferation of "free" apps, games or even memes, and other "free" services are often the means that corporations and bad actors use to steal your personal data so they can sell it to third parties or even to help guess your passwords. FLOSS software is free, so corporations often use them as a base and add their own proprietary data-gathering elements when they package and brand them for sale.

4. *Choose better software tools:* In addition to FLOSS products, many tools available are designed to maximize privacy. Signal (by WhisperSystems) is the most secure texting app available as of 2021. DuckDuckGo is a search engine that doesn't track you in the way that Google does. Mozilla Foundation has several widely used FLOSS programs, including the Firefox browser and the Thunderbird email client. The Tor browser is widely trusted software that uses an innovative technology to provide secure internet communication.

5. *Step up your password game:* Avoid the trap of re-using a simple one that's easily remembered. One option for stronger passwords is to use full sentences. Add capitalization, spaces between words, and punctuation. Password manager tools such as KeePassXC generate and manage strong random passwords.

6. *Encrypt, encrypt, encrypt:* Many devices have the option to encrypt their hard-drives to protect the full operating system, the programs, and the personal data stored on them. Be in the habit of carefully reviewing the settings of each of the services you use and be sure you are utilizing the strongest privacy options available. Encrypting messages before sharing or sending them

to others across the internet is a strong privacy step. For email, GnuPG (usually referred to as GPG) is the FLOSS version of the proprietary PGP encryption. This "end-to-end encryption" is currently the strongest available encryption method for email.

7. *Do the two-step:* This useful tool automates a second step when you log in to a system or service with a password—usually by sending you a text or email with a random code that you need to enter to continue. Enable this option wherever possible.

8. *No knowledge is good knowledge:* One approach to protecting your personal information is to only gather, store, or retain information that is necessary to keep. Called "no knowledge"— the principle is simple: design a system that does not require the service to retain any of your information. If they don't have it, then they cannot contribute to its being compromised.

9. *Party!* One of the best ways to overcome privacy threats, an ever-changing landscape, and different levels of expertise is to help each other. "Crypto parties" are gatherings where people bring their devices (cell phones and computers for example) and help each other implement these changes. This might mean having someone help you find the encryption settings in your phone or helping you change your computer's default search engine.

Privacy advocates often organize crypto-parties that are open to members of their communities. If you have a level of skill and comfort with some of these technologies you can organize one yourself. Friends don't let friends go without basic, freely available privacy tools.

THE JUDICIAL BRANCH

James Orenstein is a magistrate judge in the Eastern District of New York. In a 2019 *New York Times* op-ed he described how, in the federal courthouse in Brooklyn, prosecutors routinely ask the magistrate judge on duty to issue sealed orders authorizing use of investigative technologies or mandating tech companies to keep secret their tech-based searches.[9]

Not on his watch.

When Judge Orenstein is on duty, prosecutors wait until the next judge, who will likely sign off on their requests, is up. "This waiting game is a symptom of how new surveillance technologies are challenging a legal system that hasn't figured out how to handle them," he writes.

Because Congress lags in determining limits on intrusive police technology, the Supreme Court has heard few legal battles on the topic. Judge Orenstein says, "For the public, as a practical matter, the rules of the road are being decided by prosecutors. Your privacy is not their highest priority."

Judge Orenstein understands, firsthand, the prosecutorial mindset. He served as an assistant United States attorney for the Eastern District of New York from 1990 until 2001. During this time, he received several concurrent appointments, first as a member of the prosecution team in the Oklahoma City bombing trials from 1996 to 1998, then as an attorney-advisor in the Justice Department's Office of Legal Counsel, and finally as associate deputy attorney general from 1999 to 2001.

The role of judges as impartial arbiters in tech cases is essential because there is no one in court to represent individuals targeted for surveillance. There is no chance of appeal either. And federal prosecutors seek out judges inclined to rule favorably.

Orenstein asks the right questions. He knows the pitfalls of relying on antiquated laws that didn't anticipate the digital era: "If no such law exists, society needs to make deliberate choices about how best to balance the promise of more efficient investigative technologies against the risks to personal liberty."

That's when Congress must step in, he says.

But that's the problem: the judge notes that Congress hasn't enacted any meaningful updates of digital privacy laws governing police investigations since the internet's early days. "That's why the Justice Department relied on a law written in 1789 when it tried to force Apple to help search an iPhone by disabling the device's password protection. I ruled against the government in that case," he says.

It falls on the judiciary, Orenstein notes, to devise ways to maintain fair reviews of new technological investigative tools if Congress fails to create modern and appropriate laws. He cites the FISA court's system of engaging impartial attorneys to argue new or impactful legal issues arising from government requests for tech-based surveillance orders. Without representing the target of the investigations, these attorneys can still raise arguments in favor of the target's privacy interests.

THE EXECUTIVE BRANCH

The executive branch—including the president and state attorneys general, whose mission is to enforce the law and protect individual rights—must step up its efforts to understand technological advances and effect the right balance between law enforcement powers and privacy rights. This is just as much the case at the state level as at the federal level.

Small measures are encouraging.

In November 2016, hackers based in the US and Canada secretly told security officials at Uber Technologies that they had downloaded personal data of 57 million riders and drivers, 25 million of whom were in the US and 7.7 million of whom were drivers. The hackers demanded "six figures" to delete the data and not disclose the breach. Uber paid them $100,000.[10]

Then Uber concealed the breach, violating laws in all fifty states and taking users for a ride. When Uber's board of directors hired a forensic team on another matter, Uber gave notice of the breach, in late November 2017, a year after the ransom was paid. The New York State Office of the Attorney General independently investigated the data breach, but later joined in a multi-state investigatory process, where it took a leadership position, to reach a settlement.[11]

THE LEGISLATIVE BRANCH

There's enormous need for sensible reform ideas and privacy protection laws. But the House of Representatives and the Senate must grow a backbone.

One example of a reform is for Congress to end the artificial distinction between metadata and content data. Terry Jones, from Oak Ridge National Laboratory, says: "Any storage architecture that maintains a distinction between metadata and data has real problems that will limit its flexibility and usefulness. You may possess information about something without having the thing. There may be no pieces of content, or there may be many."[12] Those determining distinctions between data and metadata are typically computer programmers, system architects, or product managers. This gives power to a select few.

There are market solutions to help curb the urge to amass more and more personal data. Tristan Harris proposes a tax on income derived from targeted digital ads, an approach endorsed by the economist and Nobel laureate Paul Romer. Former Democratic presidential candidate Andrew Yang has also proposed taxing data aggregation for profit as well as creating a new department to regulate algorithms on social networks. The idea is to encourage tech companies to adopt business models that are less reliant on personal data. The taxes would be progressive, favoring smaller businesses. Harris likens the monetization of user data to fossil fuel extraction: "These are the most profitable business models but also the most polluting."[13]

These are just a few examples of areas that can benefit from legislative reform. The use of biometrics, legal protections for children, predictive policing, the Internet of Things, the use of surveillance drones, and virtually every other aspect of surveillance needs a tune-up and regular check-ins from lawmakers and enforcers.

CODA: SECURING THE RIGHT TO BE LET ALONE

Over two decades before joining the Supreme Court, a young Louis Brandeis wrote about the portable camera and celebrity journalism. He noted that new mechanical devices posed a threat to preserving the individual right to be let alone. With his law partner Samuel Warren, Brandeis published the first article urging a legal right to privacy, namely "The Right to Privacy" in the *Harvard Law Review* in 1890. Ever since, the article has become a staple in law school classes. Well before the digital age, Brandeis understood well the threats that technology poses to privacy.

As we consider the important role that segments of American society must play in preserving privacy, Judge James Orenstein's words resonate beyond the courtroom. They serve as an important mantra for anyone who cherishes freedom: "As the pace of technological advancement increases, the need becomes more urgent for society to balance those interests in a coherent, fair and democratic way."[14]

All four "branches," from the president to you and me, need to play a role in that rebalancing.

SURVEILLANCE
AND PRIVACY TIMELINE

1902—US authorities first use fingerprints, beginning with the New York Civil Service Commission. Use of fingerprints quickly spreads to prisons, the military, and police departments.

1924—Congress mandates the FBI to manage a national fingerprint card database, which by 1946 grew to one hundred million records.

1936—The US adopts use of social security numbers as part of the New Deal economic plan to provide citizens with financial benefits.

1952—President Harry Truman founds the National Security Agency.

1971—Seven activists break into an FBI field office in Media, Pennsylvania. Documents they discover reveal the US Counterintelligence Program, COINTELPRO.

1978—Congress enacts the Foreign Intelligence Surveillance Act establishing procedures for gathering intelligence on foreign powers.

1983—President Ronald Reagan watches the movie *WarGames* and grows concerned about cyber vulnerabilities. The FBI asks Congress to enact national computer crime–related laws.

1984—The first federal computer crime statute is contained in the Comprehensive Crime Control Act (CCCA) of 1984. After tinkering with the 1984 act, in 1986 Congress passes the Computer Fraud and Abuse Act (CFAA).

1985—Congress passes the Employer Sanctions provision of the Immigration Reform and Control Act of 1985: this resulted in widespread (and government documented) discrimination against foreign-looking American workers, especially Asians and Latinx people.

1986—UK psychologists stationed in eighteen homes welcome children on Halloween. In half of the houses they secretly record children alone with a mirror and candy bowl. The researchers' theory was confirmed: kids are less apt to sneak a handful of candy if they see their reflection.

1994—The Communications Assistance for Law Enforcement Act (CALEA) of 1994 is an early legislative effort to address FBI fears of "going dark." It requires telecommunications carriers to afford police ways to comply with court orders for real time interceptions and call-identifying information.

1994—The Republican-controlled Senate and House eliminate the congressional Office of Technology Assessment. From 1972 to 1995, this office gave representatives an analysis of science and technical issues.

1998—Congress enacts the primary law, which would be implemented by the Federal Trade Commission, protecting children from advertising: Children's Online Privacy Protection Act of 1998 (COPPA). It limits collection of personally identifiable information from children without parental consent.

2000—Kevin Ashton helps launch a line of Oil of Olay cosmetics and needs a way to track shades of lipstick. He has an idea: sticking a credit card microchip on the lipstick so a wireless network takes data from a lipstick package for inventory purposes. Ashton consults with two MIT researchers who had been seeking to miniaturize radio frequency ID technology, or RFID chips.

2001—Four coordinated attacks against the US occur on September 11, 2001, marking a new chapter in the so-called "war on terror."

2001—Congress passes the USA PATRIOT Act. The act changes FISA and ECPA and eases restrictions on wiretapping. For example, roving wiretaps and sneak-and-peek warrants are allowed, a turning point for domestic spying. The act expands the use of National Security Letters, including adding a gag order provision. Section 215 permits sharing of "any tangible thing" as part of an international terrorism investigation.

2001—Section 215 of the USA PATRIOT Act amends Title V, Section 501 of the Foreign Intelligence Surveillance Act (FISA), "Access to Certain Business Records for Foreign Intelligence and International Terrorism Investigations" (50 U.S.C. sec. 1861). This authorization concerns collection of telephony metadata, and not the content of any communication, the identity of any party to the communication, or any cell-site location information.

2001—New York's Metropolitan Transportation Authority (MTA) trademarks and implements "If you see something, say something," as an anti-terrorism campaign. The MTA later licenses it to the Department of Homeland Security for nationwide use in 2010.

2002—NSA employees Thomas Drake, Bill Binney, Ed Loomis, and J. Kirk Wiebe criticize the costly program Trailblazer, a failure for the contractor SAIC. A better program called ThinThread, developed in the 1990s, protects privacy and costs far less.

2002—Congress passes the Homeland Security Act to create the Department of Homeland Security, a Cabinet-level department aimed at unifying national security initiatives.

2003—AT&T technician Mark Klein discovers a secret room at AT&T's San Francisco office. He later testifies in an Electronic Frontier Foundation federal lawsuit against the NSA that the room was set up to conduct "vacuum-cleaner surveillance" of internet use by millions of unsuspecting Americans. AT&T's corporate relationships enabled them to turn over other internet service providers, and turn over other carriers' data, without their consent.

2004—President George W. Bush implements a directive for a mandatory, government-wide personal identification verification (PIV) card credentialing system. Through this so-called USAccess program, federal agencies issue credentials to employees and contractors after gathering and storing fingerprint and facial images.

2005—The *New York Times* reveals government surveillance going back to 2002, including warrantless wiretapping of phone and internet communications of possibly thousands of Americans.

2005—Congress passes the REAL ID Act, which closely resembles a mandatory national ID program. In late 2013, DHS announces a phased enforcement plan for the act. As of this writing, enforcement is slated to go into effect on October 1, 2021.

2006—James Risen and Eric Lichtblau of the *New York Times* receive the Pulitzer Prize for national reporting on covert domestic eavesdropping.

2006—The Center for Constitutional Rights files *CCR v. Bush* (later *CCR v. Obama*) against President George W. Bush and the heads of the major security agencies. It challenges warrantless NSA surveillance of people within the US, including CCR attorneys, as a violation of the Foreign Intelligence Surveillance Act (FISA).

2008—FISA Amendments Act of 2008 passes. Section 702 affords the NSA virtually unlimited authority to monitor Americans' communications while ostensibly targeting foreigners living abroad.

2010—The French Parrot AR Drone launches. It is the first drone that can be controlled by WiFi with a smartphone. The flight-ready drone is a commercial success.

2010—A two-year *Washington Post* investigation, "Top Secret America," reveals that, under the banner of counterterrorism, approximately 1,931 private security companies and 1,271 government organizations engage in intelligence gathering.

2011—The Federal Aviation Administration Air Transportation Modernization and Safety Improvement Act sanctions drones for domestic surveillance.

2011—Award-winning investigative journalist Sharyl Attkisson's home and work devices are hacked. In 2012, a forensic analyst determines that her computers are being monitored.

2012—The Chicago Police Department pilots a large person-based predictive policing program called the "heat list" or "strategic subjects list."

2012—The Federal Trade Commission adopts "privacy by design" as one of the three elements in a new design framework.

2012—The lawsuit *Hassan v. City of New York* claims that the NYPD violated the Constitution by surveilling mosques and local venues frequented by Muslims.

2013—Edward Snowden, former CIA staffer and in 2013 an NSA–contracted systems analyst for Booz Allen, releases documents to journalists about the NSA mass surveillance program. On June 6, 2013, *The Guardian* runs its first in a series of disclosures.

2013—Apple, Inc., makes Touch ID on several iPhones and its iPad Air 2 and iPad Mini 3 available for owners to gain access to devices. Several financial institutions follow suit. Apple's iPhone 10 model integrates facial recognition. With this move, biometric ID is on its way to normalization.

2013—SecureDrop launches. The Tor-powered software enables anonymous and secure communication between journalists and sources. The *New York Times, Washington Post*, and other global news outlets use SecureDrop.

2013—PEN American Center (which has since rebranded as PEN America) issues a report surveying nearly eight hundred writers globally on the impact of surveillance. It finds concern about surveillance nearly as high among writers in liberal democracies (75 percent) as in nondemocratic nations (80 percent).

2013—Max Schrems files numerous complaints against Facebook in Ireland, where the company's European headquarters is located. In 2015, the CJEU invalidates the arrangement governing personal data transfer from the EU to the US due to inadequate protection from surveillance. In July 2020, CJEU rules that European authorities must stop transfers of personal data made under standard contractual clauses by companies like Facebook, because the corporations don't provide sufficient protection from US surveillance to EU citizens.

2015—After Snowden's disclosures, several lawsuits challenge mass surveillance and some laws are reformed. Congress passes the USA Freedom Act to reduce mass collection of phone data.

2015—With the nonprofit Library Freedom Project, IT librarian Chuck McAndrew installs Tor browser software on Kilton, New Hampshire, library computers. Kilton is the nation's first library to provide patrons with anonymous Web surfing.

2016—The National Institute of Standards and Technology, a Department of Commerce agency, issues an internal report featuring an introduction to the concepts of privacy engineering and risk management for federal systems.

2016—The CEO of SeaWorld admits that its maritime theme park employees posed as animal rights activists to spy on People for the Ethical Treatment of Animals (PETA).

2016—The US Army War College's 2016 report on the effectiveness of anti-terrorism measures says that data suggests US efforts in the war on terror have been largely ineffective in achieving the stated objectives.

2016—The FBI tries to force Apple to unlock an iPhone after a lethal 2015 mass attack in San Bernardino, California. The FBI wants Apple to create new software for them to use to access an iPhone 5C recovered from one of the shooters.

2017—News reports surface that Samsung smart televisions recorded conversations in someone's home, and that Samsung sent those recordings to government agencies, including the CIA.

2018—Police use DNA forensics to apprehend the so-called Golden State Killer, Joseph James DeAngelo, triggering an uptick in police use of private genealogy services' DNA databases.

2018—Cambridge Analytica data scandal breaks.

2018—In *Carpenter v. United States*, the Supreme Court holds that the government violates the Fourth Amendment by accessing, without a search warrant, historical records containing physical locations of cellphones.

2018—The European Union (EU) passes the General Data Protection Regulation (GDPR), the world's most comprehensive privacy and security law. It imposes obligations on organizations anywhere, if they target or collect data related to people in the EU.

2018—President Trump renews Section 702 of FISA in January, making it, according to security expert Bruce Schneier, "effectively a permanent part of US law."

2019—Researchers from Kneron, a San Diego–based firm that develops artificial intelligence (AI) products and systems, conduct an experiment. They don 3D printed masks of other people's faces to test the strength of facial recognition security solutions. They pass through facial recognition systems at multiple airports, border crossing checkpoints, and point of sale terminals.

2019—High-profile congressional hearings involving Facebook expose the social media giant to questioning, and also illustrate lawmakers' ignorance of internet platforms.

2019—TikTok's parent company ByteDance pays a fine of $5.7 million and the Federal Trade Commission prohibits it from collecting and using data from kids under the age of thirteen.

2020—The city of Baltimore launches a wide-aerial surveillance experiment in May 2020. Its police department contracts with Ohio-based Persistent Surveillance Systems to fly Cessna aircraft over the city for six months.

2020—Sidewalk Labs of Alphabet, Inc. (Google's parent company), announces that it is canceling its billion-dollar "smart city" plan in Toronto.

2020—The Trump administration enacts a program requiring Immigration and Customs Enforcement agents to take mouth swabs of people in their custody for the FBI's DNA database.

2020—IBM, Amazon, and Microsoft announce they will pause or end sales of facial recognition technology to US law enforcement.

2020—Uprisings sweep the US in response to unjustified police killings of unarmed black persons. Demands for an end to racially biased policing trigger a rethinking of some of those practices.

2021 and on—Americans take action, demanding that federal agencies and corporations guard privacy and help users reclaim control of their data.

ACKNOWLEDGMENTS

Beacon Press represents the social conscience of the publishing world. After it published *The Pentagon Papers* in 1971, President Nixon attacked Beacon, and it was subpoenaed to appear at Daniel Ellsberg's trial. J. Edgar Hoover approved an FBI subpoena of bank records of its parent organization, the Unitarian Universalist Association. The association, from its founding in the early days of the republic, stood for abolition. Ellsberg put it best when he said: "Beacon Press has consistently shown the kind of civic courage that we must have for our country to survive as a democracy."

Gayatri Patnaik and the staff of Beacon Press carry on the legacy of "civic courage." I thank Gayatri for her enthusiasm and for her creative re-envisioning of my original project. I am grateful to be a small part of the Beacon community.

Thanks to the many groups and individuals dedicated to curbing the mass surveillance state who are mentioned in or were interviewed for this book. Their tenacity is admirable. They educate the public about data aggregation, facial recognition, marketing aimed at children, monitoring social media, and the many other facets of the surveillance state. And they litigate cases of unconstitutional practices despite a formidable opponent: the US intelligence community and its claim that its covert surveillance is a matter of national security. These surveillance sentinels are an ongoing inspiration.

Friends and colleagues were generous with their time and comments. From the outset, Julie Erickson provided creative and useful feedback. Devon Kearney helped me unmuddle many thoughts. Lesley

Alderman was a stalwart reader and counselor. Ingrid Aybar asked the right questions, always with enthusiasm. Johanna Fernández patiently challenged and supported me throughout, and suggested Beacon as a potential publisher. Susan Howard lent her eagle eye. Jonathan Stribling-Uss generously shared his thoughts about attorneys' duty to keep electronic communications private. In my home state of New Hampshire, Chuck McAndrew at the Kilton Library was a forward example of protecting library visitors' privacy by installing the Tor browser. Elizabeth Templeton has never faltered, since eighth-grade homeroom, in offering reasoned feedback. Sarah Hogarth's impeccable judgment helped close many gaps. I relied on several interviews from *Law and Disorder*, a radio program that I cohost with my dear friend Michael Steven Smith; guests such as Matthew Guariglia, Clare Garvie, Harsha Panduranga, and Shari Steele enriched this text.

Marco Lanier and Matthew Howland came to my rescue at the eleventh hour with outstanding technical assistance. They did so with grace and efficiency. I owe them a debt of gratitude.

My father, Varujan Yegan Boghosian, died as I was finishing this book. My fiercest champion, he sacrificed much to give me the opportunities he didn't have growing up in the Armenian community of New Britain, Connecticut, after his parents escaped the genocide in the early 1900s.

NOTES

INTRODUCTION

1. Therese Fauerbach, "More Valuable Than Oil, Data Reigns in Today's Data Economy," *Advanced Analytics, Big Data Blog*, https://www.northridgegroup.com /blog/more-valuable-than-oil-data-reigns-in-todays-data-economy.

2. Aliya Ram and Madhumita Murgia, "Data Brokers: Regulators Try to Rein In the 'Privacy Deathstars,'" *Financial Times*, January 7, 2019, https://www .ft.com/content/f1590694-fe68-11e8-aebf-99e208d3e521; Matthew Crain, "The Limits of Transparency: Data Brokers and Commodification," *New Media and Society* 20, no. 1 (2018): 88–104, https://doi.org/10.1177%2F1461444816657096.

3. "Cambridge Analytica: The Data Firm's Global Influence," *BBC News*, March 22, 2018, https://www.bbc.com/news/world-43476762.

4. Christopher Wylie, "Cambridge Analytica: How Did It Turn Clicks into Votes?" *Guardian*, May 6, 2018, https://www.theguardian.com/news/2018/may /06/cambridge-analytica-how-turn-clicks-into-votes-christopher-wylie.

5. "Meet Brittany Kaiser, Cambridge Analytica Whistleblower Releasing Troves of New Files from Data Firm," *Democracy Now*, January 7, 2020, https:// www.democracynow.org/2020/1/7/the_great_hack_cambridge_analytica.

6. Matt Tatham, "Identity Theft Statistics," Experian, March 15, 2018, https:// www.experian.com/blogs/ask-experian/identity-theft-statistics.

7. "Audit of the Federal Bureau of Investigation's Information Security Program Pursuant to the Federal Information Security Modernization Act of 2014 Fiscal Year 2019," Office of the Inspector General, March 2020, https://oig.justice .gov/sites/default/files/reports/a20050.pdf.

8. Emily Dreyfuss, "The US Government Isn't Just Tech-Illiterate. It's Tech-Incompetent," *Wired*, May 11, 2017, https://www.wired.com/2017/05/real-threat -government-tech-illiteracy.

9. Bob Egelko, "Stanford Graduate Student Mistakenly Put on No-Fly List Gets Redemption," *San Francisco Chronicle*, January 2, 2019, https://www .sfchronicle.com/bayarea/article/Stanford-graduate-student-mistakenly-put -on-13504267.php.

10. "Comments of the Electronic Privacy Information Center to the Department of Justice: Privacy Act of 1974; Implementation 84 FR 49073," EPIC, October 18, 2019, https://www.epic.org/apa/comments/EPIC_DOJ_NCIC_Oct2019.pdf.

11. "All Data Breaches in 2019 and 2020–An Alarming Timeline," *SelfKey Blog*, July 5, 2020, https://selfkey.org/data-breaches-in-2019.

12. Howard Solomon, "E-Learning Site Oneclass Left Subscriber Database Open, Researchers Say," *IT World Canada,* June 25, 2020, https://www.itworld canada.com/article/canadian-e-learning-site-left-subscriber-database-open -say-researchers/432427.

13. Albert Fox Cahn quoted in Natasha Singer and Choe Sang-Hun, "As Coronavirus Escalates, Personal Privacy Plummets," *New York Times,* March 23, 2020, https://www.nytimes.com/2020/03/23/technology/coronavirus-surveillance -tracking-privacy.html.

14. Matthew Guariglia, "Too Much Surveillance Makes Us Less Free," *Washington Post,* July 18, 2017, https://www.washingtonpost.com/news/made-by -history/wp/2017/07/18/too-much-surveillance-makes-us-less-free-it-also-makes -us-less-safe.

15. Bruce Schneier, "How the NSA Threatens National Security," *Atlantic,* January 6, 2014, https://www.theatlantic.com/technology/archive/2014/01/how -the-nsa-threatens-national-security/282822.

16. Mark Klein was the first to expose AT&T's role in sharing phone logs with the NSA; David Kravets, "NSA Leak Vindicates AT&T Whistleblower," *Wired,* June 27, 2013, https://www.wired.com/2013/06/nsa-whistleblower-klein.

MYTH 1: "Smart homes are more secure"

1. Mark Murison, "Smart Home Surveillance at 'Staggering' Levels—Report," *Internet of Business,* June 5, 2018, https://internetofbusiness.com/smart-home -surveillance-at-staggering-levels-report.

2. Emily Ferron, "2019 Safety.com Home Security Report," Safety.com, October 12, 2020, https://www.safety.com/home-security-survey.

3. Michael Hayden in interview with Steven Colbert: "General Michael Hayden Says the CIA Is Not Spying on Us Through Our Televisions," *Colbert Show,* March 8, 2017, https://www.youtube.com/watch?v=buI8aO7nRDM. See also Samsung Smart TV reference: Nicole Nguyen, "If You Have a Smart TV, Take a Closer Look at Your Privacy Settings," *CNBC News,* March 9, 2017, https:// www.cnbc.com/2017/03/09/if-you-have-a-smart-tv-take-a-closer-look-at-your -privacy-settings.html.

4. Karl Bode, "Yet Another Study Shows the Internet of Things Is a Privacy Security Dumpster Fire," *Techdirt,* June 11, 2018, https://www.techdirt.com /articles/20180604/07134939961/yet-another-study-shows-internet-things-is -privacy-security-dumpster-fire.shtml.

5. Ashley Sears, "'Felt So Violated': Milwaukee Couple Warns Hackers Are Outsmarting Smart Homes," *Fox6,* September 23, 2019, https://www.fox6now .com/news/felt-so-violated-milwaukee-couple-warns-hackers-are-outsmarting -smart-homes.

6. "North America Home Automation Systems Market to Generate a Value of US $17.4 Billion, 2019–2024—ResearchAndMarkets.com," Business Wire, January 13, 2020, https://www.businesswire.com/news/home/20200113005384 /en/North-America-Home-Automation-Systems-Market-to-Generate-a-Value -of-US-17.4-Billion-2019-2024---ResearchAndMarkets.com.

7. Author interview with Matthew Guariglia, *Law and Disorder*, September 16, 2019.

8. Rani Molla, "How Amazon's Ring Is Creating a Surveillance Network with Video Doorbells," *Vox*, January 28, 2020, https://www.vox.com/2019/9/5/20849846/amazon-ring-explainer-video-doorbell-hacks; see also Jason Kelly, "Amazon's Ring Enables the Over-Policing Efforts of Some of America's Deadliest Law Enforcement Agencies," Electronic Frontier Foundation, July 2, 2020, https://www.eff.org/deeplinks/2020/07/amazons-ring-enables-over-policing-efforts-some-americas-deadliest-law-enforcement.

9. Interview with Guariglia.

10. Katherine Albrecht and Liz McIntyre, *Spychips: How Major Corporations and Government Plan to Track Your Every Move with RFID* (Nashville, TN: Plume, 2006).

11. Author interview with Liz McIntyre, *Law and Disorder*, August 14, 2017.

12. John R. Quain, "Alexa, What Happened to My Car?" *New York Times*, January 25, 2018, https://www.nytimes.com/2018/01/25/business/amazon-alexa-car.html.

13. "Cybersecurity Risk Reduction Public Safety and Homeland Security Bureau Federal Communications," FCC White Paper, January 18, 2017, https://www.fcc.gov/document/fcc-white-paper-cybersecurity-risk-reduction. The large and diverse number of IoT vendors—who are driven by competition to keep prices low—hinders coordinated efforts to build security by design into the IoT on a voluntary basis.

14. Farhad Manjoo, "How Tech Companies Conquered American Cities," *New York Times*, June 20, 2018, https://www.nytimes.com/2018/06/20/technology/tech-companies-conquered-cities.html.

15. Bianca Wylie and Heidi Boghosian, *Law and Disorder*, August 20, 2018.

16. Sidewalk Labs, Wylie, and Boghosian, *Law and Disorder*.

17. Moira Warburton, "Alphabet's Sidewalk Labs Cancels Toronto 'Smart City' Project," Reuters, May 7, 2020, https://www.reuters.com/article/us-canada-sidewalk/alphabets-sidewalk-labs-cancels-toronto-smart-city-project-idUSKBN22J2FN.

18. Author interview with Matthew Guariglia, *Law and Disorder*, September 16, 2019.

MYTH 2: "I have nothing to hide, so I have nothing to fear"

1. Breonna Taylor account was sourced from several news articles including Rukmini Callimachi, "Breonna's Life Was Changing: Then the Police Came to Her Door," *New York Times*, August 3, 2020, https://www.nytimes.com/2020/08/30/us/breonna-taylor-police-killing.html; Bridget Read, "What We Know About the Killing of Breonna Taylor," *The Cut*, updated September 29, 2020, https://www.thecut.com/2020/09/breonna-taylor-louisville-shooting-police-what-we-know.html; Phillip Bailey and Tessa Duvall, "Breonna Taylor's lawyers link her shooting death to Louisville gentrification plan," *Louisville Courier Journal*, July 5, 2020, https://www.courier-journal.com/story/news

/nation/2020/07/05/breonna-taylor-louisville-gentrification-plan-lawyers /5382035002.

2. James Duane, "Why 'I Have Nothing to Hide' Is the Wrong Way to Think About Surveillance," *Wired*, June 13, 2013, https://www.wired.com/2013/06/why -i-have-nothing-to-hide-is-the-wrong-way-to-think-about-surveillance.

3. Nikole Hannah-Jones, "A Principal Is Accused of Being a Communist, Rattling a Brooklyn School," *New York Times*, May 4, 2017, https://www.nytimes .com/2017/05/04/nyregion/a-principal-is-accused-of-being-a-communist-rattling -a-brooklyn-school.html; Bloomberg v. NYC Department of Education, 17 Civ. 3136 (PGG, September 24, 2019).

4. Marcia Kramer and Frank Lombardi, "New Top State Judge: Abolish Grand Juries and Let Us Decide," *New York Daily News*, January 31, 1985, https:// www.nydailynews.com/news/politics/chief-judge-wanted-abolish-grand-juries -article-1.2025208.

5. The twenty-three states with castle laws are Arkansas, California, Colorado, Connecticut, Delaware, Hawaii, Illinois, Iowa, Maine, Maryland, Massachusetts, Minnesota, Nebraska, New Jersey, New Mexico, New York, North Dakota, Ohio, Oregon, Rhode Island, Virginia, Washington, and Wisconsin.

6. "The FBI Checked the Wrong Box and a Woman Ended Up on the Terrorism Watch List for Years," ProPublica, December 15, 2015, https://www.propublica .org/article/fbi-checked-wrong-box-rahinah-ibrahim-terrorism-watch-list.

7. Government Accountability Office (GAO) fraudnet privacy options are listed on the GAO website: https://gao-fais.entellitrak.com/etk-gao-fais-prod /page.request.do?page=page.efile.publicLanding.

8. NYPD Crime Stoppers stats are listed on the NYPD website: https:// www1.nyc.gov/site/nypd/services/see-say-something/crimestoppers.page and at https://crimestoppers.nypdonline.org.

9. Henry A. Landsberger, *Hawthorne Revisited: Management and the Worker, Its Critics, and Developments in Human Relations in Industry* (Ithaca: New York State School of Industrial and Labor Relations, 1958), https://openlibrary .org/books/OL6265029M/Hawthorne_revisited; Kathy Baxter, Catherine Courage, and Kelly Caine, "Chapter 13—Field Studies," in *Understanding Your Users* (Burlington, MA: Elsevier, 2015), https://www.sciencedirect.com/topics/computer -science/hawthorne-effect.

10. "Halloween Psychology: How Mirrors Keep Kids in Line," *Social Psych Online*, October 30, 2015, http://socialpsychonline.com/2015/10/halloween -psychology-self-awareness. Full study: A. Beaman, B. Klentz, E. Diener, and S. Svanum, "Self-Awareness and Transgression in Children: Two Field Studies," *Journal of Personality and Social Psychology* 37, no. 10 (1979): 1835–46, https:// pubmed.ncbi.nlm.nih.gov/512839.

11. Coffin v. United States, 156 U.S. 432 (1895), establishing the presumption of innocence of persons accused of crimes.

12. Michael Boyd, "Constitutional Cases Resulting from the 9/11 Attacks," *Constitution Daily*, September 11, 2020, https://constitutioncenter.org/blog /constitutional-cases-resulting-from-the-9-11-attacks.

MYTH 3: "Encryption and anonymity tools—those are for terrorists!"

1. James Vincent, "NSA and GCHQ Agents Spied on Online Gamers Using World of Warcraft and Second Life," *Independent*, December 9, 2013, https://www.independent.co.uk/life-style/gadgets-and-tech/nsa-and-gchq-agents-spied-online-gamers-using-world-warcraft-and-second-life-8993432.html.

2. Alan Hope, "Brussels Is 'Weakest Link' in Europe's Fight Against Terrorism," *Bulletin*, November 13, 2015, https://www.thebulletin.be/brussels-weakest-link-europes-fight-against-terrorism.

3. R. Dingledine, N. Mathewson, and P. Syverson, "Tor: The Second-Generation Onion Router," Center for High Assurance Computer Systems at the US Naval Research Laboratory, 2004, https://www.nrl.navy.mil/itd/chacs/dingledine-tor-second-generation-onion-router.

4. Alec Muffett, "1 Million People Use Facebook over Tor," Facebook post, April 22, 2016, https://www.facebook.com/notes/facebook-over-tor/1-million-people-use-facebook-over-tor/865624066877648. For other statistics on Tor use, see the Tor Project website, https://www.torproject.org.

5. Author interview with Chuck McAndrew on July 17, 2017, and emails on September 26, 2016, and June 2, 2020.

6. Interview and emails with Chuck McAndrew.

7. Julia Angwin, "First Library to Support Anonymous Internet Browsing Effort Stops After DHS Email," *ProPublica*, September 10, 2015, https://www.propublica.org/article/library-support-anonymous-internet-browsing-effort-stops-after-dhs-email.

8. Comey's speech available at Fred Dews, "WATCH: FBI Director James Comey on Technology, Law Enforcement, and 'Going Dark,'" Brookings, October 16, 2014, https://www.brookings.edu/blog/brookings-now/2014/10/16/watch-fbi-director-james-comey-on-technology-law-enforcement-and-going-dark.

9. James Comey, *A Higher Loyalty: Truth, Lies, and Leadership* (New York: Flatiron Books, April 17, 2018).

10. Phillip Rogaway, "The Moral Character of Cryptographic Work," Department of Computer Science University of California, Davis, December 2015, https://web.cs.ucdavis.edu/~rogaway/papers/moral.pdf.

11. CALEA, the US wiretapping law, was passed in 1994 during the Clinton administration. (Pub. L. No. 103–414, 108 Stat. 4279, codified at 47 USC 1001–1010). For more information, see https://www.fcc.gov/public-safety-and-homeland-security/policy-and-licensing-division/general/communications-assistance.

12. Bruce Schneier, "The Value of Encryption," *The Ripon Forum*, April 2016, http://www.schneier.com/essays/archives/2016/04/the_value_of_encrypt.html.

13. See more at https://www.nytimes.com/tips#securedrop and https://www.washingtonpost.com/securedrop.

14. Radio interview with author and Shari Steele, *Law and Disorder*, May 16, 2016.

15. Interview with Shari Steele.

16. Richard Pérez-Peña and Adam Goldman, "'It Finally Clicked That This Wasn't an Exercise': Report Recounts San Bernardino Shooting," *New York Times*,

September 9, 2016, https://www.nytimes.com/2016/09/10/us/it-finally-clicked-that
-this-wasnt-an-exercise-report-recounts-san-bernardino-shooting.html.

17. Katie Benner, "Barr Asks Apple to Unlock Pensacola Killer's Phones,
Setting Up Clash," *New York Times*, January 13, 2020, https://www.nytimes.
com/2020/01/13/us/politics/pensacola-shooting-iphones.html.

18. Katie Benner, "Barr Revives Encryption Debate, Calling on Tech Firms
to Allow for Law Enforcement," *New York Times*, July 23, 2019, https://www
.nytimes.com/2019/07/23/us/politics/william-barr-encryption-security.html;
"FBI's 'Going Dark' Claims Now Even More Dubious," Center for Democracy
and Technology, May 22, 2018, https://cdt.org/press/fbis-going-dark-claims-now
-even-more-dubious.

19. Radio interview with author and Shari Steele, *Law and Disorder*, May 16,
2016.

20. Devlin Barrett, "FBI Repeatedly Overstated Encryption Threat Figures to
Congress, Public," *Washington Post*, May 22, 2018, https://www.washingtonpost
.com/world/national-security/fbi-repeatedly-overstated-encryption-threat-figures
-to-congress-public/2018/05/22/5b68ae90-5dce-11e8-a4a4-c070ef53f315_story.html.

21. "FBI's 'Going Dark,'" *Center for Democracy and Technology*.

22. "Open Letter to Law Enforcement in the US, UK, and Australia: Weak Encryption Puts Billions of Internet Users at Risk," Open Technology Institute, New
America, December 10, 2019, https://www.newamerica.org/oti/press-releases/open
-letter-law-enforcement-us-uk-and-australia-weak-encryption-puts-billions
-internet-users-risk.

23. Author interview and emails with Chuck McAndrew, September 26,
2016, July 17, 2017, and June 2, 2020.

24. Interview and emails with Chuck McAndrew.

MYTH 4: "We should worry about government, not corporate, surveillance"

1. Originally released in the *Washington Post*, these investigations were
published as Dana Priest and William M. Arkin, *Top Secret America: The Rise of
the New American Security State* (New York: Little, Brown, 2011).

2. Amanda Hess, "How Privacy Became a Commodity for the Rich and
Powerful," *New York Times Magazine*, May 9, 2017, https://www.nytimes.com
/2017/05/09/magazine/how-privacy-became-a-commodity-for-the-rich-and
-powerful.html.

3. Barton Gellman and Sam Adler-Bell, "The Disparate Impact of Surveillance," Century Foundation, December 21, 2017, https://tcf.org/content/report
/disparate-impact-surveillance.

4. Kalev Leetaru, "Much of Our Government Digital Surveillance Is Outsourced to Private Companies," *Forbes*, June 18, 2019, https://www.forbes.com
/sites/kalevleetaru/2019/06/18/much-of-our-government-digital-surveillance
-is-outsourced-to-private-companies/?sh=4fb716951799.

5. For an overview of Hemisphere, "EPIC v. DEA-Hemisphere," *EPIC*,
https://www.epic.org/foia/dea/hemisphere, accessed December 13, 2020.

6. The Foreign Intelligence Surveillance Act of 1978 ("FISA" *Pub.L. 95–511, 92
Stat. 1783, 50 U.S.C. Ch. 36*) establishes procedures for the physical and electronic

surveillance and collection of "foreign intelligence information" between "foreign powers" and "agents of foreign powers" suspected of espionage and terrorism. The act created the Foreign Intelligence Surveillance Court to oversee requests for surveillance warrants from intelligence and federal law enforcement agencies. Congress passed the FISA Amendments Act of 2008 on July 9, 2008 and added a new Title VII to the act, which was slated to expire at the end of 2012. But Congress extended the provisions to December 31, 2017. In January 2018, the amendments were extended for another six years. Official Statement by President Trump is available here: https://www.whitehouse.gov/briefings-statements /statement-president-fisa-amendments-reauthorization-act-2017.

7. Phillip Knightley, *The Second Oldest Profession: Spies and Spying in the Twentieth Century* (New York: Penguin Books, 1980).

8. Mark Hertsgaard, "How the Pentagon Punished NSA Whistleblowers," *Guardian,* May 22, 2016, https://www.theguardian.com/us-news/2016/may/22 /how-pentagon-punished-nsa-whistleblowers.

9. Kimberly Wehle, "Letting Mercenaries Fight Our Wars Undercuts the Constitution," *The Hill,* September 2, 2017, https://thehill.com/blogs/pundits -blog/defense/348981-letting-mercenaries-fight-our-wars-undercuts-the -constitution.

10. Zack Whittaker, "Google Formally Settles Wi-Fi Data Collection Case in US for $7M," *ZDNet,* March 12, 2013, https://www.zdnet.com/article/google -formally-settles-wi-fi-data-collection-case-in-u-s-for-7m.

11. Associated Press, "Settlement Overturned in Privacy Lawsuit Against Google," *CBS San Francisco,* August 6, 2019, https://sanfrancisco.cbslocal.com /2019/08/06/google-class-action-lawsuit-settlement-overturned-cookies-privacy.

12. Andrew Keshner, "Appeals Court Concerned Google's $5.5 Million Settlement over Alleged Privacy Violations Won't Actually Go to Consumers," *MarketWatch,* August 7, 2019, https://www.marketwatch.com/story/appeals -court-concerned-consumers-will-be-overlooked-in-googles-55-million -settlement-over-alleged-privacy-violations-2019-08-07.

13. Private Security Advisory Council, "Law Enforcement and Private Security Sources and Areas of Conflict and Strategies for Conflict Resolution," National Criminal Justice Reference Service, June 1977, https://www.ncjrs.gov /pdffiles1/Digitization/44783NCJRS.pdf.

14. Artemis Moshtaghian, "SeaWorld Says It Spied on Animal Activists," CNN, February 25, 2016, https://www.cnn.com/2016/02/25/us/seaworld-spying /index.html.

15. "SeaWorld to Stop Spying on Activists," *Maritime Executive,* February 25, 2016, https://www.maritime-executive.com/article/seaworld-to-stop-spying-on -activists.

16. William Turton, "US Investigating Hacker Ring Paid to Target Corporate Critics," *Bloomberg News,* June 9, 2020, https://www.bloomberg.com/news/articles /2020-06-09/u-s-investigating-hacker-ring-paid-to-target-corporate-critics.

17. John Scott-Railton, Adam Hulcoop, Bahr Abdul Razzak, Bill Marczak, Siena Anstis, and Ron Deibert, "Dark Basin, Uncovering a Massive Hack-for-Hire Operation," *Citizen Lab,* June 9, 2020, https://citizenlab.ca/2020/06/dark -basin-uncovering-a-massive-hack-for-hire-operation.

18. William Turton, "US Investigating Hacker Ring Paid to Target Corporate Critics."

19. Joel Bakan, "Charming Psychopaths: The Modern Corporation," *Resilience*, February 14, 2020, https://www.resilience.org/stories/2020–02–14/charming-psychopaths-the-modern-corporation.

MYTH 5: "The USA doesn't have national ID numbers"

1. Ana Rodríguez and Glenn Garvin, "What's Wrong with a National ID Card?" *Government Technology*, April 30, 1996, https://www.govtech.com/magazines/gt/Whats-Wrong-With-a-National-ID.html.

2. National ID and the REAL ID Act, *EPIC*, 2008, https://epic.org/privacy/id_cards.

3. Jim Harper, "The New National ID Systems," CATO, January 30, 2018, https://www.cato.org/publications/policy-analysis/new-national-id-systems.

4. Julie Rovner, "'Partial-Birth Abortion': Separating Fact from Spin," NPR, February 21, 2006, https://www.npr.org/2006/02/21/5168163/partial-birth-abortion-separating-fact-from-spin.

5. Daniel King, "The Language of Climate Reporting Is Heating Up, Too," *Mother Jones*, July 23, 2019, https://www.motherjones.com/environment/2019/07/the-language-of-climate-reporting-is-heating-up-too.

6. Carolyn Puckett, "The Story of the Social Security Number," *Social Security Bulletin* 60, no. 2, 2009, https://www.ssa.gov/policy/docs/ssb/v69n2/v69n2p55.html.

7. Puckett, "The Story of the Social Security Number."

8. Tom Ridge, "Transatlantic Homeland Security Conference," Johns Hopkins University, September 13, 2004, https://www.hsdl.org.

9. REAL ID Act—Title II: Emergency Supplemental Appropriations Act for Defense, the Global War on Terror, and Tsunami Relief, H.R. 1268, P.L., 2005, 109–13, https://www.dhs.gov/xlibrary/assets/real-id-act-text.pdf.

10. Alan Dershowitz, "Why Fear National ID Cards?," *New York Times*, October 13, 2001, https://www.nytimes.com/2001/10/13/opinion/why-fear-national-id-cards.html.

11. "Mandatory National IDs and Biometric Databases," EPIC, https://www.eff.org/issues/national-ids, accessed August 30, 2020.

12. "Privacy International Report on ID-Cards and Terrorism," EDRI, May 5, 2004, https://edri.org/our-work/edrigramnumber2-9idcard; Privacy International report available on web.archive at https://web.archive.org/web/20051030083349/http://www.privacyinternational.org/issues/idcard/uk/id-terrorism.pdf.

13. Matt Apuzzo and Adam Goldman, "After Spying on Muslims, New York Police Agree to Greater Oversight," *New York Times*, March 6, 2017, https://www.nytimes.com/2017/03/06/nyregion/nypd-spying-muslims-surveillance-lawsuit.html; for further insight into NYPD's surveillance on Muslim communities check: American Civil Liberties Union, "*Raza v. City of New York*—Legal Challenge to NYPD Muslim Surveillance Program," ACLU, August 3, 2017, https://www.aclu.org/cases/raza-v-city-new-york-legal-challenge-nypd-muslim-surveillance-program; Raza v. City of N.Y., 998 F. Supp. 2d 70 E.D.N.Y. 2013.

14. "National IDs Around the World—Interactive Map," *World Privacy Forum*, July 2017, https://www.worldprivacyforum.org/2017/07/national-ids -around-the-world.

15. Electronic Frontier Foundation, "Mandatory National IDs and Biometric Databases," https://www.eff.org/issues/national-ids, accessed October 10, 2020.

16. Electronic Frontier Foundation, "Mandatory National IDs."

MYTH 6: "Surveillance drones are just for war"

1. "Drone Saves Two Australian Swimmers in World First," *BBC News*, January 18, 2018, https://www.bbc.com/news/world-australia-42731112.

2. "Software for Effective Drone Defense," *Dedrone*, Accessed October 15, 2020, https://www.dedrone.com/c/drone-protection.

3. Kris Holt, "CBP Flew a Predator Drone over Minneapolis amid George Floyd Protests," *Forbes*, May 29, 2020, https://www.forbes.com/sites/krisholt/2020 /05/29/cbp-predator-drone-minneapolis-george-floyd-aclu/?sh=437c2d9940fa.

4. FAA Transportation Modernization and Safety Improvement Act, S.223. 112th Congress, 2011–12, https://www.congress.gov/bill/112th-congress/senate -bill/223/text.

5. Conor Friedersdorf, "The Rapid Rise of Federal Surveillance Drones over America," *Atlantic*, March 10, 2016, https://www.theatlantic.com/politics/archive /2016/03/the-rapid-rise-of-federal-surveillance-drones-over-america/473136.

6. Loren Korn, "Daytona Beach Police Using Drones with Intercoms to Enforce Coronavirus Closures," *ClickOrlando*, April 7, 2020, https://www.click orlando.com/news/local/2020/04/07/daytona-beach-police-using-drones-with -intercoms-to-enforce-coronavirus-closures.

7. Dan Gettinger, "Public Safety Drones: An Update," Center for the Study of the Drone at Bard College, May 2018, https://dronecenter.bard.edu/public-safety -drones-update.

8. Jayne Miller, "Surveillance Plane Starts Flying over Baltimore, Recording Everyone's Movements," WBAL-TV, May 1, 2020, https://www.wbaltv.com /article/baltimore-police-surveillance-plane-starts-flying-recording-everyones -movements/32346318; Talia Richman, "Baltimore's Controversial Surveillance Planes Await Approval," *Government Technology*, March 25, 2020, https://www .govtech.com/public-safety/Baltimores-Controversial-Surveillance-Planes -Await-Approval.html.

9. Author interview with David Rocah, *Law and Disorder*, June 15, 2020.

10. Carpenter v. US: 585 U.S. (2018); 138 S. Ct. 2206; 201 L. Ed. 2d 507.

11. "ZenMuse Z30," DJI, https://www.dji.com/zenmuse-z30, accessed October 15, 2020.

12. For more on the spread of drones in police forces, see Jake Laperruque and David Janovsky, "These Police Drones Are Watching You," POGO, September 25, 2018, https://www.pogo.org/analysis/2018/09/these-police-drones-are -watching-you.

13. Andy Greenberg, "Hacker Says He Can Hijack a 35K Police Drone a Mile Away," *Wired*, March 2016, https://www.wired.com/2016/03/hacker-says-can -hijack-35k-police-drone-mile-away.

14. Carpenter v. US: 585 U.S. (2018); 138 S. Ct. 2206; 201 L. Ed. 2d 507.

MYTH 7: "Surveillance makes the nation safer"

1. Steven Brill, "Is America Any Safer?" *Atlantic*, September 2016, https://www.theatlantic.com/magazine/archive/2016/09/are-we-any-safer/492761.

2. Dana Priest and William Arkin, "A Hidden World, Growing Beyond Control," *Washington Post*, July 19, 2010, https://www.washingtonpost.com/investigations/top-secret-america/2010/07/19/hidden-world-growing-beyond-control-2.

3. Priest and Arkin, *Top Secret America*.

4. Erik W. Goepner, "Measuring the Effectiveness of America's War on Terror," *Parameters* 46, no. 1 (2016), https://press.armywarcollege.edu/parameters/vol46/iss1/12.

5. Seth Jones, "The Rise of Far-Right Extremism in the United States," *CSIS Briefs*, November 7, 2018, https://www.csis.org/analysis/rise-far-right-extremism-united-states.

6. Neta Crawford, "United States Budgetary Costs and Obligations of Post-9/11 Wars Through FY2020: $6.4 Trillion," Watson Institute, Brown University, Costs of War Project, November 13, 2019, https://watson.brown.edu/costsofwar.

7. Matthew Burrows, a former CIA analyst, contributed to an unclassified intelligence report called "Mapping the Global Future" that spoke to the risk of pandemics in 2004: "In recent annual public assessments, American intelligence agencies have been warning about the increasing risks of a global pandemic that could strain resources and damage the global economy, while observing that the frequency and diversity of global disease outbreaks has been rising." *Mapping the Global Future: Report of the National Intelligence Council's 2020 Project, Based on Consultations with Nongovernmental Experts Around the World, Office of the Director of National Intelligence* (December 2004), https://www.dni.gov/files/documents/Global%20Trends_Mapping%20the%20Global%20Future%202020%20Project.pdf.

8. Olivia Waxman, "Coronavirus Is Putting the US Strategic National Stockpile to the Test. Here's the Surprising Story Behind the Stash," *Time*, March 11, 2020, https://time.com/5800393/coronavirus-national-stockpile-history.

9. Ken Dilanian, Dan De Luce, and Andrew Lehren, "From Clinton to Trump, 20 Years of Boom and Mostly Bust in Prepping for Pandemics," *NBC News*, April 13, 2020, https://www.nbcnews.com/politics/national-security/clinton-trump-20-years-boom-mostly-bust-prepping-pandemics-n1182291.

10. Yeganeh Torbati and Isaac Arnsdorf, "How Tea Party Budget Battles Left the National Emergency Medical Stockpile Unprepared for Coronavirus," *ProPublica*, April 3, 2020, https://www.propublica.org/article/us-emergency-medical-stockpile-funding-unprepared-coronavirus; Matthew Brown, "Fact Check: Did The Obama Administration Deplete the Federal Stockpile Of N95 Masks?" *USA Today*, April 3, 2020, https://www.usatoday.com/story/news/factcheck/2020/04/03/fact-check-did-obama-administration-deplete-n-95-mask-stockpile/5114319002.

11. Linda Bilmes, "The Trump Administration Has Made the US Less Ready for Infectious Disease Outbreaks Like Coronavirus," *The Conversation*, February 3, 2020, https://theconversation.com/the-trump-administration-has-made-the-us-less-ready-for-infectious-disease-outbreaks-like-coronavirus-130983.

12. David U. Himmelstein and Steffie Woolhandler, "Public Health's Falling Share of US Health Spending," *American Journal of Public Health* 106, no. 1 (January 2016): 56–57, https://doi.org/10.2105/AJPH.2015.302908.

13. "New Report Shows Hamstrung COVID-19 Response Was Years in the Making," *TFAH*, April 16, 2020, https://www.tfah.org/article/new-report-show-hamstrung-covid-19-response-was-years-in-the-making.

14. Richard Fried, *Nightmare in Red: The McCarthy Era in Perspective* (New York: Oxford University Press, 1990), 138.

15. G. B. Lewis, "Lifting the Ban on Gays in the Civil Service: Federal Policy Toward Gay and Lesbian Employees Since the Cold War," *Public Administration Review* 51 (1997): 387–95, https://www.jstor.org/stable/3109985.

16. David Cunningham, "Patterning of Repression: FBI Counterintelligence and the New Left," *Social Forces* 82, no. 1, September 2003, https://www.jstor.org/stable/3598144.

17. US Senate Select Committee to Study Governmental Operations with Respect to Intelligence Activities, *Final Report of the Select Committee to Study Governmental Operations with Respect to Intelligence Activities: Together with Additional, Supplemental, and Separate Views* (US Senate, April 23, 1976), https://archive.org/details/finalreportofselo1unit/page/70/mode/2up.

18. US Senate Select Committee on Intelligence, *Report of the Select Committee on Intelligence United States Senate Together with Additional Views* (US Senate, July 1989), https://www.intelligence.senate.gov/sites/default/files/publications/10146.pdf.

19. "World Trade Center Bombing 1993," FBI, https://www.fbi.gov/history/famous-cases/world-trade-center-bombing-1993.

20. Richard Jackson, *Writing the War on Terrorism: Language, Politics, and Counter-Terrorism* (Manchester, UK: Manchester University Press, 2005).

21. William Bloss, "Escalating US Police Surveillance After 9/11: An Examination of Causes and Effects," *Surveillance and Society*, "Surveillance and Criminal Justice," part 1, 4, no. 3 (2007), https://ojs.library.queensu.ca/index.php/surveillance-and-society/article/view/3448.

22. Edward Snowden, interviewed by Ewen MacAskill and Alex Hern, "Edward Snowden: 'The People Are Still Powerless, but Now They're Aware,'" *Guardian*, June 4, 2018, https://www.theguardian.com/us-news/2018/jun/04/edward-snowden-people-still-powerless-but-aware.

23. Erik W. Goepner, "Measuring the Effectiveness of America's War on Terror"; see also A. Trevor Thrall and Erik Goepner, "Step Back: Lessons for U.S. Foreign Policy from the Failed War on Terror," Cato Institute, June 26, 2017, https://www.jstor.org/stable/resrep04912; William Adair Davies, "Counterterrorism Effectiveness to Jihadists in Western Europe and the United States: We Are Losing the War on Terror," *Studies in Conflict and Terrorism* 41, no. 4 (2018), https://www.tandfonline.com/doi/abs/10.1080/1057610X.2017.1284447.

MYTH 8: "No one wants to spy on kids"

1. "More Than 175,000 Children Go Online for the First Time Every Day," UNICEF, February 6, 2018, https://www.unicef.org/eca/press-releases/more-175000-children-go-online-first-time-every-day-tapping-great-opportunities.

2. "Kids' Advertising Will Be a $1.2 Billion Industry Worldwide in 2021," *Children's Advertising Review Unit*, June 12, 2019, https://carunews.blogspot.com /2019/06/kids-advertising-will-be-12-billion.html.

3. Sidhartha Banerjee, "Unhappy with Happy Meals, Father Allowed to Bring Class Action Against McDonald's," *National Post*, November 15, 2018, https://nationalpost.com/pmn/news-pmn/canada-news-pmn/quebec-judge -says-class-action-lawsuit-over-mcdonalds-happy-meal-toys-can-go-ahead.

4. Lois Beckett, "Under Digital Surveillance: How American Schools Spy on Millions of Kids," *Guardian*, October 22, 2019, https://www.theguardian.com /world/2019/oct/22/school-student-surveillance-bark-gaggle; Adrienne LaFrance, "The Perils of 'Sharenting," *Atlantic*, October 6, 2016, https://www.theatlantic .com/technology/archive/2016/10/babies-everywhere/502757.

5. "Kids for Privacy Campaign," Child Rescue Coalition, https://childrescue coalition.org/kids-privacy-campaign/, accessed September 13, 2020.

6. See the Kids for Privacy Instagram at https://www.instagram.com/kidsfor privacy.

7. Brooke Auxier et al., "Parenting Children in the Age of Screens," Pew Research Center, July 28, 2020, https://www.pewresearch.org/internet/2020/07/28 /parenting-children-in-the-age-of-screens.

8. "AG James: Google and Youtube To Pay Record Figure For Illegally Tracking And Collecting Personal Information from Children," NY Office of the Attorney General, September 4, 2019, https://ag.ny.gov/press-release/2019/ag-james -google-and-youtube-pay-record-figure-illegally-tracking-and-collecting.

9. Beckett, "Under Digital Surveillance."

10. Sen. Edward Markey et al., "Letter to FTC on Children's Privacy," US Senate, May 8, 2020, https://www.markey.senate.gov/imo/media/doc/Markey letter to FTC 6(B) on children's privacy.pdf.

MYTH 9: "Police don't monitor social media"

1. Rallings quoted in Bretin Mock, "Memphis: Spying on Activists Is Just Good Police Work," *Bloomberg CityLab*, August 9, 2018, https://www.bloomberg .com/news/articles/2018-08-09/memphis-spying-on-activists-is-just-good -police-work.

2. Kevin Roose, "A Mass Murder of, and for, the Internet," *New York Times*, March 15, 2019, https://www.nytimes.com/2019/03/15/technology/facebook -youtube-christchurch-shooting.html.

3. David D. Kirkpatrick, "Massacre Suspect Traveled the World but Lived on the Internet," *New York Times*, March 15, 2019, https://www.nytimes.com/2019 /03/15/world/asia/new-zealand-shooting-brenton-tarrant.html.

4. For more information on FBI's Internet Crime Complaint Center, visit their website: https://www.ic3.gov.

5. Phillip K. Dick, *The Minority Report* (London: Orion Books, 1956).

6. Brandi Vincent, "FBI Wants Tech to Track Social Media for Criminals and Terrorists Before They Act," NextGov.com, July 31, 2019, https://www.next gov.com/emerging-tech/2019/07/fbi-wants-tech-track-social-media-criminals -and-terrorists-they-act/158843.

7. Vincent, "FBI Wants Tech to Track Social Media."

8. Dell Cameron, "Dozens of Police-Spying Tools Remain after Facebook, Twitter Crack Down on Geofeedia," *DailyDot*, February 28, 2020, https://www.dailydot.com/irl/geofeedia-twitter-facebook-instagram-social-media-surveillance.

9. Lee Fang, "The CIA Is Investing in Firms That Mine Your Tweets and Instagram Photos," *The Intercept*, April 14, 2016, https://theintercept.com/2016/04/14/in-undisclosed-cia-investments-social-media-mining-looms-large.

10. Geofeedia press release is available at https://www.aclunc.org/docs/20161011_geofeedia_baltimore_case_study.pdf.

11. Matt Cagle, "Facebook, Instagram, and Twitter Provided Data Access for a Surveillance Product Marketed to Target Activists of Color," ACLU NorCal, October 11, 2016, https://www.aclunc.org/blog/facebook-instagram-and-twitter-provided-data-access-surveillance-product-marketed-target.

12. Colin Daileda, "Twitter Cuts Ties with Another Social Media Surveillance Company," *Mashable*, October 20, 2016, https://mashable.com/2016/10/20/twitter-social-media-surveillance-snaptrends.

13. Daileda, "Twitter Cuts Ties."

14. Kalev Leetaru, "Geofeedia Is Just the Tip of the Iceberg: The Era of Social Surveillance," *Forbes*, October 12, 2016, https://www.forbes.com/sites/kalevleetaru/2016/10/12/geofeedia-is-just-the-tip-of-the-iceberg-the-era-of-social-surveillence/ - 5c37a1ec5b90.

15. Glencora Borradaile, "Weed and Geotags: The Danger and Uselessness of Social Media Monitoring," *Oregon State University Blogs*, January 28, 2020, http://blogs.oregonstate.edu/glencora/2020/01/28/weed-and-geotags-the-danger-and-uselessness-of-social-media-monitoring.

16. Ms. Smith, "Beware: Surveillance Software Police Are Using to Score Citizens' Threat Level," *CSO*, January 11, 2016, https://www.csoonline.com/article/3020669/beware-surveillance-software-police-are-using-to-score-citizens-threat-level.html.

17. For more information on ConnectedCOPS, or their awards, visit their website: connectedcops.net.

18. Quotations and observations from Mara Verheyden-Hilliard are based on email interviews with author on September 15, 2020.

19. More information about Mara Verheyden-Hilliard and the Partnership for Civil Justice Fund can be found on their website: http://www.justiceonline.org/about.

20. Morgan Gstalter, "Memphis Police Accused of Making Fake Social Media Accounts to Spy on Black Lives Matter," *The Hill*, August 2, 2018, https://thehill.com/blogs/blog-briefing-room/news/400064-memphis-police-accused-of-making-social-media-accounts-to.

21. Ryan Devereaux, "Homeland Security Used a Private Intelligence Firm to Monitor Family Separation Protests," *The Intercept*, April 29, 2019, https://theintercept.com/2019/04/29/family-separation-protests-surveillance.

22. Naomi Wolf, "Revealed: How the FBI Coordinated the Crackdown on Occupy," *Guardian*, December 29, 2012, https://www.theguardian.com/commentisfree/2012/dec/29/fbi-coordinated-crackdown-occupy.

23. Colin Moynihan, "Officials Cast Wide Net in Monitoring Occupy Protests," *New York Times*, May 22, 2014, https://www.nytimes.com/2014/05/23/us/officials-cast-wide-net-in-monitoring-occupy-protests.html.

24. Chip Gibbons, "Documents Reveal ATF and US Marshals also Monitoring Occupy Movement," *Rights and Dissent*, March 15, 2016, https://rightsanddissent.org/news/documents-reveal-atf-and-us-marshals-also-monitoring-occupy-movement.

25. Author interview with Mara Verheyden-Hilliard, June 2020; see also "Exposed: ATF Spying on Occupy and 'Known Anarchists and Protestors' List," Partnership for Civil Justice Fund, March 10, 2016, http://www.justiceonline.org/exposed_atf_s_monitoring_of_occupy_and_known_anarchists_and_protestors.

26. Michael S. Schmidt and Colin Moynihan, "FBI Counterterrorism Agents Monitored Occupy Movement, Records Show," *New York Times*, December 24, 2012, https://www.nytimes.com/2012/12/25/nyregion/occupy-movement-was-investigated-by-fbi-counterterrorism-agents-records-show.html.

27. "DHS-OPS-PIA-004 Publicly Available Social Media Monitoring and Situational Awareness Initiative," Department of Homeland Security, May 13, 2015, https://www.dhs.gov/publication/dhs-ops-pia-004f-publicly-available-social-media-monitoring-and-situational-awareness.

28. Faiza Patel et al., *Report: Social Media Monitoring* (Brennan Center for Justice, May 22, 2019), updated March 11, 2020, https://www.brennancenter.org/our-work/research-reports/social-media-monitoring.

29. Quotes in this section are from author interview with Harsha Panduranga, *Law and Disorder*, June 22, 2020.

30. Details of the Brennan Center's court case against DHS are available at https://www.brennancenter.org/our-work/court-cases/brennan-center-justice-v-department-homeland-security-et-al.

31. Patel et al., *Report: Social Media Monitoring*.

32. Jon Schuppe, "Schools Are Spending Billions on High-Tech Security. But Are Students Any Safer?" *NBC News*, May 20, 2018, https://www.nbcnews.com/news/us-news/schools-are-spending-billions-high-tech-security-are-students-any-n875611.

33. See Patel et al., *Report: Social Media Monitoring*.

34. Karen Savage and Daryl Khan, "Teens Remain Squarely in Crosshairs of NYC Law Enforcement, Panelists Say," *Juvenile Justice Information Exchange*, February 13, 2017, https://jjie.org/2017/02/13/teens-remain-squarely-in-crosshairs-of-nyc-law-enforcement-panelists-say.

35. Alice Speri, "New York Gang Prosecutions Use Conspiracy Charges to Criminalize Whole Communities," *The Intercept*, June 7, 2018, https://theintercept.com/2018/06/07/rico-gang-prosecution-nyc.

36. Heidi Boghosian and Zachary Wolfe, "Prosecutors Overreach in RICO Gang Arrests," *Huffington Post*, February 13, 2017, https://www.huffpost.com/entry/prosecutors-overreach-in-rico-gang-arrests_b_58a23621e4b0cd37efcfec2a.

37. See Morgan Gstalter, "Memphis Police Accused."

38. Queenie Wong, "Police Use of Social Media Is Under a Microscope amid Protests," CNET, June 11, 2020, https://www.cnet.com/news/police-use-of-social -media-is-under-a-microscope-amid-protests.

39. See Speri, "New York Gang Prosecutions."

40. For more information on the Center for Protest Law and Litigation, visit their website at protestlaw.org.

41. William Marcellino et al., *Monitoring Social Media* (Rand Corporation, 2017), https://www.rand.org/pubs/research_reports/RR1742.html.

MYTH 10: "Biometrics technologies are foolproof"

1. Jay Peters, "Researchers Fooled Chinese Facial Recognition Terminals with Just a Mask," *The Verge*, December 13, 2019, https://www.theverge.com/2019 /12/13/21020575/china-facial-recognition-terminals-fooled-3d-mask-kneron -research-fallibility.

2. For a good study on the characteristics of biometrics, see Patricia M. Corby et al., "Using Biometrics for Participant Identification in a Research Study: A Case Report," *Journal of the American Medical Informatics Association* 13, no. 2 (2006): 233–35, https://www.ncbi.nlm.nih.gov/pmc/articles/PMC1447546.

3. Swaroop Sham, "What Is Biometric Authentication?," *Okta*, July 16, 2020, https://www.okta.com/blog/2020/07/biometric-authentication.

4. The Constitution Project's Task Force on Facial Recognition Software and Jake Laperruque, "Facing the Future of Surveillance," POGO, March 4, 2019, https://www.pogo.org/report/2019/03/facing-the-future-of-surveillance.

5. "HSPD-12," US Department of the Interior, August 27, 2004, https://www .doi.gov/hspd12.

6. "Face Recognition Grand Challenge," National Institute of Standards and Technology, December 7, 2010, https://www.nist.gov/programs-projects/face -recognition-grand-challenge-frgc.

7. "Apple Announces iPhone 5s—The Most Forward-Thinking Smartphone in the World," Apple, September 10, 2013, https://www.apple.com/newsroom /2013/09/10Apple-Announces-iPhone-5s-The-Most-Forward-Thinking -Smartphone-in-the-World.

8. Penny Crosman, "The Eyes Have It: Bank of America, Samsung Pilot Iris-Scan Logins," *American Banker*, August 8, 2017, https://www.americanbanker .com/news/the-eyes-have-it-bank-of-america-samsung-pilot-iris-scan-logins.

9. For more information on Apple's Face ID Technology, visit their website: https://support.apple.com/en-us/HT208108. For a more general history of bio-metrics, see Stephen Mayhew's "History of Biometrics" for a lengthy timeline of the technology: https://www.biometricupdate.com/201802/history-of -biometrics-2.

10. "Consumer Acceptance of Biometrics Growing," *Veridium*, June 28, 2016, https://veridiumid.com/consumer-acceptance-biometrics-growing.

11. Department of Homeland Security's website has a page dedicated to e-Passports, which rely on biometrics; see https://www.dhs.gov/e-passports.

12. Neema Singh Guliani, "The FBI Has Access to Over 640 Million Photos of Us Through Its Facial Recognition Database," ACLU, June 7, 2019, https://

www.aclu.org/blog/privacy-technology/surveillance-technologies/fbi-has-access
-over-640-million-photos-us-through.

13. Facts from this section on global integration of biometrics come from
Jayshree Pandya, "Hacking Our Identity: The Emerging Threats from Biometric
Technology," *Forbes*, March 9, 2019, https://www.forbes.com/sites/cognitive
world/2019/03/09/hacking-our-identity-the-emerging-threats-from-biometric
-technology.

14. Jennifer Lynch, "Face Off: Law Enforcement Use of Face Recognition
Technology," EFF, February 12, 2018, https://www.eff.org/wp/law-enforcement
-use-face-recognition.

15. Quotes are from author interview with Clare Garvie, *Law and Disorder*,
November 20, 2017.

16. Robert A. Kahn, "Anti-Mask Laws," Middle Tennessee State University,
2009, https://www.mtsu.edu/first-amendment/article/1169/anti-mask-laws.

17. David Lawder, "Masked White Nationalists March in Washington
with Police Escort," *US News*, https://www.usnews.com/news/top-news/articles
/2020-02-08/masked-white-nationalists-march-in-washington-with-police
-escort.

18. Avi Selk, "The Ingenious and 'Dystopian' DNA Technique Police Used to
Hunt the 'Golden State Killer' Suspect," *Washington Post*, April 28, 2018, https://
www.washingtonpost.com/news/true-crime/wp/2018/04/27/golden-state-killer
-dna-website-gedmatch-was-used-to-identify-joseph-deangelo-as-suspect
-police-say.

19. Jason Grant, "Seeking to Protect Uncharged Suspects' Rights, Legal Aid
Calls for Abolishing City's DNA Databank," *New York Law Journal*, July 7, 2020,
https://www.law.com/newyorklawjournal/2020/07/07/seeking-to-protect
-uncharged-suspects-rights-legal-aid-calls-for-abolishing-citys-dna-databank
/?slreturn=20200922161916.

20. Nomaan Merchant, "US to Start Collecting DNA from People Detained
at Border," Associated Press, January 6, 2020, https://apnews.com/article/8e7d4e
3d6e2ef24dcc4fd9e79552a3d0.

21. Human Rights Watch, "Kuwait: Court Strikes Down Draconian DNA
Law," October 17, 2017, https://www.hrw.org/news/2017/10/17/kuwait-court
-strikes-down-draconian-dna-law.

22. Andrew Perrin, "About Half of Americans Are OK with DNA Testing
Companies Sharing User Data with Law Enforcement," Pew Research Center,
February 4, 2020, https://www.pewresearch.org/fact-tank/2020/02/04/about
-half-of-americans-are-ok-with-dna-testing-companies-sharing-user-data-with
-law-enforcement.

23. Ram quoted in Lindsey Van Ness, "DNA Databases Are Boon to Police
but Menace to Privacy, Critics Say," Pew Research Center, February 20, 2020,
https://www.pewtrusts.org/en/research-and-analysis/blogs/stateline/2020/02/20
/dna-databases-are-boon-to-police-but-menace-to-privacy-critics-say.

24. "Website Security Breach Exposes 1 Million DNA Profiles," Associated
Press, July 23, 2020, https://apnews.com/article/technology-law-enforcement
-agencies-hacking-california-0def85a68f2d1d5a03d5b27dbcdd45e6.

25. Jon Porter, "Huge Security Flaw Exposes Biometric Data of More Than a Million Users," *The Verge*, August 14, 2019, https://www.theverge.com/2019/8/14/20805194/suprema-biostar-2-security-system-hack-breach-biometric-info-personal-data.

26. Brendan I. Koerner, "Inside the Cyberattack That Shocked the US Government," *Wired*, October 23, 2016, https://www.wired.com/2016/10/inside-cyberattack-shocked-us-government.

27. Ananya Bhattacharya, "A New 3D-Printed Hand Simultaneously Makes Fingerprint Scanners More Secure and Vulnerable," *Quartz*, October 21, 2016, https://qz.com/815103/3d-printed-hand-fingerprint-scanner.

28. Kaveh Waddell, "When Fingerprints Are as Easy to Steal as Passwords," *Atlantic*, March 24, 2017, https://www.theatlantic.com/technology/archive/2017/03/new-biometrics/520695.

29. Robin Harding, "Fingerprint Theft Points to Digital Danger," *Financial Times*, January 16, 2017, https://www.ft.com/content/446ac29a-dbc1-11e6-9d7c-be108f1c1dce.

30. Yi Xu et al., "Virtual U: Defeating Face Liveness Detection by Building Virtual Models from Your Public Photos," USENIX, August 10, 2016, https://gangw.cs.illinois.edu/class/cs598/papers/sec16_3d-face.pdf.

31. Cooper quoted in Waddell, "When Fingerprints Are as Easy to Steal as Passwords."

32. Complaint, Adams v. Des Plaines Dev. L.P., No. 19L893 (Will Cty. Cir. Ct. Oct. 18, 2019).

33. Bobby Allyn, "Judge: Facebook's $550 Million Settlement In Facial Recognition Case Is Not Enough," NPR, July 17, 2020, https://www.npr.org/2020/07/17/892433132/judge-facebooks-550-million-settlement-in-facial-recognition-case-is-not-enough.

34. Alex Hern, "Hacker Fakes German Minister's Fingerprints Using Photos of Her Hands," *Guardian*, December 30, 2014, https://www.theguardian.com/technology/2014/dec/30/hacker-fakes-german-ministers-fingerprints-using-photos-of-her-hands.

35. "Chaos Computer Clubs Breaks Iris Recognition System of the Samsung Galaxy S8," Chaos Computer Club, May 22, 2017, https://www.ccc.de/en/updates/2017/iriden.

MYTH 11: "Metadata doesn't reveal much about me"

1. Ryan Goodman, "Video Clip of Former Director of NSA and CIA: 'We Kill People Based on Metadata,'" *Just Security*, May 12, 2014, https://www.justsecurity.org/10318/video-clip-director-nsa-cia-we-kill-people-based-metadata.

2. "Naming the Dead," Bureau of Investigative Journalism, https://v1.thebureauinvestigates.com/namingthedead, accessed August 23, 2020.

3. Anne Gilliland, "Setting the Stage," in *Introduction to Metadata*, ed. Murtha Baca (Los Angeles: Getty Publications, 2016), https://www.getty.edu/publications/intrometadata/setting-the-stage.

4. "Metadata: What Is It and Why Is It Important?," *SecurityNewspaper*, 2018, https://laptrinhx.com/metadata-what-is-it-and-why-is-it-important-1064637543.

5. "Former CIA Director: 'We Kill People Based on Metadata,'" *RT*, May 12, 2014, https://www.rt.com/usa/158460-cia-director-metadata-kill-people.

6. Edward Felten, "Written Testimony at the US Senate, Committee on the Judiciary Hearing on Continued Oversight of the Foreign Intelligence Surveillance Act," US Senate, Oct. 2, 2013, https://www.cs.princeton.edu/~felten/testimony-2013-10-02.pdf.

7. Alisa Esage G, "Metadata: What Is It and Why Is It Important?" *Information Security Newspaper*, November 16, 2018, https://www.securitynewspaper.com/2018/11/16/metadata-what-is-it-and-why-is-it-important.

8. Ellen Nakashima, "Independent Review Board Says NSA Phone Data Program Is Illegal and Should End," *Washington Post*, January 23, 2014, https://www.washingtonpost.com/world/national-security/independent-review-board-says-nsa-phone-data-program-is-illegal-and-should-end/2014/01/22/4cebd470-83dd-11e3-bbe5-6a2a3141e3a9_story.html.

9. "The NSA's SKYNET Program May Be Killing Thousands of Innocent People," *Ars Technica*, February 16, 2016, https://arstechnica.com/information-technology/2016/02/the-nsas-skynet-program-may-be-killing-thousands-of-innocent-people.

10. Charlie Savage, "Trump Administration Asks Congress to Reauthorize N.S.A.'s Deactivated Call Records Program," *New York Times*, August 15, 2019, https://www.nytimes.com/2019/08/15/us/politics/trump-nsa-call-records-program.html.

11. Fahmida Rashid, "Lab Presents: What Data Brokers Know about Users," *Decipher*, July 9, 2020, https://duo.com/decipher/lab-presents-what-data-brokers-know-about-users.

12. For respective legislation, see CA Assembly Bill 1202, 2019–2020 reg. sess. (Cal. 2011), https://openstates.org/ca/bills/20192020/AB1202; VT LEG #333821 v.1. H.764; Act no. 171 (H.764), Sen. sess., 5/22/2018, (Ver. 2018), https://legislature.vermont.gov/bill/status/2018/H.764.

13. "Behind the Data: Investigating Metadata," available at https://exposingtheinvisible.org/en/guides/behind-the-data-metadata-investigations.

14. David Haynes, *Metadata for Information Management and Retrieval: Understanding Metadata and Its Use*, 2nd ed. (London: Facet Publishing, 2018).

MYTH 12: "The Constitution protects reporters and their sources"

1. Bruce Brown, statement in "Reporters Committee Statement on Latest Assange Indictment," Reporters Committee for Freedom of Press, May 23, 2019, rcfp.org/may-2019-rcfp-assange-statement.

2. Terry Gross with James Risen, "Journalist Talks Confidential Sources, Getting Subpoenaed and His New Book," NPR, October 14, 2014, https://www.npr.org/2014/10/14/356121289/journalist-talks-confidential-sources-getting-subpoenaed-and-his-new-book.

3. Gross, "Journalist Talks Confidential Sources."

4. "As Leak Investigations Surge, Our New Lawsuit Seeks the Trump Admin's Guidelines on Surveillance of Journalists," Freedom of the Press Foundation, November 29, 2017, https://freedom.press/news/lawsuit-seeks-government-guidelines-surveillance-journalists-leak-investigations-surge.

5. Press statement, "DOJ's Seizure of Reporter's Records Raises Questions About Status of DOJ Media Guidelines," Knight First Amendment Institute, June 8, 2018, https://knightcolumbia.org/content/dojs-seizure-of-reporters-records-raises-questions-about-status-of-doj-media-guidelines.

6. Sharyl Attkisson, *Stonewalled: My Fight for Truth Against the Forces of Obstruction, Intimidation, and Harassment in Obama's Washington* (New York: HarperCollins, 2014).

7. Attkisson v. Holder, Civil Action No. 2015–0238, D.C. 2017, Filed March 19, 2017, Docket Number: Civil Action no. 2015–0238.

8. For overview and document access, see "Judicial Watch Statement on Release of Enormous Trove of DOJ Fast and Furious Documents," Judicial Watch, November 20, 2014, https://www.judicialwatch.org/press-releases/judicial-watch-statement-release-enormous-trove-doj-fast-furious-documents.

9. Gross with Risen, "Journalist Talks Confidential Sources, Getting Subpoenaed and His New Book."

10. Michael M. Grynbaum and John Koblin, "After Reality Winner's Arrest, Media Asks: Did 'Intercept' Expose a Source?" *New York Times*, June 6, 2017, https://www.nytimes.com/2017/06/06/business/media/intercept-reality-winner-russia-trump-leak.html.

MYTH 13: "The attorney–client privilege is sacrosanct"

1. Kaveh Waddell, "When Fingerprints Are as Easy to Steal as Passwords," *Atlantic*, March 24, 2017, https://www.theatlantic.com/technology/archive/2017/03/new-biometrics/520695.

2. Author interview with Jonathan Stribling-Uss, 2017, and subsequent email messages on October 12, 2020. See also Jonathan Stribling-Uss, "Legal Cybersecurity in the Digital Age," NYCLU, September 29, 2020, https://www.nyclu.org/en/publications/legal-cybersecurity-digital-age.

3. John Napier Tye, "Meet Executive Order 12333: The Reagan Rule That Lets the NSA Spy on Americans," *Washington Post*, July 18, 2014, http://www.washingtonpost.com/opinions/meet-executive-order-12333-the-reagan-rule-that-lets-the-nsa-spy-on-ameri- cans/2014/07/18/93d2ac22–0b93–11e4-b8e5-dode80767fc2_story.html; See also Steven Melendez, "Suspicious Packages Spotlight Vast Postal Surveillance System," *Fast Company*, October 25, 2018, https://www.fastcompany.com/90257308/suspicious-packages-spotlight-vast-postal-surveillance-system-mail-covers.

4. See CCR v. Obama (formerly CCR v. Bush), Center for Constitutional Rights, https://ccrjustice.org/home/what-we-do/our-cases/ccr-v-obama-formerly-ccr-v-bush, accessed August 30, 2020.

5. Author email exchange with Michael Avery, July 17, 2020.

6. Author interview with Jonathan Stribling-Uss, 2017.

7. "Vulnerabilities Equities Policy and Process," White House, November 15, 2017, https://www.whitehouse.gov/sites/whitehouse.gov/files/images/External%20-%20Unclassified%20VEP%20Charter%20FINAL.PDF.

8. Human Rights Watch, *Dark Side: Secret Origins of Evidence in US Criminal Cases* (2018), 34, https://www.hrw.org/sites/default/files/report_pdf/us0118.pdf.

9. Paul Fletcher, "Criminal Procedure in Mayberry," *Virginia Lawyers Weekly*, July 6, 2012, https://valawyersweekly.com/2012/07/06/criminal -procedure-in-mayberry.

10. Human Rights Watch, *The Dark Side*, 38. See also John Shiffman and Kristina Cooke, "US Directs Agents to Cover Up Program Used to Investigate Americans," Reuters, August 5, 2013, https://www.reuters.com/article/us-dea -sod/exclusive-u-s-directs-agents-to-cover-up-program-used-to-investigate -americans-idUSBRE97409R20130805.

11. James Risen and Laura Poitras, "Spying by NSA Ally Entangled US Law Firm," *New York Times*, February 15, 2014, https://www.nytimes.com/2014/02/16 /us/eavesdropping-ensnared-american-law-firm.html.

12. "Model Rules of Professional Conduct, American Bar Association," 2020, https://www.americanbar.org/groups/professional_responsibility/publications /model_rules_of_professional_conduct/model_rules_of_professional_conduct _table_of_contents.

13. Millard v. Doran, no. 153262/2016 (Sup. Ct. N.Y. Cty. 2016).

14. "New NYCLU Report Guidelines for Digital Legal Confidentiality," NYCLU, September 29, 2020, https://www.nyclu.org/en/press-releases/new -nyclu-report-details-guidelines-digital-legal-confidentiality.

15. 23 NYCRR part 500 can be accessed at https://www.dfs.ny.gov/industry _guidance/cyber_faqs.

16. Albert Fox Cahn quoted in "New NYCLU Report Details Guidelines for Digital Legal Confidentiality," NYCLU, September 29, 2020, https://www.nyclu .org/en/press-releases/new-nyclu-report-details-guidelines-digital-legal -confidentiality.

MYTH 14: "They can't design products and platforms for privacy"

1. Geoffrey A. Fowler, "When the Most Personal Secrets Get Outed on Facebook," *Wall Street Journal*, October 13, 2012, https://www.wsj.com/articles/SB100 00872396390444165804578008740578200224.

2. Alena Miklasova, "Nir Eyal on the Power of Habit-Forming Products— And Why Users Have More Control Than They Think, Product Board, April 7, 2020, https://www.productboard.com/blog/nir-eyal-habit-forming-products; see also Nir Eyal, *Indistractable: How to Control Your Attention and Choose Your Life* (Dallas: BenBella Books, 2019); Nir Eyal, *Hooked: How to Build Habit-Forming Products* (New York: Portfolio, 2013).

3. "10 New Gurus You Should Know," *Fortune*, 2008, https://archive.fortune .com/galleries/2008/fortune/0811/gallery.10_new_gurus.fortune.

4. Casey Chin, "Tristan Harris: Tech Is 'Downgrading Humans.' It's Time to Fight Back," *Wired*, April 23, 2019, https://www.wired.com/story/tristan-harris -tech-is-downgrading-humans-time-to-fight-back; Bianca Bosker, "The Binge Breaker," *Atlantic*, November 2016, https://www.theatlantic.com/magazine /archive/2016/11/the-binge-breaker/501122.

5. Tristan Harris, "A Call to Minimize Distraction and Respect Users' Attention," 2013, available at https://digitalwellbeing.org/googles-internal-digital -wellbeing-presentation-transcript-and-slides.

6. Simone Stolzoff, "The Formula for Phone Addiction Might Double As a Cure," *Wired*, February 1, 2018, https://www.wired.com/story/phone-addiction-formula.

7. See https://www.humanetech.com/what-we-do.

8. John Herrman, "How Tiny Red Dots Took Over Your Life," *New York Times*, February 27, 2018, https://www.nytimes.com/2018/02/27/magazine/red-dots-badge-phones-notification.html.

9. Woodrow Hartzog, *Privacy's Blueprint: The Battle to Control the Design of New Technologies* (Cambridge, MA: Harvard University Press, 2018).

10. Shoshana Zuboff, "The Surveillance Threat Is Not What Orwell Imagined," *Time*, June 6, 2020, https://time.com/5602363/george-orwell-1984-anniversary-surveillance-capitalism.

11. Joe Fields, "Interview with Ann Cavoukian," Onalytica, March 2, 2018, https://onalytica.com/blog/posts/interview-ann-cavoukian; see also Ann Cavoukian, "Privacy by Design: The 7 Foundational Principles," Internet Architecture Board, February 2011, https://www.iab.org/wp-content/IAB-uploads/2011/03/fred_carter.pdf.

12. European Data Protection Supervisor, *Preliminary Opinion on Privacy by Design* (May 21, 2018), https://stepnews.isti.cnr.it/wp-content/uploads/2018/07/European-Data-Protection-Supervisor.pdf.

13. Hartzog, *Privacy's Blueprint*.

14. Maxy Lotherington, "Design Is Not Just What It Looks and Feels Like. Design Is How It Works," *Medium*, November 6, 2017, https://medium.com/@maxylotherington/001-design-is-not-just-what-it-looks-and-feels-like-design-is-how-it-works-36867dde11bc.

MYTH 15: "Congress and courts protect us from surveillance"

1. Mark Weinberg, *Movie Night with the Reagans: A Memoir* (New York: Simon & Schuster 2018), 84–96.

2. Julie Angwin and Surya Mattu, "Amazon Says It Puts Customers First. But Its Pricing Algorithm Doesn't," ProPublica, September 20, 2016, https://www.propublica.org/article/amazon-says-it-puts-customers-first-but-its-pricing-algorithm-doesnt.

3. Andy Greenberg, "Inside the Courthouse Break-In Spree That Landed Two White-Hat Hackers in Jail," *Wired*, August 5, 2020, https://www.wired.com/story/inside-courthouse-break-in-spree-that-landed-two-white-hat-hackers-in-jail.

4. Tim Wu, "Fixing the Worst Law in Technology," *New Yorker*, March 18, 2013, https://www.newyorker.com/news/news-desk/fixing-the-worst-law-in-technology.

5. "How Do You Sustain a Business Model in Which Users Don't Pay for Your Service," C-SPAN, April 11, 2018, https://www.c-span.org/video/?c4723131/user-clip-sustain-business-model-users-pay-service.

6. Garrett Graff, "Government Lawyers Don't Understand the Internet. That's a Problem," *Washington Post*, September 23, 2016, https://www.washingtonpost.com/posteverything/wp/2016/09/23/government-lawyers-dont-understand-the-internet-thats-a-problem.

7. Kim Zetter, "Of Course Congress Is Clueless about Tech—It Killed Its Tutor," *Wired*, April 21, 2016, https://web.archive.org/web/20160624032442/https://www.wired.com/2016/04/office-technology-assessment-congress-clueless-tech-killed-tutor.

8. Jonathan Swan et al., "Scoop: Trump Team Considers Nationalizing 5G Network," *Axios*, January 28, 2018, https://www.axios.com/trump-team-debates-nationalizing-5g-network-f1e92a49-60f2-4e3e-acd4-f3eb03d910ff.html.

9. S.918, 116th Congress (2019–2020), https://www.congress.gov/bill/116th-congress/senate-bill/918/text?q=%257b%2522search%2522%253A%255B%2522e+frontier%2522%255D%257d&r=2&s=3.

10. Lev Sugarman, "Document: Former Military and Intelligence Officials Letter on 5G Risks," *Lawfare*, April 3, 2019, https://www.lawfareblog.com/document-former-military-and-intelligence-officials-letter-5g-risks.

11. Anthony Gregory, *American Surveillance: Intelligence, Privacy, and the Fourth Amendment* (Madison: University of Wisconsin Press, 2016).

12. Al-Haramain Islamic Found., Inc. v. Bush, 507 F.3d 1190 (9th Cir. 2007), https://scholar.google.com/scholar_case?case=5006140604567331133&hl=en&as_sdt=6,41&as_vis=1; Amnesty International, 568 U.S. 398 (2013), https://www.supremecourt.gov/opinions/12pdf/11-1025_ihdj.pdf; American Civil Liberties Union v. National Security Agency, 493 F.3d 644 (6th Cir. 2007), https://www.aclu.org/legal-document/aclu-v-nsa-federal-court-decision.

13. Gregory, *American Surveillance*.

MYTH 16: "Surveillance doesn't influence how I act"

1. Timothy Snyder, *On Tyranny: Twenty Lessons from the Twentieth Century* (New York: Tim Duggan Books, 2017).

2. Debora Mackenzie, "'Big Brother' Eyes Make Us Act More Honestly," *New Scientist*, June 28, 2006, https://www.newscientist.com/article/dn9424-big-brother-eyes-make-us-act-more-honestly.

3. Jonathan Shaw, "The Watchers: Assaults on Privacy in America," *Harvard Magazine*, January–February 2017, https://harvardmagazine.com/2017/01/the-watchers.

4. Jon Penney, "Chilling Effects: Online Surveillance and Wikipedia Use," *Berkeley Technology Law Journal* 31, no. 1 (2016), https://papers.ssrn.com/sol3/papers.cfm?abstract_id=2769645.

5. "New PEN Report Demonstrates Global Chilling Effect of Mass Surveillance," PEN America, January 5, 2015, https://pen.org/press-release/new-pen-report-demonstrates-global-chilling-effect-of-mass-surveillance; see full report at https://pen.org/sites/default/files/globalchilling_2015.pdf.

6. Lee Raine and Mary Madden, "How People Are Changing Their Own Behavior," Pew Research Center, March 16, 2015, https://www.pewresearch.org/internet/2015/03/16/how-people-are-changing-their-own-behavior.

7. Elizabeth Stoycheff, "Under Surveillance: Examining Facebook's Spiral of Silence Effects in the Wake of NSA Internet Monitoring," *Journalism and Mass Communication Quarterly* 93, no. 2 (March 8, 2016), https://doi.org/10.1177/1077699016630255.

8. Keith Hampton et al., *Social Media and the "Spiral of Silence"* (Washington, DC: Pew Research Center, August 26, 2014), https://www.pewresearch.org/internet/2014/08/26/social-media-and-the-spiral-of-silence.

9. Joshua Franco, a senior research advisor and deputy director of Amnesty Tech at Amnesty International says surveillance becomes part of their psyche. He writes, "Inside Uzbekistan, surveillance is a looming threat for human rights defenders, government critics and independent journalists, but it is only one of the many human rights threats they face." Joshua Franco, "'We Will Find You, Anywhere': The Global Shadow of Uzbekistani Surveillance," *Medium*, March 30, 2017, https://medium.com/amnesty-insights/we-will-find-you-anywhere-the-global-shadow-of-uzbekistani-surveillance-254405805860.

10. Kendra Schaefer, "China's Corporate Social Credit System: Context, Competition, Technology and Geopolitics," *Trivium*, December 8, 2020, https://www.uscc.gov/research/chinas-corporate-social-credit-system-context-competition-technology-and-geopolitics.

11. Charlie Campbell, "'The Entire System Is Designed to Suppress Us.' What the Chinese Surveillance State Means for the Rest of the World," *Time*, November 21, 2019, https://time.com/5735411/china-surveillance-privacy-issues.

12. Human Rights Watch, *Tiger Chairs and Cell Bosses: Police Torture of Criminal Suspects in China*, May 13, 2015, https://www.hrw.org/report/2015/05/13/tiger-chairs-and-cell-bosses/police-torture-criminal-suspects-china.

13. Campbell, "'The Entire System Is Designed to Suppress Us.'"

14. Snyder, *On Tyranny*, 88.

MYTH 17: "Teenagers don't care about privacy"

1. Monica Anderson and Jingjing Jiang, "Teens, Social Media and Technology 2018," Pew Research Center, May 31, 2018, https://www.pewresearch.org/internet/2018/05/31/teens-social-media-technology-2018.

2. Christakis is quoted in Andrea Petersen, "Is Your Child a Digital Addict? Here's What You Can Do," *New York Times*, April 15, 2020, https://www.nytimes.com/2020/04/15/parenting/big-kid/child-screen-addiction.html.

3. Damon Centola, "The Spread of Behavior in an Online Social Network Experiment," *Science* 329 (September 3, 2010): 5996, https://doi.org/10.1126/science.1185231.

4. Suzanne Shaffer, "How Social Media Can Affect College Admissions," *TeenLife*, December 19, 2014, https://www.teenlife.com/blogs/social-media-can-affect-college-admissions; "Is Social Media Making Cliques Worse?" Netsanity, January 20, 2016, https://netsanity.net/social-media-making-cliques-worse.

5. Amy Ellis Nutt and Frances E. Jensen, *The Teenage Brain: A Neuroscientist's Survival Guide to Raising Adolescents and Young Adults* (New York: HarperCollins, 2014).

6. Sarah-Jayne Blakemore, *Inventing Ourselves: The Secret Life of the Teenage Brain* (New York: PublicAffairs, 2018).

7. Deborah Temkin, "All 50 States Now Have a Bullying Law. Now What?" *Child Trends*, April 27, 2015, https://www.childtrends.org/blog/all-50-states-now-have-a-bullying-law-now-what.

8. Author's email correspondence with Liz Geisewite, October 4, 2020.

9. Joel Bakan, *Childhood Under Siege: How Big Business Targets Children* (New York: Penguin, 2011).

MYTH 18: "Surveillance affects everyone equally"

1. Hassan is quoted in Jason Grant, "A Soldier, an American, a Muslim: NJ Man Leads Fight Against NYPD Spying," *Star-Ledger*, July 1, 2012, https://www.nj.com/news/2012/07/former_american_soldier_from_n.html.

2. "Matt Apuzzo, Adam Goldman, Eileen Sullivan and Chris Hawley of the Associated Press" Pulitzer, 2012, https://www.pulitzer.org/winners/matt-apuzzo-adam-goldman-eileen-sullivan-and-chris-hawley.

3. First Amended Complaint, Hassan v. City of New York, No. 2:12-cv-03401-SDW-MCA October 3, 2012, https://muslimadvocates.org/wp-content/uploads/2019/06/Court-Case_2012.06.06_Hassan-v.-NYC_Complaint.pdf.

4. *Hassan v. City of New York.*

5. For a timeline of the case, see the Center for Constitutional Rights, https://ccrjustice.org/home/what-we-do/our-cases/hassan-v-city-new-york.

6. Malkia Amala Cyril, "Black America's State of Surveillance," *Progressive*, March 30, 2015, https://progressive.org/magazine/black-america-s-state-surveillance-cyril.

7. Malkia Amala Cyril, "Black America's State of Surveillance."

8. Khan is quoted in Sam Adler-Bell and Michelle Miller, "The Datafication of Employment," Century Foundation, December 19, 2018, https://tcf.org/content/report/datafication-employment-surveillance-capitalism-shaping-workers-futures-without-knowledge.

9. For more information on Stop LAPD Spying Coalition's anti-predictive policing curriculum, visit their website: stoplapdspying.org.

10. For more information about the Safe Spaces Initiative, visit the Muslim Public Affairs Council: https://www.mpac.org/safespaces.

11. Asraa Mustufa, "Report: Illinois' Countering Violent Extremism Programs Struggle to Gain Community Partners," *Chicago Reporter*, March 21, 2019, https://www.chicagoreporter.com/report-illinois-countering-violent-extremism-programs-struggle-to-gain-community-partners.

12. Brennan Center for Justice, "Why Countering Violent Extremism Programs Are Bad Policy," September 9, 2019, https://www.brennancenter.org/our-work/research-reportswhy-countering-violent-extremism-programs-are-bad-policy.

13. Peter Beinart, "Trump Shut Programs to Counter Violent Extremism," *Atlantic*, October 29, 2018, https://www.theatlantic.com/ideas/archive/2018/10/trump-shut-countering-violent-extremism-program/574237.

14. For the study, see "Homeland Threat Assessment," Department of Homeland Security, October 2020, https://www.dhs.gov/sites/default/files/publications/2020_10_06_homeland-threat-assessment.pdf.

15. German is quoted in Aviva Stahl, "These LA Activists Are Showing How to Fight Surveillance Under Trump," *In These Times*, November 30, 2018, https://inthesetimes.com/article/stop-lapd-spying-countering-violent-extremism-trump-anti-terrorism.

16. "Targeted Violence and Terrorism Prevention Grant Program," Department of Homeland Security, https://www.dhs.gov/tvtpgrants, accessed October 21, 2020.

17. See Joy Buolamwini and Inioluwa Deborah Raji, "Actionable Auditing: Investigating the Impact of Publicly Naming Biased Performance Results of Commercial AI Products," MIT Media Lab, January 24, 2019, https://www.media.mit.edu/publications/actionable-auditing-investigating-the-impact-of-publicly-naming-biased-performance-results-of-commercial-ai-products.

18. See Brian Fung, "Facial Recognition Systems Show Rampant Racial Bias, Government Study Finds," CNN, December 19, 2019, https://www.cnn.com/2019/12/19/tech/facial-recognition-study-racial-bias/index.html.

19. Kade Crockford, "How Is Face Recognition Surveillance Technology Racist?" ACLU, June 16, 2020, https://www.aclu.org/news/privacy-technology/how-is-face-recognition-surveillance-technology-racist.

20. See Bobby Allyn, "IBM Abandons Facial Recognition Products, Condemns Racially Biased Surveillance," NPR, June 9, 2020, https://www.npr.org/2020/06/09/873298837/ibm-abandons-facial-recognition-products-condemns-racially-biased-surveillance.

21. Mark Morales and Laura Ly, "Released NYPD Emails Show Extensive Surveillance of Black Lives Matter Protesters," CNN, January 18, 2019, https://www.cnn.com/2019/01/18/us/nypd-black-lives-matter-surveillance/index.html.

22. See "Activists Say Chicago Police Used 'Stingray' Eavesdropping Technology During Protests," CBS, December 6, 2014, https://chicago.cbslocal.com/2014/12/06/activists-say-chicago-police-used-stingray-eavesdropping-technology-during-protests.

23. Andrew Van Dam, "Economists Conducted a $5 Million Experiment to (Literally) Shed Light on Crime," Washington Post, May 14, 2019, https://www.washingtonpost.com/business/2019/05/14/economists-conducted-million-experiment-literally-shed-light-crime.

24. "311 Service Requests from 2010 to Present," NYC OpenData, https://nycopendata.socrata.com/Social-Services/311-Service-Requests-from-2010-to-Present/erm2-nwe9/data, accessed October 1, 2020.

25. Naples-Mitchell quoted in Van Dam, "Economists Conducted a $5 Million Experiment."

26. Stevens quoted in Van Dam, "Economists Conducted a $5 Million Experiment."

27. Jake Bittle and Jasper Craven, "Do NYCHA's $80 Million Crime-Reducing Lights Actually Reduce Crime?" Gothamist, May 14, 2018, https://gothamist.com/news/do-nychas-80-million-crime-reducing-lights-actually-reduce-crime.

28. Bittle and Craven, "Do NYCHA's $80 Million Crime-Reducing Lights Actually Reduce Crime?"

29. For more information on the advocacy group Media Justice, visit their website: mediajustice.org.

30. Barton Gellman and Sam Adler-Bell, The Disparate Impact of Surveillance, Century Foundation, December 21, 2017, https://tcf.org/content/report/disparate-impact-surveillance.

31. Gellman and Adler-Bell, The Disparate Impact of Surveillance.

MYTH 19: "'If You See Something, Say Something' is a civic duty"

1. Hanson O'Haver, "How 'If You See Something, Say Something' Became Our National Motto: Is It Helping Us or Hurting Us?" *Washington Post*, September 23, 2016, https://www.washingtonpost.com/posteverything/wp/2016/09/23/how-if-you-see-something-say-something-became-our-national-motto.

2. Office of the Press Secretary, "Secretary Napolitano Announces 'If You See Something, Say Something' Campaign at Super Bowl XLV," Department of Homeland Security, January 31, 2011, https://www.dhs.gov/news/2011/01/31/secretary-napolitano-announces-if-you-see-something-say-something-campaign-super.

3. Department of Homeland Security, "If You See Something, Say Something Campaign Overview," Department of Homeland Security, https://www.dhs.gov/sites/default/files/publications/SeeSay-Overview508_1.pdf, accessed October 2, 2020.

4. Michael Price, "New Counterterrorism Program in Los Angeles: Suspicious Thought Reporting?" Brennan Center for Justice, December 1, 2016, https://www.brennancenter.org/our-work/analysis-opinion/new-counterterrorism-program-los-angeles-suspicious-thought-reporting.

5. Reeves explains how citizen watch programs work to program neighborhood detectives: "Regulating the conduct of citizen patrols becomes a matter of cultivating the seeing/saying habits of the public while preventing their behavior from escalating into vigilantism and other acts of direct physical engagement." Joshua Reeves, *Citizen Spies: The Long Rise of America's Surveillance Society* (New York: New York University Press, 2017), 183.

6. Reeves, *Citizen Spies*.

7. John Prados and Luke Nichter, "Spying on Americans: Infamous 1970s White House Plan for Protest Surveillance Released," National Security Archive, June 25, 2020, https://nsarchive.gwu.edu/briefing-book/intelligence/2020–06–25/spying-americans-new-release-infamous-huston-plan.

8. "What Is Neighborhood Watch?" National Neighborhood Watch, https://www.nnw.org/what-neighborhood-watch, accessed October 12, 2020.

9. Community Oriented Policing Services, "Community Policing Defined," COPS Department of Justice, https://cops.usdoj.gov/RIC/Publications/cops-p157-pub.pdf, accessed October 3, 2020.

10. Author interview with Joshua Reeves, *Law and Disorder*, May 18, 2020.

11. Joan Starr, "Libraries and National Security: An Historical Review," *First Monday* 9, no. 12 (December 6, 2004), https://doi.org/10.5210/fm.v9i12.1198.

12. Robert McFadden, "FBI in New York Asks Librarians' Aid In Reporting on Spies," *New York Times*, September 18, 1987, https://www.nytimes.com/1987/09/18/nyregion/fbi-in-new-york-asks-librarians-aid-in-reporting-on-spies.html.

13. "Boston's Legacy: Can Crowdsourcing Really Fight Crime?" *NBC News*, April 12, 2014, https://www.nbcnews.com/tech/internet/bostons-legacy-can-crowdsourcing-really-fight-crime-n74831.

14. Jeff Howe, "The Rise of Crowdsourcing," *Wired*, June 1, 2006, https://www.wired.com/2006/06/crowds.

15. Mark Velez, "See Something, Say Something, Send Something: Everyone Is a Cyber Detective," *Police Chief*, 2018, https://www.policechiefmagazine.org/see-something-say-something-send-something.

16. Velez, "See Something."

17. "Axon Citizen," Axon, https://global.axon.com/products/citizen, accessed October 5, 2020.

18. Amanda Cochran, "'America's Most Wanted' Host John Walsh on Cancellation: Show Needs to Be on TV," *CBS News*, May 7, 2013, https://www.cbsnews.com/news/americas-most-wanted-host-john-walsh-on-cancellation-show-needs-to-be-on-tv.

19. David Correia and Keegan James Sarmiento Kloer, "Albuquerque Police Engaged in Secret Intelligence Gathering Operation, Leaked Documents Show," *Counterpunch*, September 7, 2020, https://www.counterpunch.org/2020/09/07/albuquerque-police-engaged-in-secret-intelligence-gathering-operation-leaked-documents-show; see also, http://www.ddosecrets.com/wiki/BlueLeaks.

20. A searchable index of all BlueLeaks files is available at https://blueleaks.io/index.html, accessed December 23, 2020; files pertaining to CONNECT and ARAPA are in the file titled "azorca," and spreadsheets containing the database of private and state actors are located in "ESBE" and "ESBE00000."

21. "What Is CONNECT," Albuquerque Police Department, https://connectabq.org/default.aspx/MenuItemID/252/MenuGroup/Public.htm, accessed December 23, 2020.

22. Reeves, *Citizen Spies*, 139.

23. Julie Harumi Mass and Michael German, "The Government Is Spying on You: ACLU Releases New Evidence of Overly Broad Surveillance of Everyday Activities," ACLU, September 19, 2013, https://www.aclu.org/blog/national-security/privacy-and-surveillance/government-spying-you-aclu-releases-new-evidence.

24. Christopher Maag, "'See Something, Say Something' Plays Critical Role in Thwarting Bombings," *USA Today*, September 20, 2016, https://www.usatoday.com/story/news/nation-now/2016/09/20/see-something-say-something-plays-critical-role/90723920.

25. William Staples, "Questioning the Culture of Surveillance," *Bank Info Security*, December 2, 2013, https://www.bankinfosecurity.com/interviews/questioning-culture-surveillance-i-2117.

MYTH 20: "Surveillance can't predict future behavior"

1. Charles Duhigg, "How Companies Learn Your Secrets," *New York Times Magazine*, February 16, 2012, https://www.nytimes.com/2012/02/19/magazine/shopping-habits.html.

2. Heidi Boghosian, "The Business of Surveillance," *ABA Journal*, May 2013, https://www.americanbar.org/groups/crsj/publications/human_rights_magazine_home/2013_vol_39/may_2013_n2_privacy/the_business_of_surveillance.

3. David Shenk, *Data Smog: Surviving the Information Glut* (New York: HarperCollins, 1998).

4. "OIG Releases Advisory on the Chicago Police Department's Predictive Risk Models," Office of Inspector General, January 23, 2020, https://igchicago.org/2020/01/23/oig-releases-advisory-on-the-chicago-police-departments-predictive-risk-models; Martin Macias Jr., "Audit Finds LAPD Predictive Policing Programs Lack Oversight," Courthouse News Service, March 8, 2019, https://

www.courthousenews.com/audit-finds-lapd-predictive-policing-programs
-lack-oversight.

5. See Grace Baek and Taylor Mooney, "LAPD Not Giving Up on Data-Driven
Policing, Even after Scrapping Controversial Program," CBSN, February 23, 2020,
https://www.cbsnews.com/news/los-angeles-police-department-laser-data-driven
-policing-racial-profiling-2-0-cbsn-originals-documentary; Eva Ruth Moravek,
"Do Algorithms Have a Place in Policing?" *Atlantic*, September 5, 2019. https://
www.theatlantic.com/politics/archive/2019/09/do-algorithms-have-place-policing
/596851; for an enumeration of police departments who have dropped their predpol programs, see Mark Puente, "LAPD Pioneered Predicting Crime with Data.
Many Police Don't Think It Works," *Los Angeles Times*, https://www.latimes
.com/local/lanow/la-me-lapd-precision-policing-data-20190703-story.html.

6. *Brennan Center for Justice v. New York Police Department*, February 27,
2020, https://www.brennancenter.org/our-work/court-cases/brennan-center
-justice-v-new-york-police-department; for access to documents, visit Brennan
Center for Justice, "NYPD Predictive Policing Documents," July 12, 2019,
https://www.brennancenter.org/our-work/research-reports/nypd-predictive
-policing-documents.

7. E. S. Levine et al., "The New York City Police Department's Domain
Awareness System: 2016 Franz Edelman Award Finalists," *Interfaces* 41, no. 1
(January 2017), https://www.researchgate.net/publication/312542282_The_New
_York_City_Police_Department's_Domain_Awareness_System_2016_Franz
_Edelman_Award_Finalists; see also: Ali Winston, "'Red Flags' as New Docu-
ments Point to Blind Spots of NYPD 'Predictive Policing,'" *The Daily Beast*, July
15, 2019, https://www.thedailybeast.com/red-flags-as-new-documents-point
-to-blind-spots-of-nypd-predictive-policing.

8. Ben Green et al., "Modeling Contagion Through Social Networks to
Explain and Predict Gunshot Violence in Chicago, 2006 to 2014," *JAMA
Internal Medicine* 177, no. 3 (March 2017), https://jamanetwork.com/journals
/jamainternalmedicine/fullarticle.

9. Tim Lau, "Predictive Policing Explained," Brennan Center for Justice,
April 1, 2020, https://www.brennancenter.org/our-work/research-reports
/predictive-policing-explained.

10. Jessica Saunders et al., "Predictions Put into Practice: A Quasi-
Experimental Evaluation of Chicago's Predictive Policing Pilot," *Journal of
Experimental Criminology* 12 (August 12, 2016), https://link.springer.com
/article/10.1007/s11292-016-9272-0.

11. "Advisory Concerning the Chicago Police Department's Predictive Risk
Models," Office of the Inspector General, January 2020, https://igchicago.org
/wp-content/uploads/2020/01/OIG-Advisory-Concerning-CPDs-Predictive-
Risk-Models-.pdf; Kathleen Foody, "Chicago Police End Effort to Predict Gun
Offenders, Victims," Associated Press, January 23, 2020, https://apnews.com
/41f75b783d796b80815609e737211cc6.

12. "The Problem with LAPD's Predictive Policing," editorial, *Los Angeles
Times*, March 16, 2019, https://www.latimes.com/opinion/editorials/la-ed-lapd
-predictive-policing-20190316-story.html.

13. See above, *Brennan Center for Justice v. New York Police Department*.

14. NYPD predictive policing policies cited in "Predictive Policing in Pittsburgh: A Primer," Coalition Against Predictive Poling in Pittsburgh, https://capp-pgh.com/files/Primer_v1.pdf, accessed September 10, 2020.

15. See Andrew Guthrie Ferguson, "Predictive Policing and Reasonable Suspicion," *Emory Law Journal* 62, no. 2 (May 2, 2012): 259, https://papers.ssrn.com/sol3/papers.cfm?abstract_id=2050001; Sarah Brayne, Alex Rosenblat, and Danah Boyd, "Predictive Policing," in *Data and Civil Rights: A New Era of Policing and Justice*, October 27, 2015, http://www.datacivilrights.org/pubs/2015-1027/Predictive_Policing.pdf.

16. Rashida Richardson, Jason Schultz, and Kate Crawford, "Dirty Data, Bad Predictions: How Civil Rights Violations Impact Police Data, Predictive Policing Systems, and Justice," *NYU Law Review Online* 192 (March 5, 2019), https://papers.ssrn.com/sol3/papers.cfm?abstract_id=3333423.

17. Will Douglas Heaven, "Predictive Policing Algorithms Are Racist. They Need to Be Dismantled," *MIT Technology Review*, July 17, 2020, https://www.technologyreview.com/2020/07/17/1005396/predictive-policing-algorithms-racist-dismantled-machine-learning-bias-criminal-justice.

18. Tim Lau, "Predictive Policing Explained."

19. "'Operation Ceasefire' Takes Aim at Crime in Newark," Community Foundation of New Jersey, February 6, 2020, https://cfnj.org/operation-ceasefire-takes-aim-at-crime-in-newark.

20. Allison Steele and Sean Collins Walsh, "Camden Disbanded Its Police Department and Built a New One. Can Others Learn from It?" *Philadelphia Inquirer*, June 14, 2020, https://www.inquirer.com/news/camden-police-defund-minneapolis-george-floyd-protest-20200609.html.

21. Lee Rainie and Janna Anderson, "Code-Dependent: Pros and Cons of the Algorithm Age," Pew Research Center, February 8, 2017, https://www.pewresearch.org/internet/2017/02/08/code-dependent-pros-and-cons-of-the-algorithm-age; Charles Okwe, "How the Digital Age Is Impacting Our Personal Privacy: A Beginner's Guide to Online Privacy," *Medium*, March 5, 2017, https://medium.com/@cre8tivemediaservices/how-the-digital-age-is-impacting-our-personal-privacy-695326dd1455.

MYTH 21: "There's nothing I can do to stop surveillance"

1. Hasan Elahi, "FBI, Here I Am!" TED Talk, October 31, 2001, https://www.ted.com/talks/hasan_elahi_fbi_here_i_am?language=en.

2. Hasan Elahi, "FBI, Here I Am!"

3. Hannah Kuchler, "Max Schrems: The Man Who Took on Facebook and Won," *Financial Times*, April 5, 2018, https://www.ft.com/content/86d1ce50-3799-11e8-8eee-e06bde01c544; "The Court of Justice Invalidates Decision 2016/1250 on the Adequacy of the Protection Provided by the EU–US Data Protection Shield," Court of Justice of the European Union, July 16, 2020, https://curia.europa.eu/jcms/upload/docs/application/pdf/2020-07/cp200091en.pdf.

4. "Data Protection Commissioner v. Facebook and Max Schrems (CJEU)," EPIC, https://epic.org/privacy/intl/dpc-v-facebook/cjeu/#resources, accessed September 4, 2020.

5. David Horowitz, "US Electronic Espionage: A Memoir," *Ramparts* 11, no. 2 (August 1972): 35–50.

6. James Risen and Eric Lichtblau, "Bush Lets U.S. Spy on Callers Without Courts," *New York Times*, December 16, 2005, https://www.nytimes.com/2005 /12/16/politics/bush-lets-us-spy-on-callers-without-courts.html; see also the National Whistleblower Center's profile of Russell Tice at https://www.whistle blowers.org/members/russell-tice.

7. See Bill Binney and Thomas Drake's PBS Frontline interviews: "Thomas Drake," *Frontline*, December 10, 2013, https://www.pbs.org/wgbh/pages/frontline /government-elections-politics/united-states-of-secrets/the-frontline-interview -thomas-drake; "Bill Binney" *Frontline*, December 13, 2013, https://www.pbs.org /wgbh/pages/frontline/government-elections-politics/united-states-of-secrets /the-frontline-interview-william-binney.

8. For an overview of media coverage on Mark Klein and the Electronic Frontier Foundation's lawsuit against AT&T, including Klein's declaration in court, see "News Coverage of Mark Klein in Washington," EFF, https://www.eff.org/pages /news-coverage-mark-klein-washington, accessed December 30, 2020; "Hepting v. AT&T," EFF, https://www.eff.org/cases/hepting, accessed December 30, 2020.

9. James Orenstein, "I'm a Judge. Here's How Surveillance Is Challenging Our Legal System," *New York Times*, June 13, 2019, https://www.nytimes.com /2019/06/13/opinion/privacy-law-enforcment-congress.html.

10. Dustin Volz, "Uber Says Hackers Behind 2016 Data Breach Were in Canada, Florida," Reuters, February 6, 2018, https://www.reuters.com/article /us-uber-cyber-congress/uber-says-hackers-behind-2016-data-breach-were-in -canada-florida-idUSKBN1FQ2YO.

11. "A.G. Underwood Announces Record $148 Million Settlement with Uber Over 2016 Data Breach," Office of the New York State Attorney General, September 26, 2018, https://ag.ny.gov/press-release/2018/ag-underwood-announces -record-148-million-settlement-uber-over-2016-data-breach.

12. Terry Jones, "Metadata vs. Data: A Wholly Artificial Distinction," Fluid-Info, September 5, 2009, webpage discontinued, can be accessed at: http://web cache.googleusercontent.com/search?q=cache:jnepAPhBE4wJ:blogs.fluidinfo .com/fluidinfo/page/7/+&cd=2&hl=en&ct=clnk&gl=us&client=firefox-b-ab.

13. Harris quoted in Brian Barth, "Big Tech's Big Defector," *New Yorker*, November 25, 2019, https://www.newyorker.com/magazine/2019/12/02/big-techs -big-defector.

14. Orenstein, "I'm a Judge. Here's How Surveillance Is Challenging Our Legal System."